Cuban Cultural Heritage

Cultural Heritage Studies

UNIVERSITY PRESS OF FLORIDA

Florida A&M University, Tallahassee
Florida Atlantic University, Boca Raton
Florida Gulf Coast University, Ft. Myers
Florida International University, Miami
Florida State University, Tallahassee
New College of Florida, Sarasota
University of Central Florida, Orlando
University of Florida, Gainesville
University of North Florida, Jacksonville
University of South Florida, Tampa
University of West Florida, Pensacola

CUBAN CULTURAL HERITAGE

A Rebel Past for a Revolutionary Nation

PABLO ALONSO GONZÁLEZ

Foreword by Paul A. Shackel

University Press of Florida

Gainesville · Tallahassee · Tampa · Boca Raton

Pensacola · Orlando · Miami · Jacksonville · Ft. Myers · Sarasota

23 22 21 20 19 18   6 5 4 3 2 1

Library of Congress Cataloging-in-Publication Data
Names: Alonso González, Pablo, author. | Shackel, Paul A., author of
   foreword.
Title: Cuban cultural heritage : a rebel past for a revolutionary nation /
   Pablo Alonso González ; foreword by Paul A. Shackel.
Other titles: Cultural heritage studies.
Description: Gainesville : University Press of Florida, 2018. | Series:
   Cultural heritage studies | Includes bibliographical references and index.
Identifiers: LCCN 2017031774 | ISBN 9780813056630 (cloth : alk. paper)
Subjects: LCSH: Cuba—History. | Cuba—Social life and customs. |
   Cuba—Civilization.
Classification: LCC F1776 .A45 2018 | DDC 972.91—dc23
LC record available at https://lccn.loc.gov/2017031774

The University Press of Florida is the scholarly publishing agency for the State University
System of Florida, comprising Florida A&M University, Florida Atlantic University, Florida
Gulf Coast University, Florida International University, Florida State University, New College
of Florida, University of Central Florida, University of Florida, University of North Florida,
University of South Florida, and University of West Florida.

University Press of Florida
15 Northwest 15th Street
Gainesville, FL 32611-2079
http://upress.ufl.edu

CONTENTS

FIGURES

FOREWORD

Pablo Alonso González' *Cuban Cultural Heritage: A Rebel Past for a Revolutionary Nation* is a powerful and insightful examination of heritage building in Cuba. This compelling book explores the role that cultural heritage—in the forms of narratives, monuments, and museums—played in the construction of a national identity in postcolonial Cuba, from Cuban independence from Spain until Cuban-U.S. rapprochement. Alonso González' access to archives and interviews from the republican and the revolutionary periods allows him to develop groundbreaking research and to make this work accessible to the English-speaking world. Understanding the changing meaning of heritage in Cuba is timely, as Cuba now faces new challenges with the passing of Fidel Castro and the opening of new relations with the United States.

Throughout the book, Alonso González documents the complexities of developing a consensus about Cuban history and Cuban national identity. Much of this heritage building process is related or a reaction to relationships with Spain, the United States, and the Soviet Union. The early Castro government strove to erase colonial representations on the landscape and in monuments and museums while building many more monuments and museums than had previously existed, in an effort to create a consensual historical narrative that could serve as a vehicle for nation-building.

Cuban Cultural Heritage provides a rich description and analysis about the memory making and heritage building required to develop a national identity. Memory often presents an uncomplicated way of seeing the past. Who has control over a group's memory is a question of power. Individuals and groups frequently struggle over the meaning of memory, as the power elite often impose the official memory. Written more than a generation ago, Eric Hobsbawm's words about the relationship of memory to power still ring true: "The history which became part of the fund of knowledge or the ideology of nation, state or movement is not what has actually been preserved in popular memory, but what has been selected, written, pictured, popularized and institutionalized by those whose function it is to do so" (Hobsbawm 1983:13).

The heritage development of the early Castro government became increasingly influenced by the Soviet Union, despite Cuba's efforts to conceal its dependence on this external power. The Cuban leadership created slogans such as "Neither Yankee Imperialism nor Russian Totalitarianism" and presented itself as a Marxist humanist government. However, they relied on the Soviet Union for support, which also influenced how they interpreted and displayed their heritage. With the fall of the Soviet Union in 1991 and Cuba's need to generate income, the island nation has begun to restore its European colonial heritage, in an effort to create an image of authenticity that will satisfy the demands of European tourists. The heritage processes in Cuba have been increasingly conditioned by the requirements of global actors such as the EU or UNESCO, and Cuban authorities have changed what they believe is important and appropriate to display to the public. The government has shifted its views toward the restoration of Old Havana as a World Heritage Site, moving from a condemnation of the Spanish colonial heritage to its promotion for the purpose of developing tourism. Alonso González' research shows us how this island nation reached this point, where the government is now promoting its colonial history after spending decades trying to erase it.

Cuban Cultural Heritage details a century of heritage and nation-building and their materialization in Cuban cities and landscapes. At its core, this book is about how the Cuban government has used and continues to use heritage to support its nation-building program, although the meaning of "heritage" continues to be in flux. This book is destined to become a key work in Cuban cultural heritage and national identity.

Paul A. Shackel
Series Editor

References Cited

Hobsbawm, Eric. 1983. "Introduction: Inventing Tradition." In *The Invention of Tradition*, edited by Eric Hobsbawm and Terrence Ranger, 1–14. New York: Cambridge University Press.

ABBREVIATIONS

26-J	Movimiento 26 de Julio (Twenty-sixth of July Movement)
CDR	Comités de Defensa de la Revolución (Committees for the Defense of the Revolution)
CENCREM	Centro Nacional de Conservación, Restauración y Museología (National Center of Preservation, Restoration and Museology)
CNC	Consejo Nacional de Cultura (National Council of Culture)
CNPC	Centro Nacional de Patrimonio Cultural (National Center of Cultural Heritage)
CODEMA	Consejo Asesor para el Desarrollo de la Escultura Monumentaria y Ambiental (Advisory Board for the Development of Monumental Sculpture)
COMECON	Council for Mutual Economic Assistance
EU	European Union
HRCDH	Rescate Patrimonial y Desarrollo Cultural en La Habana: Palacio del Segundo Cabo (Heritage Rescue and Cultural Development in Havana: Palace of the Second Cape)
ICOM	International Council of Museums
ICOMOS	International Council on Monuments and Sites
MICONS	Ministry of Construction
MINCULT	Ministry of Culture
MINED	Ministry of Education
MINFAR	Ministry of the Revolutionary Armies
MININT	Ministry of Internal Affairs or Home Office
MR	Museum of the Revolution
OHCH	Oficina del Historiador de la Ciudad de La Habana (Office of the City Historian of Havana)

PCC	Partido Comunista de Cuba (Cuban Communist Party)
PSP	Partido Socialista Popular (Popular Socialist Party)
U.S.	United States
USSR	Union of Soviet Socialist Republics

1

Introduction

As I write these pages, Fidel Castro's passing is being announced by the media worldwide. While thousands of Cubans mourn the loss of their *comandante*, another side of a divided nation celebrates the departure of the last living leader of the Cold War. Only in 2015, Cuba entered another phase in its history, as Secretary of State John Kerry watched the U.S. flag rise at the U.S. embassy in Havana for the first time in more than five decades. In the background of the image, however, dozens of flagpoles that are part of the Tribuna Antiimperialista José Martí (José Martí Anti-Imperialist Tribune) remind us of the decades of Cuban hostility toward the United States. Cuba is entering a crucial period of rapid changes, the meaning of which we cannot hope to grasp without considering the dimension of heritage politics and policies. This book makes a timely contribution to such an endeavor, incorporating the study of heritage into the general question of postcolonial Cuban nation-building and thus enhancing our understanding of heritage in Socialist countries. In doing so, it provides a better understanding of the uses of heritage under different regimes and ideologies from a long-term perspective.

The book spans a significant period of Cuban history, comprising the liberal republican era and the Revolution. It sheds light on what makes heritage different from other cultural processes in the attempt to build new national communities, identities, and narratives after decolonization. This process is complicated in Cuba, as the country embarked, together with other Socialist countries, upon a project of radical transformation,

Figure 1.1. U.S. Secretary of State John Kerry watches the raising of the American flag for the first time in fifty-four years at the U.S. Embassy in Havana on August 14, 2015. Source: United States Department of State.

of national culture and politics and, more deeply, of human beings into "new men." The book focuses on three broad areas of inquiry. The first is conceptual and concerns debates about the definition of heritage, museums, monuments, and about what heritage should be preserved. The second aims to map the heritage apparatus and its main institutional, political, artistic, and professional actors. The third analyses the material and symbolic construction of Cuban national narratives, that is, the stories that Cuba, like every society, has developed about the past and that are periodically revised to address present needs. The goal is therefore to advance knowledge of the Cuban nation-building process in a long-term perspective, to explore the conceptualization and functioning of heritage in Socialist societies, and to provide a more complex account of heritage in postcolonial settings.

The book also explores the relationships between heritage and internal and external cultural and political relations. It investigates the long-term impact of heritage policies after conflicts and the role these policies can play in reconciliation processes. The examination of the various ideological and nationalist projects at work in Cuba has implications for the long-standing debate on Cuban geopolitics and relationships with the Union of Soviet Socialist Republics (USSR) and the United States. Many wonder about the endurance of the Cuban Revolution after the collapse of the USSR and the sustained U.S. economic blockade. There is also speculation about Cuba's future economic and political paths and about the potential reconciliation with Cuban exiles outside the island after the normalization of relationships with the United States. Will Cuba follow the model of Chinese state capitalism, twenty-first-century Latin American socialism, or Western democratic liberalism, or will it remain a unique political project with its own features? This book has by no means a definitive answer to these questions, but it sheds light on the current situation by providing a long-term genealogy of the shifting uses of heritage, both its narratives and its symbols.

This project opens a strand of research largely unexplored in postcolonial Cuba. While much is written about Cuba, biased geopolitical approaches prevail, and few studies in anthropology or cultural history have been carried out between the 1960s and 2000s that address the revolutionary period. Moreover, no studies have investigated the nexus between politics, ideology, identity, and heritage from a long-term perspective. Usually, studies about Cuba are restricted to single periods, owing to the radically different theoretical frameworks and data sources required to explore them. To ensure the coherence of my argument, this book delineates the genealogy of relations between heritage and Cuban nationalism. Addressing these dynamic relations proves crucial to understanding not only how heritage has influenced, shaped, or reflected sociopolitical contexts but also how the latter has transformed the meanings of heritage in the process of representing national identity.

Cuba's independence from Spain in 1898 led to a nation-building process that is ongoing and contested inside and outside the island. However, the power of nationalism associated with the notions of *patria* (fatherland) and struggle has been fundamental to the long-term survival of the Revolution. How should we interpret the changing notions of nation and their relevance for different Cuban political regimes in light of heritage? The need to create an identity that can navigate between heritage, people, territory, and state led the postcolonial Cuban state to implement hegemonic strategies of political incorporation. Following the anthropologist Ana Alonso, nationalism can be conceived of as a homogenizing project and ideology aimed at the political incorporation of the masses that produces a "sense of political community that conflates peoplehood, territory, and state" (Alonso 1994:391).

The convergence between culture and state usually involves an elite-driven imposition of values, aesthetic criteria, and beliefs that lead to cultural homogenization. In turn, cultural homogenization leads to the formation of symbolic imaginaries to ensure consent and the construction of a national character and identity that through concrete manifestations of legible form and materiality allow the state to be perceived as a reality. The state structures space to develop nationalist projects using images, metaphors, and representational practices. But states also structure time, by producing narratives that allow people to embed their personal histories within a shared temporality that provides meaning to their lives. So how can heritage mediate the fluid terrain between materiality and history that cements nationalist projects?

In many periods of Cuban history, however, Cubans were forced to assume what the nation was and the role they should play in it. Unlike Benedict Anderson's (2006) ideas of the imagined community, the state actively planned and materialized the national community and dictated political consciousness by establishing what the "deep horizontal camaraderie" should look like, through cultural politics, education, and aesthetics (Lomnitz-Adler 2001:6–13). This raises the question of ideology, for in Cuba it has functioned as both a heuristic concept and a concrete reality. Ideology has shifted from the Marxist critical description of people's false consciousness and alienation under capitalism that should be suppressed under Socialism to serving as the conscious official language of the Cuban Socialist state. Revolutionary Cuba combined ideology and nationalism in complex ways, creating a benchmark to judge political allegiance and to establish what true Cubanness (Cuban identity or *Cubanía*) was.

The study of heritage in Cuba has implications for understanding the conceptualization and functioning of heritage in Socialist countries more generally. To avoid confusion, countries will be referred to as "Socialist" when they adopted some form of Marxist ideology, lacked a free market, and the state owned most means of production. This includes those states labeled as realist Socialist, state Socialist, Socialist, and communist. Although Cuba defines itself as a Socialist republic, the archival sources often use different concepts interchangeably.

The growing body of literature addressing the different fates of Socialist legacies in post-Socialist societies most often leaves aside the uses of heritage within Socialist regimes in their historic context. How did Socialist states conceive of and use heritage in the attempt to reconcile Marxist-Leninist ideology with nationalism? The gradual disappearance of Socialist regimes (Libya) or their conversion into state-led market economies (China, Vietnam) precludes the study of heritage *as an ongoing process* rather than as history. Cuba can cast light on the differences in heritage management between the regimes that survived the Soviet collapse such as China, on the one hand, and the countries that collapsed in the Eastern Bloc, on the other. However, Cuba also differs from China in its reluctance to assume significant market reforms and facilitate digital and physical communications and has remained largely isolated until the 2014 rapprochement with the United States.

My analysis of Cuba raises further questions regarding the relationship with the USSR, the characterization of its political status, and the degree of room for internal dissent. Certainly, Cuba is a rather unique case within the spectrum of Socialist states, owing to its geographic isolation in America, its differential sociocultural and ethnic composition, and the popular rather than imposed character of its revolution. However, using the USSR as a model, recent research on other Socialist countries, such as Romania, Yugoslavia, Poland, and Bulgaria, has also revealed their distinctiveness from the USSR due to different national traditions and political configurations. Other Socialist states openly opposing the USSR, such as China and the "nonaligned" countries, also deviated from the USSR in different ways.

Nonetheless, these Socialist countries shared some concerns, ideas, and practices regarding heritage. To identify the similarities and differences between Cuba and other Socialist countries, I explore heritage under Socialism as a state-sponsored process, analyzing the role of heritage

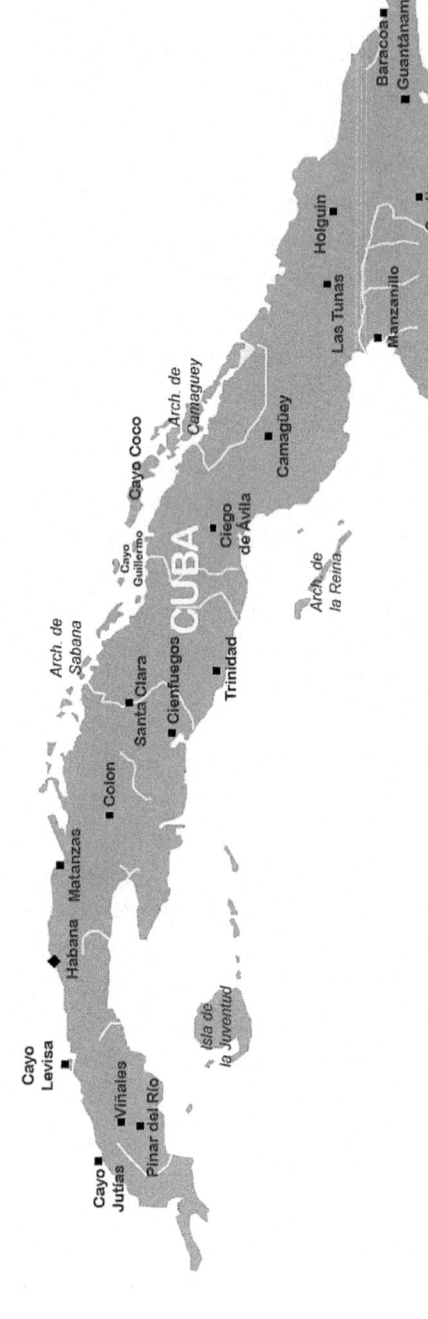

Figure 1.2. Map of Cuba. Source: Author.

in spreading the official ideology, aligning popular with state meanings, tastes, and values, and mystifying the charisma of the leadership while relinquishing tradition. It is not that capitalist, liberal, and democratic states do not use heritage to project their ideologies, but more social actors intervene in the mediation between ideology and heritage. In Socialist countries, official history and ideology are considered scientific and are explicitly considered to be constituent parts of the symbolic system of the state. This makes it necessary to carry out long-term studies, to identify the distinctive features of Socialist heritage production by comparing it with alternative logics in other periods—for example, between the republican and revolutionary periods in Cuba.

Understanding heritage in revolutionary Cuba can shed light on the complex relationships that Cuba and the USSR sustained for three decades. This touches upon another goal of this book: to provide a complex account of heritage in postcolonial Cuba with implications for postcoloniality in other contexts. If heritage is often contested, the legacies of colonialism in postcolonial settings are highly politicized and sensitive. Many postcolonial states suppress, forget, or allow their colonial pasts to crumble while assuming the heritage values of new global powers. Usually, this process leads to the suppression of competing histories and heritages, relinquishing complexity for the sake of constructing homogenous national identities. Indeed, the literature on postcoloniality and heritage studies often overlaps in the field of identity. Heritage plays a significant role in the postcolonial need to reinforce individual and collective identity and a sense of group belonging. It does this by highlighting certain aspects from the past that bound them together and differentiated them from others.

However, as Rodney Harrison and Lotte Hughes ask, "Do we even know what postcolonial heritage is, and what its role should be?" (Harrison and Hughes 2010:264). The theory of the coloniality of power developed, among others, by Walter Mignolo (2000) and Aníbal Quijano (2000) can help us answer this question in the Cuban case. This theory complicates any easy reading of postcolonial contexts by looking at the different layers of coloniality—racial, epistemic, cultural, or political—that outlived political colonialism and permitted the incorporation of local elite groups into the hegemonic Anglo and Eurocentric paradigm of modernity. The coloniality of power endures after the end of formal colonial domination by naturalizing and institutionalizing Western hierarchies of knowledge, value, and culture.

The need for postcolonial countries to address the consequences of colonialism and renegotiate heritage and tradition is complicated in Cuba by the revolutionary drive to break with the past. What are the consequences for postcolonial countries of relinquishing tradition and replacing it with a Marxist-Leninist ideology? This begs the troublesome question of the postcolonial status of Cuba. Social actors in each historic period in Cuba have seen previous periods as influenced by foreign powers and thus colonized to different extents. This led them to pass judgment and declare a tabula rasa with regard to the undesired legacies of previous eras. Thus, the Republic built its symbolic legitimacy against Spanish colonialism, the Revolution against the United States–backed neocolonial Republic, and the post-1990 period against Soviet influence.

I examine postcolonial Cuba along three lines of inquiry. First, what has been the fate of colonial heritage in each historic period since independence? Has it been actively celebrated, despised, or simply ignored? I investigate this issue by looking at the changing perceptions and policies regarding colonial city centers throughout Cuba, with a focus on Old Havana. Second, what is the meaning of the celebration of colonial heritage in Cuba after 1990? Is it a pragmatic adaptation to global tourism and multicultural policies or a sign of reconciliation with Cuba's "real history"? Or is it actually a reflection of an underlying coloniality of power that highlights European monumental heritage and adopts the global hierarchies of heritage value? The book responds to these questions through an analysis of the narratives, practices, and ideas unfolding in the restoration of Old Havana and through a case study of the project Rescate Patrimonial y Desarrollo Cultural en La Habana: Palacio del Segundo Cabo (Heritage Rescue and Cultural Development in Havana: Palace of the Second Corporal, or PSC).[1] Third, what is the underlying epistemology of the conceptualization and practice of heritage in each period, and where did it come from? Answering this question can shed light on Cuba's changing symbolic and cultural allegiances at a broader political level. I analyze these changing allegiances by looking at the various heritage legislative

---

1   See the EU project website: http://goo.gl/RNIfI2; and the Office of the Historian of Havana: http://segundocabo.ohc.cu/.

frameworks, conceptual definitions, privileged aesthetic and formal canons, and forms of institutional organization.

Although people eventually overturn, reject, and reinterpret hegemonic ideas, this book focuses on official and state-sponsored heritage. Powerful actors are the main producers of heritage, because, as Clifford Geertz affirmed, for ideas to have powerful social effects, they must be carried by powerful social groups: "Someone must revere them, celebrate them, defend them, impose them. They have to be institutionalized in order to find not just an intellectual existence in society, but, so to speak, a material one as well" (Geertz 1973:314). However, heritage is not a transparent conveyor of ideology and power. Rather, it is a present-centered process that is perpetually in the making and that plays a mediating role between power and ideology, history and materiality. Consequently, instead of providing a historical account of what "really occurred" with Cuban heritage, this book adopts a genealogical approach to address the changing configuration of power regimes and ideologies from a contextual analysis of the politics of the past in different periods. This genealogy is grounded in Foucauldian interpretive analytics. Its aim is not to identify the particular materialization of a general heritage pattern or the concretization of heritage as an abstract category but rather to analyze a series of practices and ideas assembled in action.

This genealogical perspective produces a comprehensive analysis of the ways heritage has contributed to the representation of different notions of Cubanness. Accordingly, I focus my analysis on the different social and institutional actors involved in the field of heritage and how their ideas, practices, and debates about heritage were continued, reinterpreted, or refuted in the different periods under investigation. This requires exploring the material manifestations of representations of collective identity and memory. The focus on materiality allows me to connect heritage and nationalism. Nationalism posits the existence of an essential relationship among otherwise unrelated individuals, but the definition of that shared essence often remains contested, be it ethnic, racial, cultural, or historic. As anthropologist Michael Herzfeld (Byrne and Herzfeld 2011:154–155) has argued, nationalism can be conceived as a terrain of struggle over the definition of what becomes essentialized. For him, because essentialism is closely connected to reification, and reification means to make something material, the politics of heritage can be framed and investigated as a question of ontology, that is, as a question of defining what exists in reality. Therefore, the twofold symbolic and material constitution of heritage is taken as the starting point for research.

However, the meaning of heritage is not fixed but context-specific; it is socially negotiated over time and space and subject to different interpretations that eventually become dominant by means of practice, performance, and association. This processual and meaningful phenomenon is encapsulated in the concept of "heritagization." Processes of heritagization normally involve an assemblage of history and materiality through different practices. Those include the active materialization of symbols and narratives in public space and the conservation or destruction of older material remains, but also the passive disregard for the representation of certain pasts or the preservation of the material culture associated with them.

Through processes of heritagization, different social actors endow material culture with meaning and make the past significant for contemporary purposes. These features of material culture may in turn become symbols that evocate or represent something else. Symbols are the building blocks of broader representational frameworks, including myths and narratives. When used as a public symbol, heritage can both reflect and help legitimate the hegemonic social order. Moments of change and crisis make these frameworks more explicit, rendering quotidian dynamics more visible and legible. Analyzing these practices reveals how social actors define what heritage is, what deserves preservation, and their modus operandi in the different contexts of Cuban postcolonial nation-building.

The empirical evidence that grounds this study sheds light on the power relations, meanings, and events that unfold before, during, and after the production of monuments, museums, performances, and restoration processes. The argument privileges the study of what Pierre Nora (1989:7) calls "places of memory": sites where memory is embodied and a sense of historical continuity persists. Monuments, commemorative landscapes, museums, or restorations can function as places of memory. These recurrent sites for the symbolic performance of memory and identity allow for the long-term exploration of heritage in different periods. This reveals the reasons some historic periods privilege the construction of new monuments while others emphasize restoration and the resignification of previous heritage features. Examining which elements are considered usable and what is done with them, and conversely which are neglected or resignified for new purposes, can shed light on changes in ideology and national identity.

Archival work provides documentary evidence for both the republican and revolutionary periods. Most secondary and primary documentation appearing in this book is "virgin"—I am the first to use it—and serves as excellent source material for information about revolutionary Cuba. I complemented the data provided by written sources, maps, architecture and museographic plans, and pictures with ethnographic work. This included participant and nonparticipant observation of different public events, spatial analyses, and comparative studies of museums, mainly related to the refurbishing of the Palacio del Segundo Cabo (Palace of the Second Corporal) in Old Havana. More than one hundred semistructured interviews were carried out with various aims: piecing together an image of the contemporary heritage field in Cuba, gathering oral testimonies about the historical evolution of heritage production and specific events, and understanding the shifting values, interpretations, and ideas about heritage over the long term. Because of the chronological development of the argument and the uneven availability of sources of information, I make greater use of archival data in chapters 2, 3, and 4, while chapters 5 and 6 present a more ethnographic component.

The book comprises five chapters of analysis and one concluding chapter. The second, third, and fourth chapters each correspond with a historic period. Chapter 2 examines the role heritage played after Cuban independence from Spain and the development of nationalism during the republican era, laying the foundation for understanding the changes and continuities during the revolutionary period. Chapter 3 explores the early revolutionary years, when the revolutionaries challenged previous heritage ideas and policies and adapted them to the new context. Chapter 4 addresses the institutionalization period, when an efficient heritage production machinery was aligned gradually with the tenets of Marxism-Leninism. Chapters 5 and 6 address the period between the disintegration of the USSR until the normalization of the Cuban-U.S. relationship in 2014. Chapter 5 focuses on shifts in state-sponsored heritage processes as Cuba moved from Marxist-Leninist rhetoric to cultural nationalism. Chapter 6 examines the role of the Oficina del Historiador de la Ciudad de La Habana (Office of the City Historian of Havana, OHCH) in the restoration of Old Havana World Heritage Site, looking at the differences between state-sponsored heritage and the OHCH. The case study of the Segundo Cabo provides a detailed account of the complexities of the contemporary Cuban heritage field. The conclusion lays out my main findings regarding Cuban postcolonial nation-building from a long-term perspective, summarizing the contribution to heritage theory and examining the workings of heritage in Socialist countries.

2

Negotiating the Past, Representing the Nation

The Contested Uses of Heritage during the Republic (1898–1959)

After two wars against Spain (1868–1878 and 1879–1880), Cuba acquired its political independence in the War of Independence between 1895 and 1898, a century after most Latin American countries. Nearly 10 percent of the Cuban population died during the war, including the intellectual José Martí, who became the martyr and hero of Cuban nationalism. The conflict had escalated with the involvement of the United States in the last months of the war, following the explosion of the battleship *Maine* in Havana's harbor. Spanish colonialism in America ended and the United States became the new regional imperial power, occupying Cuba and ensuring control over political and economic affairs through the Platt Amendment.

The occupation government put an end to the resolve to break with the old social order, favored by radical proindependence Cubans. Instead, it favored the interests of creole landowners and urban elites, who regained their positions of strength in the new republic. The period of political turmoil, civic revolts, and economic fluctuations between 1898 and 1959 reflected the tensions between the opposed modernizing projects of Cuban politico-economic elites, intervening U.S. authorities, intellectual and cultural elites, and the popular classes' demand for inclusion. In fact, the modernization of the Cuban state in its transition from a Spanish colonial corporatist structure to a liberal model was unable to combine the democratization of society with the expansion of culture and the redistribution of wealth. As a result, efforts to build an independent and more equitable state with social cohesion largely failed.

For most Cuban scholars, the nineteenth century witnessed the emergence of a national identity associated with a Cuban culture, a specific combination of Spanish and African traits (Pupo Pupo 2005:37). However, Cuba presented a heterogeneous ethnic and racial population. Also, it had to develop an original identity against an ex-colonial power with which it shared many sociocultural tenets and a language. To complicate things even further, "whitening" policies fostered the arrival of thousands of Spanish immigrants to Cuba during the first decades of the twentieth century (Naranjo Orovio 2001). The question of national identity was fundamental in Cuban political and cultural life during these decades, and there was a general disorientation in the construction of a national discourse. Although in Cuba the nation may have existed well before the state, the republican state played a prominent role in using heritage to construct usable pasts for grounding a discourse of national identity and collective memory. But the creation of usable pasts in Cuba proved a difficult task, as the Spanish, black, and indigenous histories did not provide useful underpinnings for crafting a distinct Cuban narrative. Ethnically, Cuban national identity had to be grounded in an abstract national spirit that combined, but differentiated itself from, the indigenous, black, and Spanish inheritances. The political situation exacerbated the difficulties, as Cubans debated whether the nation should be annexed to the United States, remain linked to Spain, or be independent.

The passage from defining Cuban identity against Spanish colonialism to doing so against U.S. imperialism after 1898 led to a deep process of reflection and redefinition of national representations and discourses. Cubans had to develop a national history associated with figures, facts, and myths from the past that would render Cuba unique. The Cuban nationalist project was led by mostly Hispanic elite groups, including political leaders, intellectuals, scientists, historians, doctors and writers, professional organizations, migrant associations, and political parties. This elite group's monopoly over the state apparatus has led José Fernández (2011) to speak of a "Republic of the elites." However, elites presented vaguely defined cultural and political identities that tended to imitate and import foreign models, first from Spain and Europe and after the 1930s from the United States.

It would be misleading to conflate Cuban elites with intellectuals, as they all came from diverse backgrounds and classes, and their political projects never lined up with one another (Bronfman 2005:6). Characters such as Emilio Roig de Leuchsenring represented the contradictory group that made up the intellectual elite. Following Jorge Duany (1997:12), this group was characterized by a combination of anti-imperialism with elitism, reformism, and paternalism and by a frustrated ambition to lead and transform the nation. For them, heritage was fundamental in the project to create a homogeneous people and culture that shared a representation of the national past to disseminate through education. As in the Puerto Rican and other Latin American nation-building processes, the construction of the national idea involved the intermixing of political and intellectual elites, with intellectuals providing legitimacy and guidance for political action.

Cuban elites sought heritage management models in consolidated nations, such as the United States, England, and France. In these countries, evolutionist ideas informed the production of monuments and museums. Heritage served to rank social groups chronologically and hierarchically and to fix the morality and tastes of the newly defined nations. In Cuba, this entailed a form of continuity with the attitudes of elites during the late colonial period. In his exploration of late colonial Cuba, Paul Niell (2015) has related the appearance of heritage policies in Havana during the eighteenth and nineteenth centuries with the emergence of a public sphere and the phenomenon of cultural modernism. For him, Cuban creole elites patronized public heritage works to ensure cultural authority through the symbolic appropriation of Western Greco-Roman neoclassicism. In doing so, Havana's elites connected their social position within the colony to the tradition of European antiquity and set the standards of human excellence that should guide the modernization process. It is therefore necessary to explore in which ways republican heritage policies continued or disrupted the late colonial phenomenon of cultural modernism.

Cultural modernism affected not only Cuba. It was a global phenom-enon related to coloniality and modernity that influenced Latin Ameri-can elites in the context of nation-building. The difficulty with Cuba, and broadly with Latin American countries, is that the distinctive tenets of nationalism are all present but in complicated ways, meaning that the key theories on nationalism only partially apply. For instance, Cuban his-torian Marial Iglesias Utset (2011:7) has shown how Benedict Anderson's (2006) approach proves only relatively useful in Cuba, as his arguments on the imaginary constitution of the nation based on printed word do not apply in agrarian societies with high illiteracy rates such as nineteenth-century Cuba. For Iglesias Utset, text is less relevant than performances such as celebrations, public ceremonies, burials, and symbolic practices, among which we can include the monumental, museum, and heritage preservation practices that are the focus of this book.

In postcolonial Cuba, heritage became a contested site for the nego-tiation of Cuban national identity and a tool for the renewal of political hegemony for the elites. There was a lack of a distinct and unambiguous authorized heritage discourse associated with a coherent narrative and image of the nation. However, the republican period witnessed a multi-plication of usable pasts and heritage narratives. This entailed the partial break with the late-colonial cultural modernism associated with neoclas-sicism and the contested emergence of a republican-heritage aesthetic canon. My argument adds nuance to the interpretation offered by Louis Pérez (1999), who considers Cuban national identity as a present-centered modern construction based on the U.S. model. For Pérez, in the process of nation-building, Cubans

looked out and forward, but hardly ever looked in and back [. . .] In a discourse otherwise rich and ranging, dedicated almost entirely to identity and nationality, a coherent approximation of history was conspicuous by its absence. The idea of history as a narrative framework of a common past, to be shared and celebrated, a way to validate the authenticity of nationality, was not invoked in the con-struction of "Cuban" [. . .] Much of what became usable as "Cuban" was derived or appropriated from the present [. . .] Cubans did not situate themselves in a past, in fact, they lacked a coherent notion of an instrumental past. They invoked few symbols from which to claim continuity and derive legitimacy. (Pérez 1999:84)

Indeed, in 1914 liberal politician Juan Gualberto Gómez expressed his concern about a growing forgetfulness regarding the Cuban past: "We are abandoning the remembrance of those great events in our history that ushered in independence, because we are losing the religion of memory, because we are turning our backs on the past" (quoted in Horrego Estuch 1954:220). Nonetheless, rather than a general state of public amnesia, there were various social actors engaged in different processes of memorialization. This process might have lacked a coherent approximation of history, as Pérez argues, but Cubans did "look in and back" when attempting to construct a national identity. The analysis of heritage policies and practices at various levels shows that this process was incomplete and contradictory owing to the ideological disconnection between intellectuals and sociopolitical elites uninterested in investing in culture, in addition to the endurance of the coloniality of power in Cuba.

Negotiating a Contested Past

During the Republic, social actors used the memorializing function of heritage to legitimize different political projects and power positions within the new state. Choices about what to memorialize or to forget in the creation of a usable past inevitably reflected the governing assumptions of the republican times. I explore these choices by following the diverse trajectories of different heritage objects and sites in Havana, focusing on relevant processes such as urban expansion and the meaning of new symbolic spaces and their transformations.

The first example of a neglected monument in postcolonial Cuba was the statue of Spanish Queen Isabel II that dominated Parque Central (Central Park) until it was violently removed and replaced in 1899. After its removal, in 1902, the statue was claimed by the new museum Oscar María de Rojas in Cárdenas. If the introduction of material culture into museums can be a form of iconoclasm that radically alters the meanings and memories attached to objects, placing the statue of the Queen in the Oscar María de Rojas changed its semiotic status: from public symbol to aesthetic object, presented for contemplation and as a representation of an undesirable past. Spanish colonialism thus was transformed into aesthetics and became part of a past deemed appropriate for symbolic display.

The lack of a statue to replace one of the Queen created a political challenge that became a matter of national concern, not because of a lack of funds but because of the uncertainty of Cuba's political future. The magazine *El Fígaro* organized two surveys in 1899—the first among intellectuals and the second among its readers—asking which historic character should replace the Queen. In both surveys Martí came first, but only by a small margin compared to other Cuban heroes (de Leuchsenring 1939a, b). More importantly, the symbols of Liberty and of Colón, representing supporters of U.S. and Spanish domination, respectively, were almost as popular as Martí. In fact, in 1902, the government erected a copy of New York's Statue of Liberty in Parque Central, with a U.S. shield in its arm in a clear symbolic display of allegiance to the United States.

Figure 2.1. Different locations of the statue of Isabel II. *Above, left*: before the removal. *Above, right*: being removed in 1899. Source: de Leuchsenring (1942a). *Below, left*: inside the Museum Oscar María de Rojas in Cárdenas in 1902. Source: Torriente Govín (2012). *Below, right*: outside the museum, after 1977. Source: Author.

EL FÍGARO

Periódico Literario y Artístico

PREGUNTA DE "EL FÍGARO"
¿Qué estatua debe ser colocada en nuestro Parque Central?

Figure 2.2. Which statue should preside over Parque Central? Source: *El Fígaro*, "Pregunta" (1899).

Meanwhile, a civic commission had raised money by popular collection in 1900 to create a monument to Martí. The monument was made in Italy and brought to Cuba in 1903, but the uncertain political climate, and consequently Cuba's uncertain future as an independent nation, prevented the state from allocating the statue any public space. Today, the existence of an intrinsic link between Martí and Cuban nationalism seems apparent, but at the turn of the twentieth century it was not so clear. Only in 1905, on the tenth anniversary of the call to arms against Spain, was the

Figures 2.3 and 2.4. Statue of Liberty
in Parque Central in 1902 (*above*) and
detail (*right*). Source: de Leuchsenring
(1939b).

statue of Martí erected where it stands today, thus linking Martí with the birth of the nation. The ceremony was charged with religious symbols glorifying Martí as an immortal spirit and apostle of the freedom of the patria. Moreover, it was a display of power and status by Havana's urban elites in front of the lower classes that crowded Parque Central. Cuban elites used heritage to appropriate Martí, who became the foundational myth, national hero, and material symbol of Cuban nationalism. In doing so, they also reproduced the hegemonic order and negotiated their position in the national hierarchies of power.

The removal of colonial symbols was a process of selective remembrance in terms of place and historic significance. The exchange of letters between Emilio Roig de Leuchsenring, prominent liberal leftist intellectual and city historian of Havana since 1935, and various intellectual, cultural, and political personalities and institutions show both the relevance of heritage in public debates and its contestation. From as early as the 1930s, a heated debate emerged about heritage preservation. There were demands for the removal of the statue of King Fernando VII from the Plaza de Armas and its relocation to Havana's City Museum. While it had been considered a priority to remove Isabel II from Parque Central, which was perceived as the new city center of modern Havana, it was considered appropriate to preserve Fernando VII in the Plaza de Armas, which had been the symbolic center of colonial power and was therefore associated with Spanish domination.

De Leuchsenring considered that preservation issues should be discussed based on rational historic accounts of the meanings of each specific heritage feature, the historic characters it commemorated, and their relationship with Cuba, and not on aesthetic or commonsense criteria. In the case of Fernando VII, de Leuchsenring affirmed that there was no reason "to pay public homage to the worst of the Spanish Kings" (1955c:294). It was not until 1945, on the fiftieth anniversary of Cuba's independence from Spain, that the statue of Fernando VII was substituted by another "father of the patria," Carlos Manuel de Céspedes, and taken to the City Museum. A similar situation took place in the city of Matanzas, where de Leuchsenring supported local intellectuals in their attempt to relocate the statue of Fernando VII to a museum. According to de Leuchsenring,

> even if those [monuments] had—and they have not—some artistic value, their proper place is the museum and not the public square,

because even if artists can turn ignoble individuals into works of art, when those are displayed in a street or a square, the individual represented in the monument is paid respect, admiration and recognition. (de Leuchenring 2013[1945]:435)

While he considered that these statues had no artistic value, de Leuchsenring did not call for their destruction but rather their public display in museums, where they could function as symbols of an undesirable past already overcome. Conversely, he and many others thought that the monument to King Carlos III should be preserved. In a letter to the subsecretary of public construction, de Leuchsenring affirmed that the statue deserved "preservation for what his government meant to Cuba, and because it was erected by public popular subscription" (de Leuchsenring 2013[1942]:332). In this way, de Leuchsenring projected the existence of the nation backward, as if Carlos III had favored Cuba and as if the public popular subscription had been made by Cubans, to as early as the eighteenth century.

The fates of the statues of three different Spanish monarchs have shown the intricate connection between historical interpretation, material culture, and heritage. They have also reflected the tension between the processes of coopting versus neglecting past monuments. In these processes, Cubans selected which values and meanings from the past should reinforce the new postcolonial national identity. Other attempts to extricate the colonial symbols were less successful. For instance, the Comisión Nacional de Monumentos (National Monuments Commission) had been asking for the removal of the Spanish royal coat of arms from the town hall since 1938, on the grounds of a necessary "decolonization," but it was still there in 1958. Similarly, the most symbolic Spanish public spectacle, bullfighting, proved an enduring tradition in Cuba, although it had been officially abolished in 1899 (Riaño San Marful 2002). In a letter to President Fulgencio Batista, de Leuchsenring bitterly complained that bullfighting "is against Cuban traditions and reminds us of the vices and indignities of colonial times," which, he felt, were "contrary to national sentiments and [. . .] undermine[d] public customs" (de Leuchenring 2013[1941]:308). Even in 1959, de Leuchsenring (2013[1959]:513–514) complained to Fidel about the inappropriateness of hosting bullfighting spectacles in Havana. What transpires from the work of de Leuchsenring and his colleagues is a form of continuity with the cultural modernism that prevailed in late colonial times. They contested not the previous aesthetics, criteria, and canon of representation but rather the meaning of the contents represented by heritage in relation to the present needs of national construction.

The contested nature of heritage processes illustrates that the material and symbolic cleansing of the colonial past was far from complete and unambiguous and that the removal of the colonial symbols were a palliative for mitigating overall uncertainty. This uneven process reflected the poorly defined identities of Cuban intellectual elites throughout the republican period, caught as they were in the dilemma of establishing symbolic associations with cultural Pan-Hispanism and U.S.-inspired liberal modern schemes while maintaining a national cultural core. But contestation about heritage and the past also reveals the significant political and popular continuity that existed between colonial and postindependence collective identities, as had happened in other postcolonial Latin American contexts (Roniger 1998). Also, discussions about heritage served to negotiate and represent Cuban identity and to define the "others" that should remain outside the national imaginary.

The end of political colonialism also led to an ambiguous but gradual process of neglect of the colonial city that transformed the symbolic spaces of power in Havana. The early republican years replicated the former colonial areas of power by placing the Senate, presidency, and Havana's city council in the two most symbolically powerful colonial buildings of Old Havana: the Palaces of the Segundo Cabo and of the Capitanes Generales (Captains-General). It was only during the economic thrust of the 1920s that the Republic developed new spatial policies emulating those of Washington, D.C., which provided a modern example of the implementation of monumental spaces of power. The creation of a North American–inspired center of power outside the colonial city, in Parque Central and Prado Street, culminated with the construction of the Palacio Presidencial (Presidential Palace) and Capitolio in 1920 and 1929, respectively. The newly constructed Malecón swiftly became another key area for symbolic display.

The government used heritage to reassert the constitution of the new republican city center around the Capitolio in the inauguration of the Parque de la Fraternidad (Park of Brotherhood) by President Gerardo Machado in 1928. The ceremony involved the erection of statues of relevant rulers from South and North America. More importantly, Machado planted a ceiba tree like the one in Plaza de Armas, which had been one of the most important places of memory in the colonial era. The symbolic intent of the act was clear, as the tree was planted on the centennial of the inauguration of the original monument and tree in Plaza de Armas, in 1828 (Lachatañeré 1992[1942]:113–114). Following Niell (2015:233), this symbolic act can be interpreted as a heritage process that served to coopt the cultural authenticity of the tree and place it in the new city center, thus disavowing the former colonial center symbolically. But, as Joseph Hartman (2011) has shown, the use of the ceiba tree in an urban space also enabled Machado to enact a symbolic negotiation with the Afro-Cuban population by bringing together Spanish civic traditions, references to elements of Afro-Cuban religiosity, and Cuban national identity. Machado enacted the whole ritual in ways that resonated deeply among people of African descent, the ceiba tree being a key symbol in Afro-Cuban religions.

The symbolic ritual performed during the inauguration of the Parque de la Fraternidad shows that the complexity of heritage politics in Cuba goes beyond a simple dichotomy between approval or disavowal and requires an understanding of the multivocality involved in the public uses of heritage (Niell 2015). Indeed, as Ivor Miller (2000) has demonstrated, Cuban politicians from Machado to Fidel Castro have used symbols associated with Afro-Cuban religions to generate different meanings aimed at diverse audiences, both in public rituals and in the articulation of public space. This raises the question of the ambiguous status of Afro-Cubans in Cuban national identity: they are sometimes incorporated into the master-narratives of the state and elites and other times negated as disinherited subalterns who must bend to the authorized discourse of power. With different degrees of intensity, all periods of Cuban history have witnessed the negotiation of the Afro-Cuban legacy through heritage policies, an underlying issue that will resurface at different moments throughout this book.

A more monumental symbolic and material transformation was taking place in Parque Central, which became the scenario of a symbolic negotiation between the old order and the new order. The construction of state buildings evolved in parallel with a growing presence of symbols of the Spanish immigrant community, with the construction of the Disabled

Center (1907), the Spanish Casino (1912), the Galician Center (1915), and the Asturian Center (1927). In a further example of the complexity of the Cuban postcolonial nation-building process, the "Hispanicizing" style exemplified by these buildings became fashionable not only among the Spanish immigrants but also among Cuban elites and politicians. The Spanish immigrant associations also promoted the construction of monuments to Cervantes and Columbus in Havana and other cities. The association of Columbus with Spanish power was an inheritance of the late colonial period, when his remains were secured and his figure commemorated to reassert the symbolic power of the Spanish Empire (Niell 2015:162–163). However, this should not be interpreted exclusively as an assertion of Spanish power, for it is also a strategy Spanish immigrants used to negotiate their new Spanish-Cuban identities. This was a process that recalls Michelle Bogart's account of the relation between public sculpture and civic ideals in the United States, where migrants in New York "saw gifts of statues for Central Park as an appropriate way to beautify their city and to legitimate their heritage as well as their newfound status as Americans" (Bogart 1989:18–19).

Heritage also became a contested terrain for the negotiation of national identity against a neocolonial power. The U.S. intervention government not only implemented broad plans of urban modernization and hygiene but also actively tried to attract the support of Cuban elites for its positions via different means. One strategy was the establishment of a powerful new symbolic public space that could be associated with the ideas of freedom and modernity that the United States had traditionally embodied for Cubans. For instance, the replica of the Statue of Liberty substituted for Isabel II in Parque Central, until a cyclone tore it down. Similarly, a copy of the U.S. Capitol, in Washington, D.C., became the most visible landmark of Havana's urban landscape, and local governments and associations built statues and busts to U.S. leaders throughout the country.

At the same time, the provisional government of the U.S. intervention saw new Cuban historic museums as a threat to U.S. domination. For instance, during the 1907 U.S. military intervention, the museum Oscar María de Rojas was closed by the government and its building expropriated ("Monumento a Cristobal Colón" 1916). In addition, acts of disrespect for the symbols of Cuban nationalism were common; for instance, a group

Figure 2.5. U.S. soldiers on the statue of Martí in Parque Central. Source: De la Osa (1949).

of marines desecrated the statue of Martí in Parque Central in 1949, an aggression that Cubans unsuccessfully attempted to counter with the demolition of the monument to *Maine* (Iglesias Utset 2014:46).

What lurked behind U.S. heritage works was an attempt to impose a national narrative that suited U.S. plans for the annexation of Cuba. According to the version of history promoted by U.S.-intervention government and pro-U.S. Cuban politicians, Cuba was in debt to the United States for having provided Cuba its freedom, a debt that legitimized claims for U.S. annexation. This narrative highlighted the United States' role in the war against Spain and the Cuban dependence on the United States for freedom and modernization, and ignored Cuba's decades-long struggle for freedom. The control over history was assured by the creation of a

National Archive during the first U.S. military occupation (1898–1902) and then of a highly positivistic and conservative Academy of History in 1910 that adopted a pro–United States line of argument. The landmark events that functioned as key sites of memory for the relationship between Cuba and the United States were the explosion of the battleship *Maine* in Havana and the victory in the Battle of San Juan Hill in Santiago.

The explosion of the *Maine* in 1898, which caused hundreds of U.S. casualties, served as a pretext for the U.S. declaration of war with Spain. A monument to this event was first planned by the government in 1913. The aim was to integrate it into the symbolic scenery of the Malecón, which was, and still is, a site for the negotiation of Cuban-U.S. relationships. Initially planned as a simple obelisk, the final monument of 1925 dominated the square and incorporated two large *Maine* cannons and the U.S. bald eagle at the top.

The event was a symbolic statement of Cuban subordination to the United States. The Cuban sculptor Félix Cabarrocas considered that "Maine's remains could only rest in the peace of the eternal, majestic and harmless Cuban soil, grateful and happy to support their weight" (quoted in del Castañal 1913:10). The authorities launched a commemorative book, written in English and Spanish, soon after the inauguration, which was conceived as a demonstration of "the Cuban gratitude towards the majestic U.S. nation" (Santovenia 1928:124). The book provides an in-depth account of the alleged U.S. support of Cuban freedom, which "throughout at least a half-century and with different intensities, was one of the factors that concurred to the liberation endeavor" (Santovenia 1928:124). The monument and the book were intended to be read as reminders of Cuba's debt to the American citizens who perished in support of Cuban freedom.

Different monuments were built throughout Cuba to commemorate U.S. military events: the first disembarkation of the marines in Daiquirí or the ten-year anniversary of the seizure of Santiago (Iglesias Utset 2014:32; Society of the Army of Santiago de Cuba 1906). In Santiago, the central symbolic area was San Juan Hill. Here the Cuban-U.S. victory that marked the end of the war against Spain took place in 1898. The area remained under U.S. military control until 1927, becoming a contested landscape of memory where many overlapping and conflicting interpretations of events took place. The United States made a strong investment in symbolic practices to transform the site into an icon of the U.S. view of the

Figure 2.6. *Above*: U.S. Marines at the inauguration of works at the *Maine* monument. *Below left*: the first *Maine* monument, which was destroyed by a cyclone. *Below right*: the second *Maine* monument. Source: Santovenia (1928).

liberation of Cuba. U.S. officials erected monuments before 1902 and then again in 1906, 1923, and 1926, and in 1906 they put up plaques in English, imposing their interpretation of the conflict ("Monument in Cuba" 1926; "Monuments in Cuba" 1906).

The overt intention of these heritage works was to disregard the Cuban role in the war. For instance, the first obelisk erected commemorated the U.S. soldiers who died in the "war between the United States and Spain." After the Hill once again became Cuban property in 1927, the government in the following years erected three Cuban monuments glorifying their army. However, the symbolic ambiguity of the place endured until Fidel inaugurated an obelisk in 1998 that reinterpreted the site and put an end to the U.S. narrative of the liberation of Cuba at the Hill and presented Cubans as active actors in the war. The obelisk reads "Hispanic-Cuban-American war" and demonstrates the Cuban revolutionary interpretation of the war (see chapter 6).

In sum, heritage was a contested terrain between competing representations, symbols, and narratives of Cuban national identity, demonstrating that Cubans engaged with the past in many ways. However, this does not mean that they managed neither to extricate the colonial past completely nor to oppose U.S. hegemonic narratives. Rather, elements from both were always ambiguously and partially incorporated or rejected according to the political situation and the intellectual climate. What mattered was the construction of a usable past in the service of a new nation, which shared some elements with Spain and the United States but differed from both.

Representations of Nation and Identity

Beyond the negotiation of Cuban identity negatively against Spanish colonialism and U.S. imperialism, the Republic also managed to create different affirmative representations of national identity. Instead of resignifying or neglecting preexisting heritage, the creation of newly made representations required choosing new contents and forms. These representations were functional instruments for the powerful classes and the state to educate Cubans into what national heritage was and the values it embodied. Republican heritage representations reflected the values and beliefs of an elite group that adopted European and North American patterns of culture and consumption, which they saw as models for articulating successful civilizing projects. Indeed, as Kapcia (2005:19–20) has argued, it seemed easier and safer for Cuban elites to ground and develop a differential identity in the consumption and appreciation of firmly established and more prestigious cultures.

This form of cultural colonialism represented a continuation of late colonial cultural modernism and neoclassic aesthetics. It led to the creation of material representations of the Cuban nation that resembled previous European experiences in which "statuomania" was a key process. Statuomania, the use of public spaces for embodying senses of national history, was particularly pronounced in France, Germany, and elsewhere in Europe throughout the nineteenth century (Agulhon 1978). Cuba combined this European model with those of countries with stories of foreign domination, wherein dominant groups sought to reinforce their legitimacy by highlighting their connection with the heritage of struggles for national independence. Resorting to the War of Independence against Spain and its main heroes and villains was unavoidable in Cuba, owing to the lack of a glorious indigenous past that could be instrumentalized, as was the case in Mexico and Peru. Moreover, the celebrations and speeches surrounding the inauguration of monuments allowed elite groups to reassert their connection with the Independence War heroes, thus reinstating the legitimacy of their claim to power in front of Cubans (e.g., Miró Argenter 1918).

In the main Cuban cities, and especially Havana, the various European-inspired urban plans contemplated the creation of interconnected areas of symbolic and monumental display in relation with urban expansion. The monument to Martí in Central Square built in 1905 was the first of a series of monuments celebrating the heroes of the War of Independence. Then, the monuments to Antonio Maceo in 1916 and Máximo Gómez in 1935 were inaugurated with great public fanfare along the Malecón. They represented the height of the European-style monumental art, placing the heroes at the top of a pedestal and a park or a square surrounding it. The monuments to *Maine* and to Calixto García in 1958 consolidated the symbolic area of the Malecón, which also connected with the lavish Avenida de los Presidentes (Avenue of the Presidents). This monumental street was ornamented with statues of different presidents and crowned by the monument of José Miguel Gómez in 1936. Dozens of monuments scattered throughout Havana completed the republican heritagescape.

The similarities between most republican monuments point to the existence of an aesthetic canon. Two main groups prevailed: those dedicated to military heroes of the War of Independence and those celebrating contemporary presidents, political figures, or intellectuals. The public relevance of heritage became apparent in Julio Villondo y Bertrán's radio talks about Havana's monuments, wherein he emphasized that monumentalizing the heroes was fundamental to reinvigorating the "decadent and almost inexistent national spirit" (Villoldo y Bertrán 1938:10). Typically, monuments had a base, a pedestal, and a sculpture and were placed at the

Figure 2.7. The republican monumental canon: monument to Alejandro Rodríguez in Rome, just before embarking for Havana. Source: *Bohemia*, "Alejandro
Rodríguez" (1917).

center of squares. The urban plans of Havana stipulated that statues of
mayors had to be equestrian and look toward the sea, while presidents had
to be represented standing and facing inland (Martínez Inclán 1925:159).

The materials employed were intrinsically related with the constitution
of national identity and values. Bronze and Italian Carrara marble were

considered high-quality models that could encourage the national spirit (Lauderman Ortiz 1951). As the sculptor Emeterio Santovenia argued, these materials and the monuments built with them served "to praise the practice of sublime acts" (Santovenia 1915:2). Most monument sculptures were made in Italy, and many Italian sculptors, such as Domenico Boni, Aldo Gamba, and Giovanni Nicolini, settled in Cuba, attracted by the high number of works and high wages (Gutiérrez May 1919). The participation of Spanish sculptors in monument competitions garnered contempt and, for different reasons, was criticized both in Cuba and in Spain ("Monumento a Máximo Gómez" 1919; Freyre de Andrade 1919).

Most Cuban provincial cities replicated Havana's model of heritagization, most notably after President Alfredo Zayas' legal requirement in 1922 that sculptures or busts of Martí be erected in the central park of each municipality (Tamames Henderson 2012). This is one of the various signs revealing Catholic influence—including Afro-Cuban syncretic Catholicism—in the construction of Cuban symbols of national identity since independence until present. Not only were images of Martí reproduced metonymically in different locations, as a saint with similar altarlike shrines surrounded by trees, but his image was also worshipped and he was often referred as a saint.

The main heritage actors in both Havana and the provinces were social and cultural associations, often comprising elite individuals seeking public self-representation for political purposes. These groups played a central role in representing notions of national identity in the public sphere, promoting the construction of monuments through popular collection, with most donors coming from the civic elite. This pattern of monument construction was a continuation of that late colonial period and was common until the 1930s.

After the withdrawal of the Platt Amendment in 1934 and the end of political U.S. control over Cuba, there was a significant shift in politics that affected heritage policies. The state assumed a greater role in the promotion of national culture and symbols through heritage works, although with limited resources. The heritage dynamics of this period can be encapsulated in the construction of the huge Plaza Cívica (Civic Square) and the new monument to Martí, which took more than two decades to be conceived and built. The construction of the Plaza Cívica started in 1937 and was completed shortly before the Revolution in 1958, when it became world-famous as Revolution Square. Plaza Cívica and the monument became the focus of heated intellectual and political debates that placed the national question at center stage. These debates called into question the late colonial neoclassic canon and its suitability for representing the postcolonial national identity. Without going into the history of the planning and construction of the monument, the various contests held, and the debates about urban and architectural planning, my analysis privileges those elements that affected later developments in the Cuban heritage field: aesthetics, nation, and representation.

The project to build a monument to Martí in the Plaza Cívica emerged from the convergence of three elements. First, the state was interested in developing a solid symbolic power through the iconic representation of Martí. Second, there was the belief, at least from 1921 onward, that the old monument to Martí in Central Square was too modest and inappropriate. Third, the completion of modern urban and monumental plans in Havana connected the new city center with the monumental area of the Malecón. This spatial connection was also a symbolic reassertion of the temporal continuity of national identity. The monument had to materialize a connection between Cuba's past, present, and future, concretizing a symbolic affirmation of Cuban independence through the figure of Martí. Indeed, the project affirmed that the monument served to "preserve the legacy of the past and signal the historical connection of Martí with Céspedes and Maceo" ("Plaza Cívica" 1951:14). At the time, one close collaborator with de Leuchsenring, architect Luis Bay Sevilla, considered the monument to Martí "a sign of deep Cubanness, of patriotic sentiment [. . .] It is probably the higher symbol of our nationality" (Bay Sevilla 1940:21). Thus, as Rafael Rojas puts it, whereas the first decades of the Republic "placed Martí in a heroic pantheon shared with Antonio Maceo and Máximo Gómez," the last three decades "crowned Martí as the prince of all heroes, the sole monarch of the Cuban nation" (Rojas 2006:10).

A national commission created for the purpose launched an international competition calling for monument proposals to represent Martí. The project of architect Aquiles Maza and sculptor José Sicre came first, after multiple stages, in 1942. Their project envisioned a monumental open-air temple emulating Greco-Roman classical forms with neoclassic standards, with friezes representing Martí's life and a large statue of a muscular nude Martí of Olympian proportions. They conceived the

Figures 2.8 and 2.9. *Top*: half-nude classic Martí designed by Sicre. *Bottom*: dressed Martí, following the requirements of various members of the jury. Source: MICONS Archive.

project as a metamonument, with a library and a museum that would contain previous monuments, relics, documents, and offerings to Martí, including Martí's original monument in Parque Central.

The competition's committee, composed entirely of military men without the input of any artists, sculptors, or architects, suggested changes to the project and paralyzed it. Finally, in 1953, during the celebration of the centenary of the birth of Martí, the dictator Batista dismissed the winning project, and a national commission decided to build the project that had ranked fourth in the original competition: a star-shaped tower designed by Juan Labatut, a shape that, according to the intellectual Jorge Mañach, "greatly pleased those members of the jury with stars" (Mañach 1953:98), referring to the military members of the jury. Contrary to Maza's project, Labatut's envisioned a monument that precluded individual reflection and self-identification with Martí. His emphasis on visual aspects and motion reflected his conception of the citizen as a passive observer, as revealed in his theorization of monuments. For Labatut, monuments

> create an architectural air space or small visible man-made world of which *each individual is a center, an observer* [. . .] The quality of man's judgment [. . .] will depend on many factors [. . .] the size of the elements and their shape, texture, and relationship; the motion of the *observer's eyes*; the time spent *looking*; the motion of the *observer's* body in relation to the environment; the successive distances from the elements of the environment to the *retina*; the *visual sensibility* of the *observer* and his knowledge, feeling, and imagination; the influence of preceding *visual experiences*. (Labatut 1952; emphasis mine)

After various corruption scandals, an agreement was achieved: the star-shaped monument would be complemented with the statue of Martí designed by Sicre in the original project. But the dissonance created by Martí's monument reached the university and political movements. Radical intellectuals and architecture students fiercely opposed the star-shaped project favored by Batista, arguing that it had been conceived as a vulgar imitation of the national flag, which copied elements from U.S. buildings (Estévez 1953a, b; La futura Plaza Cívica 1950). Anticipating the large process of resignification implemented by the Revolution after 1959, they criticized the monument, arguing that it was a fascist pastiche emulating

Figures 2.10 and 2.11. *Above*: Labatut's original project in 1943. *Right*: design of the project without the statue of Martí at the top, 1953. Source: MICONS archive.

the architectural eclecticism promoted by Hitler, Franco, and Mussolini in Europe. Thus, if the monument was built as projected, it could only be seen as "the expression of a backward and uncultured people" (Porro Hidalgo et al. 1958:46).

For these students and intellectuals, the representation of Martí should be figurative and modest: a Martí for and of the people. Anticipating the functionalist and antiaesthetic ideas pervading monument production that would linger during the early years of the Revolution, radical architects considered that if a monument had to be erected, "it should never be ornamental, but functional and useful, which would be in tune with the thoughts and desires of the master [Martí]" (de Quesada and Bay Sevilla 1943:396). More deeply, critics of the project were challenging the monument concept as such. In doing so, they deviated from both the models conceived in the Western tradition of commemoration: the religious version adopted by moderate intellectuals and the modernist-fascist one supported by Batista and his followers.

The most prominent moderate Cuban intellectuals, instead, supported the original Maza and Sicre project of the Olympian Martí temple. Analyzing their understanding of heritage sheds light on what they considered the appropriate representation of national identity. Their praise of European neoclassicism was a clear manifestation of continuity with late colonial cultural modernism and an acknowledgement of the Cuban inferiority that evidenced the intellectual elites' coloniality of power. For instance, architect José Cortina argued, referring to the European tradition, that Cuba "should not deviate from that consecrated aesthetic current to create new monument styles, a matter in which we are only humble amateurs" (Cortina 1953:331–333).

Opening a long-standing debate in Cuba between abstract and realist art, and reflecting the elitist and pedagogic aims of their project, Maza and Sicre argued against those calling for an abstract approach to representation. For them,

a people [Cubans] with such fragmented cultural basis and beliefs can associate abstract forms [. . .] with a fact [. . .] but it cannot go beyond that [. . .] The monument should be understandable for all Cubans and Americans generally. That is, it has to fulfill an educative mission [. . .] It must be an educator of the people, as artworks should not be made to praise the masses, but to guide them. (Maza and Sicre 1953:320)

We have seen that radical intellectuals and students considered that the monument should be for and by the people. Instead, Maza and Sicre saw it as an elite instrument for guiding the uneducated masses and articulated its pedagogic intent in religious terms through the idea of the temple. Moderate republican intellectuals wholeheartedly supported this view. For Mañach, the idea of the temple "deeply concurs with Martí's apostolate, a mystic of Freedom, and with the spiritual attitude of almost religious veneration peculiar to the worship to Martí" (Mañach 1944:62). The historian and specialist in Martí's life and works, Félix Lizaso, similarly thought that Martí's monument should function as an altar and that Martí should be equated with God: "a man redemptory of men" (quoted in Maza and Sicre 1953:320). Lizaso considered it an error to represent a humble and simple Martí, because "monuments are erected in the posterity to reflect what the celebrated man represents" (Lizaso 1953:215). Therefore, he charged against those promoting a modest, functional, and realistic representation of Martí, advocating a symbolic representation that aimed to "present not the person, but the ideas that he embodied [. . .] in a transcendental form" (Lizaso 1953:218). For de Leuchsenring, this justified representing Martí as an "idealized figure, with muscles of a hero, wrapped in a toga proper to geniuses or apostles" (de Leuchsenring 1955a:38).

The centenary of Martí's birth in 1953 entailed the beginning of a process of resignification of his figure that would continue after the Revolution in 1959. However, as a heritage intervention that aimed to transform civic consciousness, the negotiation of the monument also involved a profound debate about modes of heritage representation, and not only about the contents being represented. Maza and Sicre's project and their supporters saw Martí as a timeless figure outside history. The temple design created a sacred internal space that directed the focus of the public toward the statue of Martí as a personification of the nation. The project envisioned a celebration of the transcendental ideas of Martí, who, for Timothy Hyde, was "extracted from the coarse confines of body, contemporaneity, and contingency, and transferred to a timeless, quasi-religious realm" (Hyde 2012:232). In contrast, the proposal by Labatut was embedded in

Figures 2.12 and 2.13. *Top*: assemblage of the huge statue of Martí in 1958. Source: "Editorial Arquitectura" (1958). *Bottom*: final view of the monumental complex. Source: MICONS archive.

the progression of history. A historical artifact and an iconic relationship symbolized the core of the national identity: the Cuban flag embodying the Cuban nation. Labatut's modern forms and historical contents contrasted with the classic forms and timeless contents of Sicre and Maza's proposal. The final monument to Martí, however, was an ambiguous hybrid of modernist architecture with neoclassical figurative sculpture ("Editorial Arquitectura" 1958).

The interpretation of the monument to Martí revealed not only the dissociation between political elites and moderate intellectuals but also how both disregarded radical heritage views and saw themselves as the true representatives of the national spirit. Whereas Batista's state machine was concerned with building a solid symbolic power, Cuban moderate intellectuals aimed at celebrating Martí in mystic and religious terms. The fascist architecture of the star-shaped project supported by the state created an iconic relationship between Martí, the nation, and the monument. The tower forced citizens to experience the abstract grandeur of a national symbol, which imposed its meaning by its scale and conveyed a sense of human subservience to power. In turn, the neoclassic temple supported by moderate intellectuals offered an alternative architectural environment for popular engagement. It aimed to sacralize Martí and put him in a macro-temple, drawing on metonymy rather than metaphor: it attempted to create a place where Cubans and their master Martí could establish a sacred interaction. The architectural configuration of the monument encouraged the interaction and circulation of citizens, who could learn the history and life of Martí within its walls. Instead of an imposition of an iconic symbol, the temple represented Martí as an educator and a guide for the people.

The monument to Martí was an attempt to develop a physical representation of a coherent national identity. As such, it had to reconcile the demands of various social actors. Its representation had to keep up with the greatness of Martí's ideas but also had to be modest; it had to transcend his mere human embodiment but also had to be figurative; it had to be symbolic but easily understandable, so it could be pedagogic; and it had to follow European neoclassical canons to be regarded as a symbol of modernization. In representing Martí, Cuban elites replaced his revolutionary ideas by promoting him as a national icon and a secular saint. This displaced attention from the potentially problematic political interpretation of his writings under a dictatorship to the creation of an iconic monument of uncomplicated reading. The open-ended interpretation of Martí's ideas was arrested to create a fixed representation of national identity. In the context of dictatorship, Martí could provide a usable past only as a silent and reified icon, not as a guiding mystic or apostle and even less as a modest revolutionary. By making him appear as the symbol of certain transcendent and ahistorical ideas, he could easily be set aside from the competing and contested narrations of the nation that—quite literally—fought for hegemony during the 1950s.

Nation and Tradition: Heritage Preservation as Nation-Building

As in other postcolonial countries, the identification between the state and the diverse national cultures emerging after independence was troublesome in Cuba. The resignification of past material culture and the incorporation of "folk cultures "were other attempts at connecting tradition with a vision of the nation's future prospects. Recovering the sorrowful materiality of the colonial times necessarily implied a parallel process of sanitization and selection of the past to highlight Cuban features while neglecting Spanish elements. Intellectuals and professionals intrinsically connected the selection of which past to preserve to the definition of "real" Cubanness. They conceived of the endeavor as a civilizing and pedagogic mission, whereby past monuments and traditions could provide guidelines for determining proper Cuban behavior, morality, and even racial composition.

The group of intellectuals guiding the preservation efforts was strongly influenced by modern European and Enlightenment ideas. This is not a surprising attitude of cultural elites; the French Revolution had signified destruction as retrograde and equated preservation with progressive values. Their fondness for preserving the colonial past was related to the attempt to highlight the European roots of Cuban culture, which led them as far as supporting whitening policies against the so-called Africanization of Cuba (de Leuchsenring 1925). Whitening policies involved the promotion of white emigration (mostly from Spain) to "improve" the racial component of Cuba. In this sense, intellectuals like de Leuchsenring adopted the eugenic and racist criteria prevailing in Western countries that associated the prevalence of nonwhites in Latin America with backwardness.

However, as Christabelle Peters (2010:18) has noted, this tendency was counterbalanced by a shift after 1930 toward celebrating the contributions of black people and Africanía (Africanness) as part of the essence of Cubanness.

But whitening policies were also related to the debates among republican white intellectuals in the fields of music, art, history, literature, and architecture about whether they should build a Hispanic cultural community, rather than only a Cuban one. These debates were especially heated after the end of formal U.S. political control over Cuba, in 1934 (González Aróstegui 2003). The rise of Pan-Hispanism in Cuba and Latin America during the first half of the twentieth century facilitated the recovery of a colonial past that was proudly regarded as a source of cultural and symbolic inspiration. This revealed the continuation of the coloniality of power among Cuban intellectuals, a feature they shared with their Latin American counterparts. As Walter Mignolo (2000) has shown, Latin American nations built their identity by neglecting their relationship with local popular cultures and associating themselves symbolically with Europe.

At the same time, the symbolic abandonment of Havana's colonial area raised an awareness of the differences between the new city and the old city, and nostalgia for the latter. Old Havana started to be seen as something unique that could be preserved as a symbol of national identity (Hill 2012:191). The urban plans for Havana projecting the partial destruction and modernization of the old city heightened the contradiction between preservation and modernization. The constant refurbishing and tearing down of colonial buildings similarly put Old Havana in the spotlight. As late as 1955, the Asociación de Propietarios de La Habana Vieja (Old Havana's Homeowners Association) demanded the widening of streets and the creation of green areas, which would require the destruction of most of its colonial architecture ("Habana Vieja" 1955).

A growing interest in "the past" in all academic disciplines and cultural organizations counterbalanced this modernizing thrust. Cuban intellectuals and especially historians started to function as self-conscious builders of national identity, looking for the national roots in the past. Led by de Leuchsenring and the renowned anthropologist Fernando Ortiz, they raised preservation awareness in different newspapers and promoted the creation of most of the heritage-related institutions and legislation in Cuba during the Republic. This includes the Junta Nacional de Arqueología (National Archaeology Board), Patronato Pro-urbanismo (Pro-Urbanism Trust), Corporación Nacional de Turismo (National Tourism Corporation), and the Comisión de Monumentos, Edificios y Lugares Históricos y Artísticos Habaneros (Commission of Monuments, Buildings, and Historic and Artistic Places of Havana), among many others. Ortiz exemplified the figure of a public intellectual who was also a leading representative of the pan-Hispanic cultural community. He directed the Sociedad Económica de amigos del País (Society of Friends of the Country), the Sociedad del Folklore Cubano (Society of Cuban Folklore), the Sociedad Hispano-Cubana de Cultura (Cuban-Spanish Society of Culture) and the Cuban Academia de Historia (Academy of History) and was also a member of the Spanish Academy of History.

The Academia de Historia was established in 1910. It was closely connected with the government and promoted the creation of an epic national narrative based on the War of Independence. The Academia Nacional de Artes y Letras (National Academy of Arts and Letters) was created in the same year to promote the arts and "to veil for the conservation of the artistic monuments of the nation" (Roldán Oliarte 1940:1048). Although some of the intellectuals leading these institutions were openly critical of different governments, these same governments granted them the necessary support to maintain their autonomy and performance. The role of culturally aware politicians such as Mario García Kohly was fundamental in the promotion of these institutions (Dihigo 1937). This reveals the complex relations that existed between cultural and political elites and shows that heritage served to negotiate the relationships between them.

The most salient event in terms of heritage management was the creation of the OHCH in 1938. The OHCH played a primary role in terms of heritage preservation, historical publications, archive and library work, and musealization, that is, the operation that extracts physical or conceptual realities from their context and brings them to the field of the museum. The OHCH director de Leuchsenring defined it as a "cultural institution with a national scope, responsible for the promotion of the culture of Havana, the nation and the Americas, with an eminently popular projection" (quoted in Mola Fernández 1985:75). The OHCH faced the contradiction of promoting the preservation of traditions and colonial remains while affirming that this was a contribution to the modernization of Cuba. In doing so, it sought to select and aestheticize the past according to those practices conceived as "modern" or up-to-date at the time. De Leuchsenring encapsulated the heritage principles of the OHCH in the following paragraph:

> Few colonial Cuban cities have been spared from a misled conception of progress and renovation, either unconscious or perverse, an awkward iconoclasm of a past which, in a timely fashion, the liberating revolution tried to wipe out regarding its political and administrative system [. . .] but which should have been respected in its historic and artistic values, its traditions and legends, thus conceiving as material and spiritual documents the monuments, buildings, squares, quarters, streets, corners, furniture, paintings, sculptures, artworks, plaques, sinks, railings and traditional leisure, civic and religious fairs, created and maintained by the people. (de Leuchsenring 1943b:38)

The OHCH clearly differentiated between the "political and administrative system" and the cultural legacies of the colonial times that were considered a valuable heritage to incorporate into the new national identity. To ensure the preservation of that heritage, the OHCH created the City Museum in the palace of the Capitanes Generales of Havana in 1942. De Leuchsenring also encouraged the recovery of hundreds of colonial street names and traditions, leading various initiatives in defense of the preservation of the colonial architectural style and of particular colonial buildings, most famously the church of Paula and the Santa Clara convent. He raised public awareness and influenced decisions concerning the selection of colonial symbols and buildings, traditions, and customs. A letter to the Minister of Education reveals his interest in promoting a nationalist turn in Cuban education through the selection of historical texts for schooling (de Leuchenring 2013[1944]:397).

The hundreds of letters preserved in the City Archive reveal the close bond he established with intellectuals and politico-economic elites. These connections, as well as the government's interest in promoting tourism, resulted in a project to restore Old Havana under the presidency of Gerardo Machado after 1929. The relocation of the institutions of power from the Plaza the Armas to the Parque Central area paved the way for the restoration of the Capitanes Generales, El Templete, the cathedral, and other key buildings. The idea was to heritagize Old Havana, creating an aesthetic colonial coherence to suit the expectations of tourists coming from the United States. This involved, for instance, the removal of the colored plasters covering buildings and leaving the grey stone in sight, which is today perceived as the sign of colonial authenticity by both visitors and locals (Segre 2003:130). Not all intellectuals approved of the heritage recovery process, however. For instance, Ortiz (1987:40) considered the cathedral and the convent of San Francisco as ugly buildings that lacked interest and relevance—especially the former, which was refurbished and lavishly ornamented to attract tourists (Bay Sevilla 1937; Patronato 1941).

In newspapers and academic journals, professionals, journalists, and intellectuals constantly argued for the creation of heritage legislation, especially after 1934 (e.g., Bens Arrarte 1935). De Leuchsenring considered heritage preservation "an urgent necessity of our nascent nation," fundamental to "foster love for history and tradition" and to "move forward towards Cubanness" (de Leuchsenring 1941:46). The sophistication of some OHCH initiatives is surprising for their time, such as the highly developed Ley de los Monumentos Históricos, Arquitectónicos y Arqueológicos (Law of Historic, Architectural and Archaeological Monuments), written in 1939 with the support of the OHCH. But the OHCH also promoted legislation for heritage protection during war, promoted cultural exchange with foreign institutions as a representative of Cuba, developed a complex system of book borrowing between private libraries and the public, and denounced touristification processes. Moreover, the OHCH expanded its institutional framework and functioning to other cities such as Trinidad, Santiago, and Cienfuegos. Thus, the OHCH functioned as a semipublic institution that influenced local and nationwide decisions and promoted its own institutionalization and legislative processes.

In its quest to raise heritage preservation awareness and to expand culture, the OHCH never untangled questions of national identity, history, materiality, and morality. The cultural modernist ethos underpinning the OHCH was apparent in its self-description as a pedagogic entity inculcating Cubans' nationalist and universalist values. Indeed, de Leuchsenring considered it his main duty "to bring the people the benefits of culture and education" (de Leuchsenring 1942b:50). Intellectuals close to the OHCH situated the mission of the institution beyond contemporary political struggles: "Because we are eclectic due to our different education, we believe in *universal reason,* which can apply to every man in any latitude" (García Serrato 1938:36; italics in original). This preservationist, universalist, and Enlightenment perspective was not devoid of contradictions in a country with high illiteracy rates and lacking most modern facilities and infrastructures. For instance, for de Leuchsenring (1945), the reconstruction of the city of Bayamo should reconcile the construction of sewers and other basic infrastructures with the preservation of its colonial aesthetic charm. Preserving tradition was deemed fundamental because modern countries did so, but Cuba was not yet a modern nation in terms of socioeconomic development. This generated a contradiction between the values of popular classes and those of elites.

The OHCH carried out the metacultural and rational selection of heritage in parallel with a pedagogic and civilizing task aimed at the education of Cubans in terms of taste, behavior, and hygiene. For de Leuchsenring, the love for "the homeland and the belief in it as a heritage from our ancestors" was linked with notions of "public good and altruist spirit [...] whose absence is a fatal defect of the Cuban, turning him a miserable egoist" (de Leuchsenring 1943a:38). De Leuchsenring was also concerned about the noisy, superficial, and festive Cuban character. This led him to fiercely advocate the suppression of Cenas Martianas, popular dinners in honor of Martí where people danced, drank, and ate (de Leuchsenring 1955b). He considered it appropriate to reinterpret Martí's heritage as worship or a mystic devotion but not as a popular party.

This attitude reveals a key feature of the nation-building efforts of intellectuals: they were interested in the "popular" only when they could frame it as a folkloric expression of a civilized and modern national identity. Not only the OHCH but also the members of the Sociedad del Folklore Cubano (Society of Cuban Folklore) studied traditions as contemporary manifestations of a deeply rooted Cuban spirit that they had to recover. As an editorial of the Society's journal read, "In Cuba, the moment one cuts through the surface of the mentality of the People, one finds the rich veins of ancestral tradition because in the subsoil of Cuban popular culture lie unknown deposits of very different civilizations" ("Editorial Archivos" 1924:5–6). Alejandra Bronfman (2005:34) and Ricardo Quiza (2014:273) have shown in multiple instances how anthropologists and archaeologists engaged in this search and in the "feverish imagining" of the national past in the present.

The analysis of heritage illustrates how Cuban intellectuals assumed what Madina Tlostanova and Walter Mignolo describe as the "civilizing and developmental mission of modernity" (Tlostanova and Mignolo 2009:133). They fulfilled this mission through two convergent tasks: the imposition of criteria of taste and aesthetics among the masses, and the reinterpretation and negotiation of a problematic colonial past. By using heritage to connect origins with manners, Cuban intellectuals established a hinge between ethics and aesthetics, virtue and beauty, that was instrumental to the disciplining of the bodies and minds of Cubans. Heritage provided an effective material and symbolic support for Cuban intellectuals in the development of a modern ideology that aestheticized the past and naturalized a model of cultural and heritage production imported from Western countries. As in other postcolonial contexts, intellectual elites assumed the values of foreign dominant powers as "theirs"—both from the ex-metropolis and the new neocolonial power—while imposing these values locally to reproduce epistemic, political, and economic hierarchies. In this sense, the OHCH represented a form of continuity with the cultural modernism that characterized the late colonial period, but one now pervaded by nationalist rhetoric.

There were differences between the modern and Enlightenment ethics of intellectuals and the authoritarian and imposing ideology of politico-economic elites. For both groups, however, the past was becoming a "foreign country" to be overcome, either by its resignification or its incorporation into national identity or through its destruction for the purpose of modernization. The result from this combination of interests was a postcolonial process whereby the nation was performed in the present by both erasing and recuperating the past. Nonetheless, even if intellectuals aimed at the expansion of education and culture to inculcate the national idea among people, the politico-economic elites were reluctant to do so, a common contradiction in most Latin American countries. Intellectuals often established alliances with politico-economic groups and technocratic modernizers in government. However, the inability of the latter to develop a coherent project of a modern and educated Cuban nation led most intellectuals to support the revolutionary struggle against Batista. When the Revolution came, de Leuchsenring openly backed Fidel and claimed that he had run out of enemies against which to fight (quoted in Mola Fernández 1985:84). His post-Revolution letters reveal an intense exchange with people and institutions from the Eastern Bloc. With his death in 1964, the OHCH faded away. It was only in 1993 that the institution regained its former splendor, becoming again an ambiguous but powerful actor in Cuba's political, social, and cultural life.

The Timeless Nation: Museums

In an attempt to magnify the accomplishments of the revolutionary government in the area of museums, Cuban heritage director Marta Arjona Pérez (2004 [1986]) famously affirmed that the Republic had managed to create only six museums. Although the exact number escapes us, there were certainly more than twenty museums in the Republic (Stephen Thomas and Rodríguez Morey 1954:7). Museums played an important, if erratic and inconsistent, role in the Republic's construction of a national identity. Indeed, Cuba was at the forefront of museum building and development among Latin American countries at the time. The creation and naturalization of shared visual representations of the essence of Cuba and their socialization in museums was a key instrument for establishing national communal bonds by linking citizenship, culture, and the nation-state.

The main historical museums were born soon after independence. Rich businessmen and intellectuals created the Oscar María de Rojas in 1899 in Cárdenas and the Emilio Bacardí in 1901 in Santiago. Both shared a similar panoptical structure and received most objects from donations made by Cuban people through popular collections (Leyva 1922). The U.S. occupation government initially supported their establishment but soon became suspicious of them as symbols of Cuban national identity, even closing the Oscar María de Rojas in 1907. Indeed, postcolonial Cuban museums served as key spaces for the preservation of memory and for the political and cultural negotiation of the images of the national past. They were part of a nationwide phenomenon consisting of the collection of historical relics, a fashionable entertainment and self-appointed national duty among postindependence Cuban elites and middle-class professionals. This process spurred the creation of many historic collections throughout Cuba, most notably in Matanzas, Remedios, Camagüey, and Holguín. Eventually, only some of those collections became museums, like the García Feria in Holguín, between 1930 and 1954, the Ignacio Agramonte in Camagüey,

Figures 2.14 and 2.15. *Top*: Museum Bacardí in 1918. *Bottom*: Oscar María de Rojas in 1918. Source: Torriente Govín (2012).

between 1941 and 1955, the José María Espinosa in Remedios, the Maritime Museum in Mariel, the City Museum of Havana in 1942, and various museums at the University of Havana.

These museums shared their difficulties with achieving institutional stability and their focus on the recovery of relics from the War of Independence and its heroes. They also imitated Western taxonomic and colonial museums and collected a wide variety of objects, including paintings and artworks and archaeological, ethnographic, and exotic artifacts and rarities, such as the Egyptian mummy in the Bacardí and the tropical stuffed animals in the Oscar María de Rojas. A secondary interest of these museums was the recovery of indigenous material culture. Emilio Bacardí was an enthusiastic collector of Amerindian artifacts, and a group of amateur archaeologists searched for indigenous artifacts and sold them to Emilio for decades. The interest in the Amerindian legacy for building an alternative historic lineage to that of the Spanish was related to the creation of the museum of anthropology Montané at the University of Havana in 1903 (Rangel Rivero 2013). The Montané broke with traditional colonial museums that focused exclusively on natural science, botany, and zoology for teaching purposes, considering its own task of preserving the anthropological heritage of the nation, which included the "Cuban" indigenous. The Montané preserved objects from archaeological excavations and taught extensively about Cuban history under an evolutionist framework (Bronfman 2005:59).

Recent Cuban scholarship has defined these museums as "modern," in opposition to the "traditional" colonial museums, owing to their public, didactic, and nationalist character as well as their attempts to classify and identify the elements on display (Martínez Carmenate 2010). This perspective, however, contrasts with that of witnesses to the time, such as José Bofill (1900), the first director of the Bacardí, who considered his activity to be the collection of objects, or Fernando Boytel, his successor in 1944, who wrote a report describing the museum as chaotic, disordered, and devoid of "any pattern of classification, which disorients the visitors" (Boytel ca. 1945). Certainly, the scientific discipline and profession of modern museology as understood in Western countries started only with the Revolution. However, Cuban museums in the Republic were epistemologically modern in the sense of attempting to create relations between history, people, and the nation and incorporating nature, aesthetics, and culture into the national framework.

The colonial museums did not display historical narratives, because these could raise political controversy in Cuba and threaten the interests of Spain. In contrast, postcolonial museums aimed at the institutionalization of patriotic memory and history from an openly nationalistic perspective. History museums served to define historic stages and to connect them with specific objects as symbols to be associated with a national heritage. This process helped to both reject the Spanish legacy and to establish a view of national history and identity that could be shared by the various Cuban regions and social classes and inculcated in the younger generations through education. Most republican intellectuals and historians, such as Miguel Varona and Ramiro Guerra, agreed that history served to generate patriotic feelings among children mainly because it transmitted knowledge about the War of Independence and its heroes (Cordoví Núñez 2012:101). Historians referred to the museum as the perfect complement to the school, and history handbooks devoted attention to museums (e.g., Cano 1918; González del Campo and Azcuy 1950; Trujillo 1914). Some historians proposed the creation of museums in schools and of one museum in each municipality (García Castañeda 1945). By 1920, in the Pinar del Río Province, there were 100 school museums and 250 showcases funded and managed by teachers to preserve animals and historic objects (García Valdés 1923:268).

The accumulation of historic objects as a result of the work of collectors and the second U.S. invasion of Cuba increased the public claims for a national museum (Bobadilla 1910). The government conceived the National Museum initially as a national history museum, whose aim was to collect "objects and relics [. . .] primarily those from our War of Independence" and to "strengthen the worship of our heroes and of the patriotism that characterizes our people" (G.C. 1910:2030). The official legislation reflected the coloniality of Cuban intellectuals at the time, as it explicitly affirmed that the National Museum should be "analogous to others that exist abroad" (G. C. 1910:2030). Also, the director of the National Museum between 1918 and 1967, Antonio Rodríguez Morey, strove to acquire reproductions of artworks of universal relevance, mainly from the Museo del Prado and other European museums ("Rodríguez Morey" 1920). Similarly, the promoters of the National Museum emphasized the modernist connection between aesthetics and morality, arguing that museums were institutions serving "to awaken among the people the love for beautiful things" (Bobadilla 1910). The letters between intellectuals and curators of the time, such as Emilio Heredia and Oscar María de Rojas, reflect their conception of the National Museum as an elite instrument for educating and civilizing Cubans (see Torriente Govín 2012:81). Antonio Rodríguez Morey would affirm some decades later that, through the celebration of its heritage in the National Museum, Cuba could now "be at the forefront in the tradition of universal civilization" (Rodríguez Morey 1944:6).

Eventually, the National Museum was expanded to comprise more topics and collect more relics, as the number of historic objects donated by Cubans increased (Museo Nacional de Cuba and Heredia y Mora 1913:4). The National Museum regulations proceeded to classify which objects went into each category and established practical guidelines for their recollection. Objects had to be historic ("related with the Fatherland, to stimulate the worship of the past"), scientific ("to promote public culture"), and artistic ("to encourage the affirmation of the fine arts") (G. C. 1913). Although the state apparently supported the National Museum and by 1925 had designed a new building for it, in reality it was underfunded and changed locations in Havana constantly, occupying three different buildings between 1913 and 1954 (Alonso González 2012). The official indifference could also reflect a broader lack of social interest in the National Museum at the time. This became apparent in its inauguration in 1913, which was attended by very few individuals and by no government dignitaries or indeed the president (Chroniqueur 1913). Nonetheless, the social support for the National Museum increased gradually over the course of the Republic, and even public rallies and funding campaigns were organized to these ends (Arroyo de Hernández 1947).

In its origins, the appearance of the National Museum was shocking, "forming a homogeneous pile of objects, one over the other [. . .] dusty and in dark rooms" (Gerardo Castellanos, quoted in García Santana 2010:66). It was viewed with contempt among intellectuals, for whom the quest for a national museum that matched Western standards was constant during the Republic. Furthermore, the lack of an adequate national museum was deemed harmful to national pride (Ruiz 1956). As the architect Enrique Caravia argued, "Only the museum shows us what we have

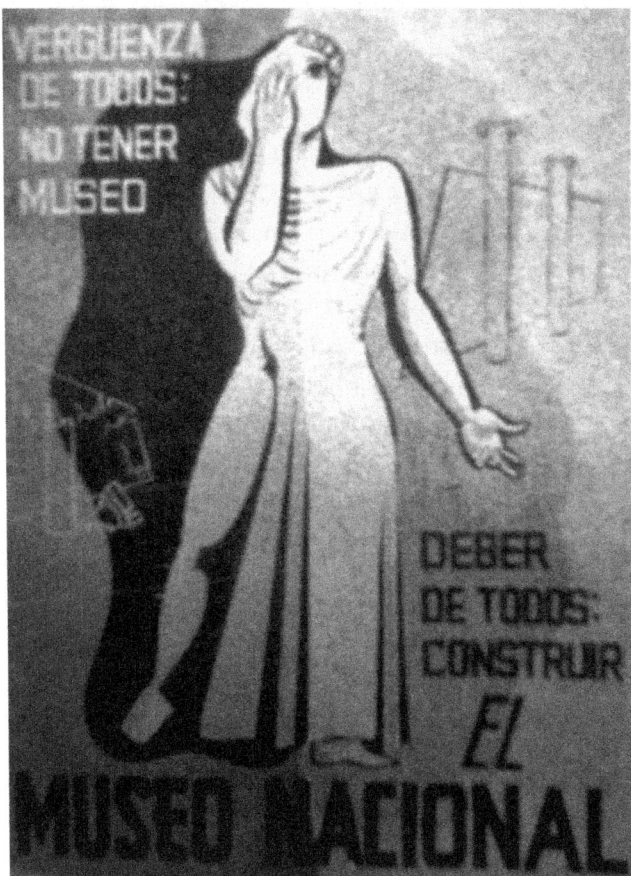

Figures 2.16 and 2.17. *Above*: public demonstrations and posters reclaiming the creation of a national museum. *Left*: poster reading "A shame for us all: not to have a museum: our duty is to build the National Museum." Source: Loose newspaper clippings from the magazine *Carteles*.

been to understand how we must be" (Caravia 1951:231). Not only could a museum connect past, present, and future, but it was also a powerful nation-building instrument, a pedagogic device with which to inculcate the idea of nation into the people. For architect Bay Sevilla, it could help to civilize the Cubans, because "from a moral viewpoint, museums contribute to improving the human condition" (Bay Sevilla 1941:19–20). The museum could improve the morality of Cubans by transmitting the national narrative to their children. For Rodríguez Morey, children could learn a lot in a museum: "In front of the relics of our heroes, of our martyrs, which would infiltrate their brains with the narration of the glorious deeds of our War of Independence, to venerate those who gave their lives in them" (Rodríguez Morey 1944:6).The passivity of the state led some civic actors to create organizations in support of the National Museum, including the Patronato Pro-museo Nacional (Pro-National Museum Trust) in 1946, then renamed the Sociedad de amigos del Museo Nacional (Society of Friends of the National Museum) in 1953, and the Patronato de Bellas Artes y Museos Nacionales (National Board of Fine Arts and National Museums) in 1954. Also, there was a Comité de Damas Pro-Museo Nacional (Board of Ladies Pro-National Museum), which consisted mainly of the wives of the richest and most politically powerful men in Cuba.

The Cuban state ultimately assumed the task of developing the National Museum, which was inaugurated in 1954. The dominant rhetoric of Cubanness among the elites emphasized the connection with Western countries, and the museum presented an opportunity to exhibit a symbol of progress and modernity. The tearing down of a traditional popular market to construct a new building for the National Museum accentuated the modernizing ethos behind the project and sparked criticism from UNESCO (Ichaso 1954). The institution was harshly criticized, and many did not consider it to be a proper museum due to its lack of facilities (Arjona Pérez 1981). Others liked it, such as the Nobel prize winner Alejo Carpentier (1993[1957]:213), who praised its modern design. More importantly, the National Museum shifted from its original conception as a history museum to a fine arts museum. Indeed, there were plans to transfer the historic collections from the National Museum to the City Museum (Zéndegui y Carbonell 1957), although this would occur only after the Revolution. As in nineteenth-century Europe, history museums were considered traditional, while art museums were considered symbols of modernity.

In conclusion, postcolonial museums in Cuba broke with traditional colonial museology. This does not necessarily mean that they became modern in the sense of Western museology, which they strove to emulate. Cuban museums resulted from intellectual elites' interest in contributing to the creation of a national identity, the pedagogic civilization of Cubans, and the expansion of public culture. The existence of museums is most significant when seen in light of the fact that Cuba was a largely rural and illiterate country; that it had museums at all reflects the elite character of urban intellectuals. Men like José Bofill, Oscar María de Rojas, and José García Castañeda made significant contributions to Cuban museology and museography that would shape future developments in the field. They conceived of museums as promoters of modernity that developed scientific and pedagogic criteria of classification and norms of taste in the arts. Those behind the promotion of museums were also aware that politico-economic elites were reluctant to sponsor cultural institutions, as would be expected of them in light of the philanthropic attitudes of elites in other Western countries. In a letter to José Bofill, Rodríguez Morey stated, "It is pointless to think that our wealthy men will support these institutions; the case of Bacardí is probably unique" (1928, quoted in Laguna Enrique 2013:146).

The development of museums in the Republic was inconsistent and partial, and museums generally lacked institutional support. This reflected the scant interest of politico-economic elites in cultural investment and their lack of a coherent identity as a group. Thus, museums in Cuba were only partially incorporated into what Michel Foucault (2007) describes as the process of governmentalization, through which the state assimilates and employs forms of cultural and social management developed by voluntary philanthropic associations. In terms of content, museums were articulated into separate fields, such as archaeology, rarities, or biology, rather than made to present a linear narrative. Museums linked the origin of the nation to the War of Independence through objects that established iconic relations with events or characters in the past. If modern Western museums were characterized by a civic ideal and the shift from showing rarity to showing representativeness (Bennett 1995:39), Cuban museums only partially matched these characteristics. Most museums were in fact private collections belonging to wealthy individuals, which was far from the ideal of public museums in modern societies. Similarly, the aim of museums to show representativeness in the attempt to become scientific and modern, and to develop a coherent representation of the nation, coexisted with an understanding of museums as repositories of rarities, such as Egyptian tombs or exotic animals. Like the ideal of an autonomous nation, the demand for modern museums according to Western standards remained elusive in Cuba.

Conclusion

The inception of Cuban national identity was intrinsically connected to the attempt to develop a modern conception of heritage that addressed the past in various ways. Accordingly, the interpretation that Cubans in the construction of the nation "hardly ever looked in and back" (Pérez 1999:93) needs to be more nuanced. Cubans dealt with the past in manifold ways and constantly invoked the past in their process of nation-state building. They also contested the U.S. attempt to create a narrative that legitimized its hegemony over Cuba.

However, the efforts to imitate Western standards by any means reflected the underlying coloniality of republican heritage policies. This form of cultural nationalism, which mirrored foreign models, was the response of Cuban elites to the twofold task of developing a modern nation-state while reproducing the differences between themselves and other social groups in terms of knowledge, taste, and values. To this end, cultural modernism and the neoclassic canon inherited from the late colonial period continued to function as the most common principles behind the creation of monuments and museums. However, the neoclassic canon merged with alternative heritage models. The clearest example of this was the monument to Martí and its combination of a neoclassic statue with modernist architecture. Cuba was not unique in this regard, however, and similar uses of the neoclassical idiom are to be found in many countries, including countries as far away as Taiwan or Thailand, with similarly complex relationships with Western colonialism.

The lack of a coherent, rich, and highly developed approximation to history was less the outcome of indifference to the past than of the deep contestation involved in the negotiation and representation of that past. Because heritage is constructed and defined through present circumstances, and because in Cuba those circumstances were highly contested during the Republic, heritage itself could not be otherwise. Moreover, heritage played a central role in the negotiation, selection, and preservation of the past and in representing the nation and generating national symbols and shared frameworks of communication for Cubans. This modernizing endeavor implied both the erasure and folklorization of tradition and the creation of a representation of the past that was consistent with elite criteria of culture, manners, knowledge, and taste. The powerful nationalist ideology that emerged lingers in present-day Cuba, especially in its emphasis on self-sacrifice and participation in battle as a prerequisite for access to state benefits and political inclusion. As in other postcolonial contexts, heroic action in the national myths generated a sanctified view of the nation and a sacred view of the heroes who sustained the meaning of rituals (Kapferer 1988).

Forms of cultural and social management first arose autonomously from the state during the Republic's first decades. They emerged via notions of civic virtue, including voluntary civic committees for building monuments or commemorating certain events and heroes, via philanthropic intellectuals concerned with the preservation of the national heritage, or via collectors who turned their houses into informal museums. Only after the 1930s did the state assume some of these tasks and take a leading role in most heritage processes, however inconsistently. Indeed, most projects remained only partially accomplished, from the creation of modern museums to the establishment of functional heritage legislation. Heritage was subject to the politics of passion: cultural policies relied on the actions of isolated patrons and the individual decisions of certain politicians or civic associations. Cuban elites managed to order only some areas of society, creating elite cultures rather than national cultures, as their Latin American counterparts did at the time. And as with most Latin American countries, culture and heritage remained the privilege of elites, who saw them as tools for the expansion of education among the masses, who the elites considered to lack civilization, manners, and hygiene.

Similarly, while Cuban elites tried to develop a national narrative, they established only an iconic relation with the heroes of the War of Independence and a mystic worship of Martí that was closer to religion than to history. Elites used heritage to establish symbolic links between the heroes of the War of Independence and contemporary politico-economic figures and to connect the nationalist agenda with a project of state modernization and the construction of an imagined community. A specific narrative emerged that included information about concrete places, actors, and actions, but a coherent narrative template was lacking. For James Wertsch and Doc Billingsley, narrative templates provide general and schematic forms of representation "used by members of a community to emplot multiple specific events" that "constrain people to see the world from a particular bounded perspective, precluding the recognition of alternatives" (Wertsch and Billingsley 2011:33).

This suggests that the Republic failed to provide an interpretation of collective events and identity shared by all Cubans. To begin with, large numbers of black Cubans were excluded both socially and politically, and by 1959 there was open discrimination against black Cubans. Cuban heroes were all white, and when they were black, like Maceo, their monuments represented them as white. Cuba's black population continued to be a symbol of barbarism, while Spanish immigrants symbolized colonialism and traditionalism. In turn, despite the fact that archaeology had been providing usable pasts for decades in the form of "discovered" indigenous cultures, these cultures were hardly represented or reflected in heritage and history. The indigenous past was used only as a decontextualized rhetorical device. As Ortiz acutely signaled at the time, "Cuban independentists exalted the indigenous peoples [. . .] because they had disappeared and therefore there was no need to subjugate them" (Ortiz 1948:186–188). The competing discourses and narratives around monuments, museums, and historic preservation in Cuba reflected the impossibility of abolishing sociopolitical contradiction and of creating a linear and teleological narrative template for plotting the national story.

All these endeavors, as well as the prospect of a modern and civilized independent nation, would be assumed and only partially accomplished by the Revolution. Nonetheless, the Republic conditioned revolutionary heritage policies in at least three ways. First, the Revolution actively rejected almost everything associated with the Republic. Accordingly, republican museums and heritage forms and contents became synonymous with "bad practice" and had to be avoided, suppressed, or resignified. Second, the Revolution passively inherited republican heritage and museums, a community of professionals, and a public used to certain canons, practices, aesthetics, and contents. Third, the history of the freedom struggle and its heroes could not be changed and therefore had to be resignified in both symbolic and material terms. Enacting this resignification and coping with the thorny question of continuity and change would become fundamental endeavors for the Revolution in its attempt to realize the possibility of an independent Cuban nation.

Heritage as Passion

The Early Years of the Cuban Revolution (1959–1973)

In May 1958, the dictator Batista launched a massive military offensive in the Sierra Maestra to wipe out the revolutionary guerrillas of the Movimiento 26 de Julio (26-J) movement led by Fidel Castro. In the midst of this offensive, Celia Sánchez, guerrilla and lifelong secretary to Fidel, sent a letter reminding him of the importance of preserving war documentation for the future. To Sánchez, it was necessary to preserve a material trace of the past, so that when "history will be written about this [the Revolution], it will be told as it really is" (Sánchez 1958:n.p.). Just after the victory over Batista, in January 1959, while summary trials and executions were taking place, Sánchez started to collect materials from guerrilla leaders Camilo Cienfuegos, Ernesto "Che" Guevara, and Fidel himself, a task that she passionately carried out until her death in 1980.

These materials were to be displayed in a future museum that would tell the story of the Revolution, beginning with the assault of the Moncada Barracks in 1953. Tellingly, she refers to this museum as "our museum" (Sánchez 1959), which implies that it symbolically belonged to the relatively small core of guerrilla revolutionaries who planned the *Moncada* attack and thereafter led the revolutionary struggle. The inner circle that constituted the leadership was a group of closely connected friends and guerrilla companions that has dominated Cuban politics to the present day. This renders the Cuban Revolution unique compared to other revolutionary processes and regimes of the twentieth century. The Revolution declared itself to be not only a Socialist regime but also a struggle of liberation and a postcolonial nation-building process. Although many institutions and political ranks slowly adopted a reified and Soviet Marxist-Leninist ideology as official discourse, this discourse always coexisted with the radical nationalism of the revolutionary leaders. Both Fidel and Guevara promoted an informal style of government during the early years, wherein emotion, charisma, personalism, experimentation, and voluntarism played a more important role than rational decision-making, bureaucracy, and institutionalism. This was not only the result of a lack of standards to follow and a partial rejection of Soviet models but also due to specific and culturally based Cuban behavior (Fernández 2000:77).

The complexity of the early revolutionary years cannot be encapsulated in any brief account. The leadership oscillated between Soviet models, the radical nationalism of the 26-J movement, and the ideas of Guevara and Marxism-Humanism. In a shifting internal and international context, the revolutionaries attempted to combine their vision of the future of Cuban politics with the views of Cubans. This required dealing with contradictory and complex processes that involved the reshaping of national identity and the subjectivity of Cubans. Fidel (1987[1959]:4–5) publicly affirmed that the fundamental aim of the Revolution was to transform the consciousness of the people. The main objective was to transform human consciousness through the suppression of prerevolutionary culture and the creation of a Socialist culture through new cultural and educational institutions. The result of this transformation would be the creation of the "new man," a selfless, hardworking, internationalist, nonmaterialistic, cooperative, gender and race blind, and obedient human being. Guevara was the embodiment of this ideal, as a convinced anti-imperialist willing to sacrifice himself in the pursuit of high moral ends. He symbolized the unification of the national and revolutionary projects that were promoted through culture, education, and the arts (Sarusky and Mosquera 1979:20).

The revolutionary leaders made many concrete efforts to transform Cubans into new men and women, believing this would automatically spur rapid economic growth and the stabilization of the new institutional order. This required conveying a new political culture and new values while erasing the old. As the boundaries between culture and politics faded, heritage became a fundamental tool for accomplishing this goal. Because heritage production required large economic investments, political will, and ideological commitment, it remained under the rigid and exclusive control of the state and its bureaucracy. For this reason, heritage reflected the projection of the regime's self-image and its internal functioning. It became an instrument for the articulation of the national-revolutionary building process and the establishment a new symbolic order—one that provided legitimacy to the revolutionary process. I examine this process by looking at the theoretical underpinnings of heritage, the forms of relating to previous republican and colonial pasts, and the material and symbolic ways in which revolutionary Cuba was constructed.

The questions that arise are whether Cuban heritage production can be addressed using a similar theoretical framework to that of other Socialist countries and whether any comparisons apply. Any potential examination is complicated by the ambiguity of the Cuban leaders' discourse and geopolitics, the precarious coexistence of the core guerrilla group with the members of the Communist Party, and the mixture of Cuban nationalism with an imported sovietized Marxist-Leninist ideology. The tensions between these processes pulled policies and politics in different directions. On the one hand, the Revolution demanded passion, the spread of culture based on humanist values, the expansion of participation, the pursuit of Enlightenment and humanist values, and high moral ends. On the other, the consolidation of the state required a disciplinary regime grounded in institutionalization, rationalization, and solid economic grounds and legitimized by a rigid ideology and symbolic order.

To understand this contradictory process, I first present the role of ideology in Socialist countries and their relationship with heritage—mainly in the USSR—with the aim of understanding the extent to which Cuba assumed or rejected these heritage ideas in different periods, given that Soviet influence was not immediately significant. Indeed, during the early revolutionary years, the ideas developed throughout the Republic by radical left-wing nationalist intellectuals and professionals confronted the slow, but gradually increasing, influence of a group of social actors advocating pro-Soviet stances within culture. In addition, when looking for inspiration for developing alternative and noncapitalist heritage concepts and policies, Cubans resorted to the practices of Socialist countries with longer experience than they had. Therefore, it is necessary to analyze how the gradual assumption of Soviet ideas took place, what it meant for Cuban heritage, and whether comparisons with other Socialist countries is useful for the study of revolutionary Cuba.

The New Symbolic Order: Ideology and Heritage in Socialist Countries

The inculcation of a new set of values, behaviors, and beliefs through political socialization led Fidel to affirm that the Revolution was an extraordinary process of education. As with any of the great revolutions of our times—the French, the Russian, or the Chinese—the Cuban Revolution triggered a substantial transformation of culture, requiring Cubans to learn new patterns of action, power relations, values, and behaviors. Given the important role of heritage in this process, it is necessary to situate it in the broader revolutionary endeavor of transforming the public sphere. This begs the questions of how ideology served as a way of achieving consensual hegemony for this transformation and the role ideology played within the Cuban political system in comparison to other Socialist countries.

Studying ideology means understanding how signification and meaning serve to reproduce social relations of domination. As the theory of the coloniality of power maintains, this applies to both Socialist and capitalist societies, because the two systems are the result of Western Enlightenment values and a process of capital accumulation, which they impose on other societies (Mignolo and Escobar 2009). As Moishe Postone (2004:54–55) has argued, "actually existing" Socialist countries during the twentieth century were part of a broader trajectory of state-centric capitalism starting with World War I and the Russian Revolution and declining after the 1970s, comprising not only Western countries and the USSR but also colonized and decolonized countries. Thus, the USSR can be seen retrospectively as an alternative and failed form of capital accumulation, rather than a political regime that negated and attempted to overcome capitalism.

In this regard, it is a common misconception that Socialist countries lack an ideological system. Hillel Ticktin (1992), for instance, argues that the USSR was a regime lacking ideology and a specific system of production. This fallacy derives from a traditional reading of Marxist theory, whereby capitalism is understood simply as a system based on private property and market exchange rather than as an abstract form of domination that subordinates individuals and societies to the law of value and commodity fetishism. According to this view, the need for an ideology would disappear as soon as it was no longer necessary to represent the interests of a particular social class, that is, when the proletariat ruled and pursued the general interest. However, this circumstance did not apply in the USSR and most Communist countries. Not only was the proletariat exploited and its interests subsumed under the rule of the party, but the law of value, the market, bourgeois property ownership, and class relations continued to apply.

The USSR was an ideocratic system with a monistic ideology developed by a class of bureaucrats, intellectuals, and technocrats. As an ideological dictatorship, it resisted the autonomy of art, alternative jurisdictions, and explanation by the social sciences. Contrary to autocratic and military dictatorships, citizens not only lacked democratic rights but also were forced to affirm that they possessed them in the best form. Ideological dictatorships like the USSR similarly differ from pluralist systems, whose legitimacy rests on the conviction of its advocates, individual and institutional approval, the relative autonomy of the ideological apparatuses of the state, and a certain coherence between facts and reality.

Ideology is a body of principles, ideas, values, and arguments that aim at the symbolic constitution of society, containing a view of historical development and its deficiencies and providing guidance about a future, more desirable reality. For Marx, ideology was a false consciousness alienated from real life that had to be unveiled and eradicated. Early in the history of the USSR, however, Marxism and historical materialism became the ideology and strategic consciousness of an established system of domination that claimed to be scientific. For most of its life, this ideology was known as Marxism-Leninism, a set of texts from Lenin, Marx, and Engels codified, formalized, and expanded by a number of exegetical texts by Soviet authors. Because of the difficulty of transmitting such a complex ideology, a master-narrative was developed that simplified ideology into its essentials, avoiding the philosophical nature of Marxism-Leninism, and that could be communicated to the masses. This vulgarized master-narrative based on Marxism-Leninism, emphasizing sacrifice, class struggle, and proletarian labor, is what the USSR exported to satellite states.

When talking about Marxism-Leninism in the Cuban context, this book refers specifically to this master-narrative of Soviet import.

Following Graeme Gill (2011:3–4), whereas ideology provided the transcendental referent for the Soviet order, its social projection required the development of other closely related dimensions: history, myths, and symbols. Socialist regimes emphasized history and narration. History underpinned ideology and served to articulate individual and collective experience through education, ritual, and commemoration, creating consciousness by giving meaning to events and rituals. Myths provided a meaningful interpretation of the formation of society, which was associated with a symbolic narrative structure. A number of simple but meaningful symbols embodied the entire symbolic order. These stood for the ideology, the master-narrative, and the myths while also drawing their meaning from them. Heritage was a key instrument in the creation and dissemination of these meanings by giving them tangible form.

The uses of heritage in Socialist states were conditioned by the belief that the new symbolic order would transform individual consciousness. Because personal identity was related to private property, and thus counter-revolutionary, Socialist states tried to collapse individual identities within a collective identity based on class. The paradox was that new notions of identity grounded most revolutionary movements. Consequently, the system faced the challenge of blurring personal identity and at the same time articulating a new collective identity. This made heritage production problematic, because monuments and museums were considered remnants of bourgeois identity and were therefore challenged during the radical early years of most revolutions, including the Russian, Chinese, and Cuban cases. This view is encapsulated by Proletkult Soviet poet Vladimir Kirillov: "In the name of our morrow, let us burn Raphael, destroy the museums, and trample underfoot the flowers of art" (1918 quoted in Baller, 1984:115). At the same time, Socialist states could not do without heritage, because it was considered a key governmentality device for enforcing the acceptance of the new order.

However, neither Marx nor Engels provided guidelines for action regarding heritage. How, then, did heritage rhetoric develop in Socialist countries? The basis of the theoretical understanding of heritage under Socialism can be found in George W. F. Hegel's (2010[1812]) theory of dialectics. From this perspective, Soviet philosopher Eleazar Baller brought together the main ideas concerning heritage in *Socialism and the Cultural Heritage* (1966), then reedited as *Communism and Cultural Heritage* (1984), half of which is devoted to the dialectics of change and continuity. For Baller, "the negation perceived dialectically suggests not only abolition, destruction and annihilation of the past, but also preservation, retention and development of the rationale which has been achieved at the preceding stage of development" (Baller 1984:10). That past "rationale" achieved in previous stages was judged in terms of its "compliance with the objective criteria of social progress" (Baller 1984:66), which were determined by ideology.

In other words, the heritage preservation depended on its compliance with Marxist-Leninist ideas of progress. Consequently, for Baller, heritage had to be hierarchically classified according to its level of reliability as "absolutely authentic; relatively authentic; absolutely untrue" (Baller 1984:58). In all cases, Socialist states needed to exorcise heritage from their capitalist past through a process of resignification that enabled its incorporation into the new symbolic order. Once sanitized and resignified, such heritage could be used as raw material for the production of new Socialist culture. In other words, "cultural heritage [. . .] always comprises both *incorporated and newly-created cultural heritage*" (Baller 1984:66; emphasis in original). Two key heritage processes stem from this theoretical conception: the selection and resignification of heritage, and the construction of new Socialist heritage through monuments and museums.

Vladimir Lenin's (1972[1913–1914]-b) stance on heritage can be interpreted in the light of Baller's ideas. Lenin attempted to counter accusations that Communists were implementing a total break with the past. To do so, he deemed it necessary to guarantee some form of historical continuity, drawing on the best models provided by feudalism and capitalism for the development of proletarian culture—a stance that Guevara would advocate in Cuba. Lenin opposed both advocates of Proletkult, who wanted to break with the past and destroy everything from preceding epochs, and conservatives, who wanted to preserve tradition and ensure continuity. Lenin set a middle course and developed his theory of the two national cultures. He argued that it was necessary to break with part of the national heritage only, because "there are two national cultures in every national culture," that is, the culture of the exploited people and "a bourgeois culture […] in the form […] of the *dominant* culture" (Lenin 1972[1913–1914]-a:32).

Notwithstanding this, Lenin passed a decree in 1918 that wiped out most monuments to figures from previous periods (USSR 1918). Lenin's view ended with the arrival of Stalinist heritage policies, which promoted gigantism and the cult of personality. Stalinist monumentalism and socialist realism endured in Soviet ideology and significantly influenced other Socialist countries. Indeed, the so-called aesthetic offensive based on socialist realist orthodoxy was firmly in place when the Cuban Revolution began (Tasalov 1980). It is therefore necessary to analyze heritage during the early years and understand the extent to which Cuba adopted Soviet ideas, shedding light upon the contradictory directions of the Revolution, which was trapped between the weight of a past to be erased and the need to develop a new symbolic order from scratch.

Cuban Ideology and Cultural Debates during the Early Years

For a number of geopolitical and economic reasons, Cuba developed close relationships with the USSR in a number of areas soon after 1959. Soviet advisors started visiting the island, and many Cuban heritage academics and professionals studied in the USSR and other countries of the Council for Mutual Economic Assistance (COMECON). However, heated internal debates about culture in Cuba conditioned the reception of Soviet ideas, the Cuban position being more pragmatic than ideological, with Castro constantly highlighting the nationalistic and independent character of the Revolution.

The revolutionary process was led by an ideologically diverse leadership made of ex-guerrillas around Fidel and, later on, the Partido Comunista de Cuba (Cuban Communist Party, PCC). They reorganized and controlled the state, which concentrated the means of production and dominated political activity, coercion, education, and the economy. Ideology in Cuba was not, however, a plain replica of elite-imposed Soviet Marxism-Leninism, as many foreign commentators and scholars have argued. Complex debates among multiple social actors were involved in defining Cuban ideology during the following decades, turning it into a well-developed, adaptive, flexible, and artful product, fixed neither in content nor in its praxis.

Ideology became a form of measuring allegiance, commitment, and, ultimately, enemies and friends. But its role in shaping Cuban policies cannot be overestimated.

The leadership was pragmatic in its attempt to sustain the revolutionary nation-state building process and constantly reinterpreted and promoted or marginalized advocates of different ideologies as conditions changed. Nonetheless, the stability and consistency of ideology increased in parallel with the institutionalization of the state. After the 1960s, Marxism-Leninism, largely unknown in Cuba before the Revolution, started to be inculcated among Cubans (Moreno Fraginals 1983). Cuban Marxism-Leninism was an alien import that was extensively taught and slowly took hold among members of the mass organizations and the PCC),[1] though never significantly among the people.

Ultimately, the key signifiers of revolutionary ideology could be encapsulated in the equation of Martí/Nation, Fidel/Revolution and (later on) Marxism-Leninism—that is, a blend of a radical historic national tradition, a charismatic figure, and an official ideology. While civic nationalisms gain support from their doubling with religious narratives, it could be said that the radical, popular, and humanist sources of revolutionary nationalism were doubled with Marxism-Leninism in Cuba. Thus, the Cuban ideology developed in similar ways to that in countries where revolutions were based on strong national traditions and popular support, such as China or Vietnam, and largely differed from the development of ideology in Eastern European countries, where Soviet ideology was enforced. But ideology is not a symbolic construct alone, and its inculcation requires a belief system and support at an individual level. The most powerful way to internalize an ideology is not through its imposition from above but rather when its collective experiences bind individuals together under a symbolic system. To become meaningful, ideology needs to be practiced through different mechanisms, such as rituals of collective belonging that allow for its adaptation to changing circumstances.

An important characteristic of Cuban ideology was that it evolved and was intimately interwoven with a number of popular and collective

---

1   The PCC was created in 1965, but its first congress took place in 1975. The PCC merged various revolutionary groups under a single structure that only partially resembled Soviet-style Communist parties.

experiences, which were gradually incorporated into the symbolic structure of revolutionary ideology in the form of myths. Ideology thus adopted a mythical narrative structure characterized by the pervasiveness of three topics: the evil conspiracy against the community, the redeemer liberating the community from evil, and the coming of a golden age. Read in this light, the government has always posited an external and internal threat to Cuba: U.S. imperialism, neoliberal globalization, or internal counter-revolution. The leadership identified itself with the savior that released Cuba from those threats and would lead the masses to the future-oriented prophecy of a coming golden age: Communism. A series of individual myths explained and ingrained in society specific aspects of Cuban national-revolutionary ideology:

- The birth of the Cuban nation, explained through the narrative of the 100 years of struggle, which posited the source of Cuban national identity in an abstract "rebellious spirit."
- The origins of the Revolution, identified with the 26-J guerrilla movement led by Fidel and epitomized by the assault of the Moncada Barracks in 1953.
- The building and progress of Socialism, represented in museums as the "accomplishments of Socialism," praising the regime's advances in terms of education, agriculture, and industry.
- The idea of threat and siege that legitimizes victimization, emphasizing the idea of struggle against enemies both external (e.g., victory of Playa Girón) and internal (e.g., the fight against bandits or internal counter-revolutionaries).
- Internationalism, underscoring Cuba's international solidarity and support of anticolonialist movements abroad.
- The idea of massive popular participation and *lucha* (struggle). Almost every social reality was conceived in military and sacrificial terms: from the Campaña de Alfabetización in the 1960s to the Batalla de Ideas (Battle of Ideas) in the 1990s.

Therefore, the codification of ideology was dynamic and sometimes contradictory; it must be read as an evolving process rather than as a fixed set of ideas. This process went beyond the leadership and state cadres to involve a significant number of national and international intellectuals and institutions. This was especially so during the 1960s. The complex and controversial Cuban debates about culture that took place during the 1960s concealed an underlying question of political power that conditioned the reception of Soviet ideas, and consequently heritage production. Debates revolved around the troublesome question of change and continuity, and thus about the "right" national tradition and which heritage should be preserved and promoted. Cuban intellectual Graziella Pogolotti (2006) provides an in-depth account of these debates. She shows that most intellectual debates eventually became political, and even geopolitical, as Latin American and European left-wing parties and intellectuals were involved. For her, the underlying debate was about Socialist construction: Was the Revolution a pretext for dogmatism and exclusion, or a space of openness, experimentation, and convergence? In other words, should the Revolution adopt a dogmatic or a critical Marxist-humanist approach?

At the time, Cuba lacked a coherent cultural policy, while the practice was quite chaotic, unclear, and, to a certain extent, improvised. However, there were some general traits that defined the positions of the different actors. Roberto Fernández Retamar (1974:154) considers that the debates could be summarized as a struggle between supporters of artistic freedom, on the one hand, and institutional and political actors, on the other. This, he admits, would already be an oversimplification, as one could hardly describe critical individuals working in cultural institutions, like Alfredo Guevara or Haydée Santamaría, as "bureaucrats." It is clear, then, that Cuban cultural policy was a complex and changing terrain of debate. Throughout the six decades of the Revolution, the orientations and positions of the state were not monolithic, and there were internal discrepancies, with leaders of cultural institutions possessing a certain freedom of action in decision-making. In addition, although Cuban governmentality was inspired by Soviet ideas, these were often softened and interpreted in the light of Martí's humanism, and the search for the essence of Cubanness remained a deep-rooted cultural concern, even during the more sovietizing years.

The importance of these debates for heritage is that they dealt with the contradiction of change and continuity, and with the issue of the "two national cultures." Should revolutionary Cuba embrace universal culture and continue with tradition or should it create a new Socialist culture and break with the cultural inheritance? Although the boundaries between factions were fluid and changing, there was an underlying conflict between, on the one hand, those that supported freedom and were inspired by critical Marxist-humanist ideas that endorsed continuity, and, on the other, those that advocated a break with the past, pro-Soviet stances, socialist realism, and political orthodoxy. Cuban scholars Ambrosio Fornet (2009) and Alberto Abreu Arcia (2007) establish a similar division. Fornet identifies the two factions as "dogmatists" and "liberals," while Abreu Arcia refers to Marxist-humanists as "autonomous" social actors, which he opposes to the "heteronymous" actors, who he described as a group of individuals that were heir to "the Soviet cultural experience and thought. They constitute a space of mediation between the spheres of power and culture. They operate through the discourses of ideology and politics as a set of regulations and dispositions that attempt to control the directions and characteristics of artistic creation" (Abreu Arcia 2007:47). The intensity of the debates and the balance of power between factions changed in each period. According to Desiderio Navarro (2002:120), the broad phases were 1959–1968, which was characterized by experimentation and intense debates; 1968–1983, a period of limited room for critical debate and experimentation; 1984–1989, when cultural and artistic debates were revived; and the post-1990 period, when critical attitudes were again discouraged but the weakness of the state led to a lack of constraints on creativity. This division aligns with Ernesto Menéndez-Conde's (2009) analysis of debates about abstract art.

Marxist-humanists invoked Martí, and after 1965 Guevara, to support artistic freedom and continuity with universal culture, arguing that all humanity shares a common nature. Guevara (2005) advocated Marx's view that Socialists should embrace the entire wealth of previous civilizations, while Armando Hart Dávalos described Cuban cultural policy as an effort to promote national culture within a universal framework:

> The cultural policy we have followed since 1959 is one of cultural relations with the whole world [. . .] The fact that we defend national culture and at the same time open ourselves up to the rest of the world may seem like a contradiction between what is national and universal, and even if it were, that contradiction would be fruitful. (quoted in Century 1991:9)

In a similar vein, the poet Nicolás Guillén defended the continuity with previous cultural traditions at the First National Congress of Writers and

Artists. Guillén considered it "a grave error to deny the important part played by the bourgeoisie in the birth and development of Socialist culture. Ambitious as our forces may be [. . .] it would be impossible to endow Cuba with a proletarian culture, as if by prescription, without taking into consideration the former culture in its most developed and progressive forms" (Guillén 1962:55). Similarly, the Preliminary Plan developed by the Consejo Nacional de Cultura (National Council of Culture, CNC²) argued that "for Marxists, the cultural past, assimilated by the development of humanity over the years, constitutes an active and influential element [. . .] of the cultural life of society" (quoted in Gordon-Nesbitt 2012:180–181). Cuban artists could reject colonialism, imperialism, and racism while incorporating the best scientific and cultural traditions of humankind. Marxist-humanists thought that not all artistic production had to embrace social commitment and revolutionary contents and forms, and thus they considered abstract art legitimate (Otero and Martínez Hinojosa 1972).

On the contrary, an ideological faction constituted by pro-Soviet, ex-members of the Partido Socialista Popular (People's Socialist Party, PSP) advocated socially committed contents and socialist realism in art and culture. They considered that preserving the purest Cuban heritage and tradition was necessary to ensure order and continuity but that the Revolution required a new culture, in line with its ongoing commitment to Socialism and a classless society. It is useful to provide a brief account of their ideas, because, although never fully implemented, they loomed large into the 1970s and 1980s, influencing heritage production. In addition to the texts of Edith García Buchaca (1961), Mirta Aguirre (1963), and Juan Marinello (1961), the writings of José Antonio Portuondo were key in setting the limits of artistic expression. For him, it was not supportive of the

> revolutionary process nor of the aesthetic formation of our people if a political slogan, however correct it is, is expressed with an anti-aesthetic and incorrect form [. . .] Form should be in entire harmony with content, and content must be loyal to the new conception of reality emerging with our Socialist Revolution. (Portuondo 1963b:69)

---

2   Former Dirección de Cultura (Directorate of Culture) of the Ministry of Education (MINED), between 1959 and 1961.

Portuondo classified artistic traditions according to which features and styles should be remembered and which forgotten. He described the abstract art that thrived during the pseudo-republic as the product of an alienated "nation out of itself" that was dominated by U.S. imperialism. Abstract art should be avoided because revolutionary art, the art of the "nation for itself," should be "understandable for everyone, essentially communicative, [and] concrete [. . .] manifesting reality in its historical and social transcendence" (Portuondo 1963a:57). His stance regarding historic change and continuity was clear: he demanded a break with the bourgeois past and the construction of a new Socialist culture. Central to the argument of PSP hard-liners was that only heritage with class character should be preserved, while bourgeois elements should be extricated. This standpoint was closer to that of Stalinism and deviated from Lenin's stance on heritage, which encouraged the preservation of the best bourgeois heritage to build the new Socialist culture.

Portuondo advocated Soviet socialist realism as official doctrine and defined abstract art as a sign of ideological deviation by artists. Soviet socialist realism demanded that artists give a proletarian and party vision of reality, Socialist in content and realist in form. Art that did not reflect the "objective conditions" of Socialism was considered traditional and as belonging to the museum (Baller 1984). As Abreu Arcia (2007:50–51) points out, the irony of this argument was clear: the affirmation of socialist realism as the proper aesthetic paradigm of Cuba as a "nation for itself" presupposed the neglect of national traditions and the assumption of a foreign style. Nonetheless, socialist realism was never the official artistic doctrine of the Revolution, no matter how much its advocates pressed for its adoption, and most Cuban intellectuals and artists rejected it and the restraints on critique and creativity that it entailed. Indeed, Navarro (2002:114) has shown how the early 1980s witnessed the last—and failed—attempt to enforce socialist realism in Cuba by some groups within the government.

Early in the 1960s, Fidel articulated what became the main reference for the limits of freedom in his famously ambiguous statement, "Inside the Revolution, everything goes, against the Revolution, nothing" (Castro 1961c:14–15). This meant that cultural manifestations could not go against the Revolution but did not necessarily have to express revolutionary themes or principles. Fidel ensured freedom in terms of artistic *form* but not in terms of *content*. Contrary to the orthodox position, Fidel did not see forms as dangerous in themselves and did not condemn abstract art. However, in the fields of culture, art, and heritage, the question of formal freedom cannot be artificially disconnected from content, or from the many other aspects that condition it, including institutional, political, and economic contexts. Indeed, the gradual fading of abstract art after the late 1960s cannot be explained purely in terms of a shift in the preferred expressive forms of artists (see Cabrera Infante 2013:244–245). Thus, it is necessary to overcome "the simple tendency to see restraints on creativity as identifiable with political obstacles" (Kapcia 2005:155) and to analyze the specific realities conditioning artistic and heritage production.

Fidel assumed a nationalistic and revolutionary position close to Martí's ideas but far from Guevara's radical criticism of socialist realism. Even if Fidel played a central role in settling controversies at the time, he preferred not to intervene in most debates, leaving the door open for ambiguous interpretations. As Jorge Domínguez argues, "Disputes ordinarily go on without his interference both within intellectual associations and institutions and between them and the bureaucracies or the armed forces. Neither side consistently wins or loses" (Domínguez 1978:394). The complex nature of these debates partially explains the contradictory character of heritage policies at the time. The following sections address this complexity by examining the processes that decided what heritage was, what was to be erased, preserved, monumentalized, and musealized, and how these decisions naturalized notions of Cuban national-revolutionary identity.

The Past as "Raw Material": Erasing, Resignifying, and Reordering Reality

The end of the war in Cuba did not signal the end of violence, which has endured until today in different forms, both physical and symbolic. Direct violence to those who have different visions of a country is often concomitant with the development of a system of structural violence. Revolutionary Cuba employed both strategies to shape a new symbolic imaginary and transform Cuban society. In this section, I investigate how the transformation of the old symbolic order to suit the new political needs triggered a process of cultural violence. To do so, I present the main episodes of iconoclasm and neglect of places of memory and heritage sites that were considered representative of the "bourgeois past," the resignification of key heritage sites and museums, and the meaning behind the transformation of the main heritage institutions.

The physical aspect of Havana has remained largely unchanged since the advent of the Revolution. This is the result of the revolutionaries' rural leanings, derived partly from Marxist ideas about reducing rural-urban inequalities and partly because of the rural provinces' support for the Revolution and the association of urban Havana with vice, corruption, and bourgeois values. Nonetheless, the spatial and symbolic configuration of Havana remained fundamental to determining power relations and affirming authority. The revolutionaries focused on the resignification of preexisting heritage, rather than on constructing new features. Processes of heritage resignification can involve destruction, material additions, or the reworking of certain elements, the inscription of specific features into a new symbolic order, or the performance of rituals that transform the social interpretations of places. The government strove to rework those areas that had a strong symbolic connection with the republican era: the Avenida de los Presidentes, Parque Central, Plaza del *Maine* (*Maine's* Square), Plaza Cívica, and the area around the National Museum and the Palacio Presidencial.

The destruction or preservation of heritage allowed the revolutionaries to publicly express their interpretation of the new Cuba. Monument expert Sanford Levinson (1998:69) has shown that the destruction of monuments as a way of forgetting is at odds with any prospect of reconciliation or conflict resolution. In Havana, the initial bursts of postrevolutionary violence revealed that the approach to the republican past did not seek any form of symbolic resolution through resignification but rather complete erasure. The revolutionaries destroyed most monuments to historic figures associated with the republican period, especially those that symbolized Cuban subjection to U.S. imperialism. The monuments of the first and second Cuban presidents were hammered down in the Avenida de los Presidentes in January 1959. Both Tomás Estrada Palma and José Miguel Gómez were considered symbols of the Cuban subordination to U.S. imperialism, and Gómez was deemed responsible for the massacre of thousands of black Cubans. The statue of the Christ of Havana, representative of the Catholic faith associated with political conservatism, lost

Figures 3.1 and 3.2.
Above: monument
to Estrada Palma
before the Revolution.
Source: Cuba Mate-
rial by María Cabrera,
http://cubamaterial.
com/blog/tag/espacio-
publico/. *Right*: monu-
ment of Estrada Palma
after the removal of
the body. It is popu-
larly known as the
"monument of the
shoes." Source: Author.

its head the day that Fidel entered Havana. Unlike the symbols of Spanish colonialism, or the monuments removed by policies of monumental iconoclasm in the early years of the USSR, these statues were destroyed instead of being placed in museums.

These isolated forms of destruction were part of the political turmoil following the revolutionary coming to power. They represented what Brenda Schildgen (2008:9) defines as "expressive iconoclasm," which she contrasts with premeditated and planned "instrumental iconoclasm." The removal of the bald eagle was a case of instrumental iconoclasm for its overt political intentionality. The eagle situated on top of the *Maine*'s monument in Plaza del Maine was an icon of U.S. imperialism. The Council of Ministers agreed to tear down the eagle and all statues of U.S. politicians in January 1961, but the law was not enforced until May 1, 1961. That day, a crane removed the Eagle, and the monument's plaque was changed to affirm Cuban sovereignty, reading: "To the victims of the Maine, who were sacrificed to a voracious imperialism in its eagerness to seize the island of Cuba." Picasso was supposed to design a cubist dove to replace the eagle, but the gradual influence of socialist realism prevented its implementation (Iglesias Utset 2014:47–48). Eusebio Leal Spengler, future director of the OHCH, recovered the fragments of the iconic eagle, which he uses today as a symbolic resource in diplomatic affairs with the United States. The orchestrated destruction of heritage on a key commemorative date set the stage for the revolutionary regime to express its interpretation of the past in front of thousands of Cubans. Indeed, May Day was going to become a key date in the calendar of revolutionary feasts, when Fidel delivered long speeches to the masses in Revolution Square.

The resignification of Parque Central was closely linked to the interpretation of the figure of Martí. Fidel considered Martí the father of the *patria* and the mastermind behind the Revolution, and he actively transformed the meaning attached to his figure. Martí underwent an extensive process of resignification because the Revolution inherited a country densely populated by busts and monuments dedicated to him. Taking up the symbol of Martí and attaching new meanings to it was a straightforward way of embedding revolutionary values in a powerful and familiar symbol for most Cubans. The first monument to Martí in Parque Central, one of the main Cuban places of memory, provides a good example of revolutionary resignification of republican heritage and its relation with geopolitics. Although the monument remained unchanged, the official reading holds that the arrival of the Revolution changed its meaning. It was considered the "heritage of our people, who, through militant demonstrations, protests, patriotic ceremonies and revolutionary affirmations, has endowed it with historical, patriotic and ideological values" (Fonts Catá 1995:18). This illustrates how the early revolutionary years emphasized performance to transform the meanings elicited by heritage and to resignify the republican past.

However, the resignification of the monument was contested. The visit in 1960 of the Soviet high-rank bureaucrat Anastas Mikoyan marked a turning point in the Revolution and laid open the various interpretations of the monument by different social actors. Mikoyan became the central figure of the Cuban lobby, a group of bureaucrats supporting Cuban positions in the USSR. Many in Cuba feared that his visit confirmed that the Revolution was shifting allegiance from the United States to the USSR (Franqui 1984:66). In this context, before inaugurating a Soviet exhibition titled "Science, Technique and Culture" in the National Museum, Mikoyan made a floral offering to Martí in Parque Central ("Exposición" 1960). What garnered attention and concern, however, was the form of the offering: a globe wrapped by a ribbon with the Socialist symbol of the hammer and sickle (Mikoyan 1960).

Later on, hundreds of catholic protesters belonging to the Directorio Revolucionario Estudiantil (Student Revolutionary Directorate) brought another offering to Martí, with a banner stating, "To you, our Apostle—to make amends for the visit of the assassin Mikoyan" ("Agresión" 1960). The catholic demonstrators claimed to embody the true anti-imperialist stance of Martí. Their signs read "Viva Fidel, down with Mikoyan and communism" and "Neither Yankee imperialism nor Russian Totalitarianism." The official support for Mikoyan's act, and the harsh repression of the protesters, was a clear statement of the government's allegiance to the USSR. However, the political might of Fidel presented it as the only way to ensure Cuban sovereignty while emphasizing that his political program was humanist rather than Socialist, which most Cubans believed ("Bienvenida" 1960). Although Cuba was ensuring its formal political independence at the price of massive economic dependence on the USSR, the leadership used heritage to portray the alliance with the USSR as a national triumph and to emphasize their allegiance to Martí's ideas rather than to Marxism-Leninism.

The destruction and resignification of heritage had a clear impact on the public perceptions of the Revolution and reflected the ongoing sociopolitical changes of the time. At a structural level, however, less spectacular but more profound changes were taking place in relation to heritage ideas and practices. The regime intended to elaborate its own places of memory in connection with the events of revolutionary history while enacting a break with the republican and colonial past. Roberto Segre, probably the most influential theoretical architect in the Cuban Revolution, considered that the aim was to create an emotive reconstruction through material culture that could make "the reality of history forged in revolutionary struggle take on a grip in the dynamics of social life, in every city and every village" (Segre 1970:205–207). This led to the reworking of Cuban iconic museums such as the Oscar María de Rojas, the Ignacio Agramonte, and the Emilio Bacardí during the 1960s. According to Cuban museology professor Nérido Pérez Terry (interview, April 23, 2013), most local museum curators in the provinces rejected what they saw as an imposition from Havana but had to adapt their collections to the new requirements. The changes were often minor, but they transformed the whole meaning of the museum exhibitions.

For instance, museum workers added republican objects to the exhibition of the museum Bacardí, explaining that they "demonstrate the defining traits of that society: private property, gambling and fraudulent elections." In turn, they represented the Revolution by adding weapons that symbolized the idea of "struggle." The intention was to instill among the younger generations a sense of a debt to the revolutionary martyrs who sacrificed themselves for their well-being. The symbolic aim was to establish categories of good and evil, us and them, between the Revolution and the Republic. If every revolution needs to set itself in struggle against an ancien régime (Touraine 1983)—reminiscent of Lenin's idea of the two national cultures—in Cuba, this regime was the Republic. The republican past became analogous to vice and corruption and the Revolution was associated with redemption, progress, and *conciencia* (political consciousness).

The centralization of cultural production entailed the disappearance or cooptation of many heritage institutions, including the OHCH, UNESCO, the Academia de Historia, the Academia Nacional de Artes y Letras, the Patronato de Bellas Artes y Museos Nacionales, and the various commissions of heritage, monuments, and museums. The Departamento Nacional de Cultura (National Department of Culture) was replaced first by the Dirección de Cultura at the Ministry of Education and then by the CNC in 1961, which centralized cultural revolutionary policies (Universidad de La Habana 1970:91–92). The CNC was first presided over by Vicentina Antuña, until 1963. Supported by García Buchaca and Aguirre, Antuña played a central role in the Cuban heritage field, becoming Cuban UNESCO representative after 1975.

The CNC created a section on museums and monuments presided over by Arjona Pérez. She would become the central figure of Cuban heritage, representing in this field what Alfredo Guevara meant to cinema or Haydée Santamaría to literature. What Arjona Pérez, Antuña, Aguirre, and García Buchaca had in common was their activism in the old Communist party, or PSP. In turn, the OHCH, a key heritage institution during the Republic, faded away with the death of its director, Emilio Roig de Leuchsenring, in 1964. The OHCH collection and library were dismantled and dispersed among the new centralized state institutions. The OHCH would reemerge only later, with the figure of Leal Spengler, who collected some historic objects and reopened the City Museum in 1968.

Just after taking power, the revolutionaries targeted another key heritage institution: the National Museum. A group of artists led by Arjona Pérez and Natalia Bolívar, members of the Directorio Revolucionario Estudiantil (Student Revolutionary Directorate), took it over in January 1959. Bolívar assumed the reorganization of the Museum while learning museology from the Soviet specialist Eugenia Georgievskaya. The CNC later started to manage the museum. In turn, most members of the Patronato de Bellas Artes y Museos Nacionales fled the country, and a new board and regulations were established. The National Museum was renamed as Museo Nacional de Bellas Artes (National Museum of Fine Arts) after 1967. This fulfilled the long-awaited Cuban dream of having an art museum in line with contemporary Western standards. The new policy was to select suitable artistic and nonartistic objects, such as historic, archaeological, or ethnographic collections, and transfer them to other sites. Most historic collections went to the City Museum led by de Leuchsenring (de Leuchsenring and Sierra Boudet 1959). Stamps were transferred to the

Museum of Communications, relevant pictures, newspapers, and correspondence to the Archivo Nacional (National Archive), weapons to the Comisión Nacional de Monumentos, and archaeological, ethnological, and folkloric pieces to the Department of Ethnology and Folklore of the CNC, among others.

The decision to devote the museum to art was partly related to the huge number of pieces collected from the Cuban bourgeoisie, whose properties were confiscated when they fled Cuba or who donated them out of fear if they decided to stay. The government created the Departamento de Recuperación de Valores del Estado (Department of Recovery of Values of the State), starting a process of confiscations and nationalizations whose focus included members of the Batista regime, those who had opposed the revolutionary process, and those who left the country legally or illegally. The confiscations endowed the National Museum of Fine Arts with a valuable collection of European paintings. More significantly in terms of heritage policy was that Cuban and Latin American archaeological and ethnographic collections were removed. At the same time, however, the museum devoted rooms to Egyptian, Greek, Roman, and Oriental archaeological objects. Those were considered part of the artistic realm, and not part of "history," in a clear attempt to imitate Western models. This is one more illustration of the coloniality of early revolutionary Cuba and its commitment to universal values of Western civilization. To be modern and educated, revolutionary Cuba had to inscribe itself with the evolutionist colonial narratives of the European Enlightenment, wherein having a collection of classic art was a marker of cultural achievement.

Science was also put under government control. The Academia de Historia was abolished in 1962. Academic departments and institutions related to disciplines such as anthropology, archaeology, folklore, or theater were put under direct control of the new Comisión Nacional de la Academia de las Ciencias (Cuban National Commission of the Academy of Sciences) (Ortiz García 2003). The academy was symbolically placed in the Capitolio, another icon of republican corruption and subordination to the United States. The decision metaphorically implied that the Revolution had substituted political corruption with the promotion of science. The academy imitated the Soviet science system, and academic exchanges of all kinds started immediately with the USSR.

Within the academy, the Centro de Estudios Folklóricos (Center of

Folklore Studies) became the Instituto de Etnología y Folklore (Institute of Ethnology and Folklore), which was put in charge of the reevaluation of national tradition and folklore. This was related to the early debates about change and continuity and the "good" national culture to be preserved. A plan of the CNC from 1962 set out ten cultural objectives for the following year. The first three aims were:

> To study and re-evaluate cultural tradition, especially that of the nineteenth century in which Cuban national identity had arisen.
> To study and research cultural roots, recognizing the Black contribution to Cuban culture.
> To divest folkloric expressions of their non-essential elements.
> (quoted in Gordon-Nesbitt 2012:288)

The center's stated objective was to create a pure Cuban revolutionary culture through the transformation of Cuban customs. In an article titled "The Revolution Will Transform the Customs of Cubans," Enrique González Manet explained that this uncontaminated culture would be "based on an intact heritage expurgated of foreign elements" (González Manet 1960:75). If previously "overshadowed and looked down on because of the pernicious influence [. . .] of imperialism,[. . .] the creole way of being and feeling will be now promoted and studied freely in the future" (González Manet 1960:75). In line with the theory of the two national cultures, the revolutionaries considered it necessary to purge Cuban heritage symbolically from foreign and bourgeois contamination to incorporate it into the new Socialist culture. From then on, traditions, legends, customs, songs, dances, and literature were evaluated in terms of their perceived authenticity as uncontaminated Cuban heritage.

The museum Felipe Poey of Natural Sciences at the University of Havana was first nationalized and then closed down. Its name was given to the new Natural Sciences Museum created by the new Academia in the Capitolio. Various bourgeois archaeological collections were donated to the new museum, including the famous exhibition of García Feria in Holguín and objects from the National Museum. The closure of some provincial and academic private or municipal collections was consistent with the revolutionary effort to centralize institutions. From the center, the government could design narratives and exhibitions and project them nationally.

One of these narratives was the tendency toward an interpretation of the indigenous as part of the natural realm. This was an attitude that would change substantially in subsequent periods, when the indigenous heritage started to provide a usable past as another of the Cuban subaltern classes under the Marxist-Leninist scheme of historical progress. For instance, the Felipe Poey developed a narrative of the natural richness of Cuba in terms of flora, fauna, and soils that included indigenous cultures. The indigenous material culture previously removed from the Bellas Artes museum was brought here and displayed as an essential part of Cuba's nature. As archaeologist José García Molina confirmed later on, the revolutionary developments at the time served to expand the knowledge of "our fatherland in Natural History broadly and especially in Indigenous anthropology" (García Molina 1989:n.p.). The rearrangement of the museum of anthropology Montané in 1962 and 1969, and the inauguration of the Museum of Archaeology Guamá in 1975, confirmed this tendency.

The Revolution transformed the ways of retrieving, selecting, and organizing heritage. The frantic circulation of objects and collections, however, took on meaning only in relation to a larger transformative process infused with modernist and epistemologically colonial values. The Revolution criticized the Republic for being neocolonial and referred to that period as the "neocolony," even after the withdrawal of the Platt Amendment. At the same time, however, the Revolution assumed the coloniality of power in the form of an epistemic continuity with previous periods. Revolutionary heritage politics often equated modernity and progress with national narratives, heritage institutions, and policies aligned with Western standards of taste and historic development. The racial composition of the leadership and the revolutionary cultural discourse demonstrated the persistence of Hispanicism, which disavowed any connection with the indigenous past and considered that Cuban identity emerged from the Hispanic spirit (e.g., UNESCO Cuba 1973). This Hispanicism reveals the continuity with deeply rooted cultural behaviors and conceptions of culture, which would change only gradually as Soviet ideas permeated revolutionary theory and practice.

The revolutionary process of resignification also brought about significant changes to the Cuban public and symbolic landscape. However, most republican material and symbolic places remained untouched, especially in the provinces. Cuban scholars and professionals have struggled to reconcile the ideological requirement to exorcise the heritage that belonged to the "bad" national culture and presence of this heritage in the physical space, as happened with Martí's monument in Parque Central. The analysis of the evolution of Camagüey's city center by Cuban historian Marcos Tamames Henderson (2012:90) is paradigmatic in this regard. For him, the traditional bourgeois city center presided over by the Agramonte Square represents republicanism. Therefore, he harshly criticizes the embellishment of the square that took place during the Republic as a hegemonic imposition of bourgeois values and aesthetic criteria, as political legitimization, and as a reflection of economic corruption. However, as if by magic, during the Revolution, his interpretation of the square changes, despite the fact that no transformations were made to the square itself. The square is no longer interpreted as a symbol of the official republican hegemony but as a symbol of rebelliousness. This is justified because "the revolutionary dynamic of ideas, thoughts and criteria modified the interpretation of the symbols erected" (Tamames Henderson 2012:90). Similar paradoxes emerge in the official interpretation of other heritage sites throughout Cuba.

Thus, official discourses of urban and architectural planning maintained the idea that the advent of the Revolution entailed in itself a symbolic transformation of a previously oppressive and hegemonic public space. This complicates the interpretation of the resignification process and raises the question of whether a completely unchanged physical environment can have an opposite symbolic meaning to its original meaning. This recurrent situation can be interpreted in terms of Jacques Derrida's (1976) concept of the "undecidable." Until Cubans were educated into the new symbolic order that would enable them to ascribe certain meanings to past heritage sites and public spaces, they could not be reconciled with the dichotomous interpretation of the past put forward by the regime. This also explains the rhetoric about educating the younger generations, which would be able to fully understand revolutionary symbols. The same public cannot accept that the same square was a hegemonic representation of power yesterday and the outcome of popular will today. Insofar as the difference with the past is undecidable, and the original articulation of meaning has been destabilized, it becomes impossible to tell whether it is the past, the present, or the future that is being experienced. Although it was probably more the result of a lack of institutionalized cultural policies than of a carefully orchestrated plan, the undecidability of heritage proved useful for the regime: it created a sense of estrangement from the past that enabled the creation of new meanings via heritage.

Reworking José Martí: The Revolution Square as a Display of Passion

If revolutionary states are often worried by identity and establishing a sense of continuity with a certain part of their past, while breaking with another (Marris 1974), Cuba was no exception. This becomes clear in the analysis of one of the key elements that the Revolution used to convey its interpretation of the past: the resignification of key places of memory. For Nora (1989:6–7), when a nation is under threat or undergoing rapid political transformations, it takes refuge in certain places of memory. The Revolution showed that the monument to Martí in the Plaza Cívica was the quintessential Cuban place of memory. As we have seen, radical students and professionals had criticized its construction during the Republic. They argued that the personality of Martí was opposed to the idea of a monument and that if a monument had to exist it should be functional and humble. However, the revolutionary regime did not do away with the monument and instead decided to use it for its own purposes. Also, the revolutionaries could not let the ambiguity over the monument to Martí last, because of its close association with the Batista dictatorship; thus, the monument required a large-scale process of resignification. As Leal Spengler recalls, the Square was seen at the time as "a void space [. . .] tainted by its aesthetic connection with the designs of Fascism" (quoted in Gonçalves 2001:30). Today, however, the link between Revolution Square and the Revolution itself is so inexorable that for most Cubans, knowledge of its troublesome republican past comes as a surprise.

The question that emerged, however, was, How could a space perceived as fascist turn into the hub of revolutionary fervor? Or, as Cuban art historian María Pereira has put it, "How can an artwork, without changing its material structure, form, or geographical location, transform its semantic and expressive content in three decades?" (Pereira 1985:2). In the case of Martí, the official narrative that emerged maintained that his figure was rhetorically usufructed during the neocolonial Republic (Portuondo 1982). Therefore, only the Revolution could implement Martí's true ideals, because these were now subject to "scientific analyses." In any case, the

continued use of the monument to Martí as a site of political socialization proves the variety of meanings that sites of memory can assume and
reveals the hold that Martí's ideas and iconography had on Cuban social
life across different ideologies (López 2006:56).

Different institutions representing diverse power groups during the
early years targeted the Plaza Cívica and the monument to Martí for their
projects. While Fidel and his team planned the speeches and rallies associated with regime feasts, the Fuerzas Armadas Revolucionarias (Revolutionary Armed Forces, MINFAR) projected the creation of the Museo
de la Revolución (Museum of the Revolution, MR) in the basement of
the monument to Martí. Meanwhile, the Ministry of Public Works (MI-
CONS) planned urban and architectural projects and continued referring
to the square by its republican name, Plaza Cívica. If the power to name
is a fundamental form of political power that creates particular categories
within the symbolic order, then the name and shape of the new square
was a contested terrain, at least at the very beginnings of the Revolution.
Only a few months after taking power, the civic commission that managed
the Plaza Cívica and Martí's monument was suppressed and MICONS
was put in charge. The same month, a podium, electricity, and a micro-
phone were installed. Gradually, cabins for radio and TV were added to the
monument, and buses were transformed into mobile toilets, cafeterías,
and ambulances deployed for mass rallies and concentrations (MICONS
1962–1964).

In parallel, MICONS kept designing a series of utopian projects whose
implementation would have led to the total transformation of the square
and the destruction of the monument to Martí—in line with the harsh
critiques of the monument by radical architects during the republican
period. A confidential 1962 report addressed to the leadership reflected
the uncertainty of urban planners over the square, as well as concern
over the role that MICONS, architecture, heritage, and urban planning
should play in the Revolution. After elaborating a technical analysis of the
square, MICONS experts affirmed that "although we do not know which
are the future prospects for the Plaza Cívica, in our opinion it should remain the administrative and cultural centre of the city" (MICONS 1962).
Meanwhile, MINFAR had sent architect Raúl Oliva to study museology in
the USSR. Oliva played a major role in the development of revolutionary
heritage policies and in the representation of the symbols and myths of

Figures 3.3 and 3.4. Addition of a podium to the monument to Martí in the Plaza Cívica in October 1959 (*top*) and June 1960 (*bottom*). Source: MICONS archive.

the leadership. He worked closely with MINFAR and designed the MR and other key museums such as the museum-school Moncada 26 de Julio, Granjita Siboney, the museum-park Abel Santamaría, and the Museum of Clandestine Struggle. Under his supervision, the MR was transferred to the basement of Martí's monument in the square in 1963, until it was dismantled in 1968.

Eventually, the contestation around the square ended with its transformation into the central symbolic hub of the Revolution. Fidel started to use it exclusively in his encounters with the masses, during which he performed what he and Jean-Paul Sartre called a form of direct democracy (Castro 1961b; Sartre 1961) that others have interpreted as "participatory totalitarianism" (Hedin 2004). Gradually, the Plaza Cívica became associated with the Revolution and started to be popularly known as Revolution Square. This reveals the power of heritage to create meaning and to support the symbolic constitution of societies. For instance, Pereira considered, as many others did, that in Revolution Square Fidel's personality was able to "multiply itself whenever he presides each act of revolutionary affirmation in such a majestic scenery" (Pereira 1985:17). The interesting shift was that the personality of Fidel was combined with the monumental space to produce meaning. This broke with the previous republican emphasis on the separation between a passive observer and a monument to be observed. What had mattered in Labatut's design of Martí's monument was the visual relation of the citizen with the monument. For Fidel, however, what counted was the participation of the observer and the establishment of ritualized procedures of participation. Fidel employed rituals to frame political legitimization because they serve to associate the repetition of practices with a certain symbolic order.

Fidel specifically wanted the square as a stage setting for its strong symbolic and commemorative power. However, as Paul Connerton (1989) has argued, performative rituals only reinforce the bonds between people and the ruling class and among each other when they involve large numbers of people. The first massive speech in the square occurred on May 8, 1959. However, the mass speeches were ritualized only a year later, when Fidel gathered a million peasants as a demonstration of power for his first May Day speech. Showing his mastery of the theatrics of power, Fidel included in the standardized calendar of celebrations the highly symbolic date of July 26 to commemorate the Moncada assault of the guerrilla

Figure 3.5. One million peasants commemorated the 26 July in 1959 at Revolution Square. Source: MICONS Archive.

group Movimiento 26 de Julio, which he led. The square allowed Fidel to convey the official version of the past that shaped an idea of the future the revolutionaries envisioned: the coming of Socialism rooted in the autochthonous ideals of Martí.

The creation of the desired symbolic effect required the material transformation of the monument. Not randomly, the monumental podium designed by MICONS placed Fidel in front of the sculpture of Martí and

Figure 3.6. Fidel used Revolution Square to reinstate the symbolic connection between himself and Martí. Below Fidel, the podium displayed large portraits of Martí, Marx, and Lenin. Source. Deena Stryker, "Speaker's podium, military parade [Item ID 1092531-R3-E418], January 2, 1964, Deena Stryker Photographs, David M. Rubenstein Rare Book & Manuscript Library, Duke University.

at its highest point among the other people standing on it. This created what Herzfeld (1997:56) would describe as a display of order. Displays of order combine modern spectacle and ritual and in this case allowed Fidel to transform and define the normative social order and ground his legitimacy in the symbolic relation between himself and Martí. His symbolic performance in the square allowed him to articulate the national-revolutionary narrative, affirm the unity of Cubans, and provide a sense of continuity and belonging. The kind of ritual performed in the Square bridged the gap between individual faith and social interconnectedness and may also be interpreted in Catholic terms. Indeed, as David Kertzer (1980) has shown in the case of Bologna, Catholic models might have influenced Castro's ritual activities more than he or the revolutionaries cared to admit.

According to James Thrower, the "symbolical nature of ritual lies in the fact that what it stands for has to be interpreted by reference to a transcendental principle outside the relationship of a means to a goal" (Thrower 1992:35). In Cuba, this transcendental reference was Martí's anti-imperialist nationalism and, increasingly, Marxism-Leninism. Taken together, the strategies employed to transform the Plaza Cívica into Revolution Square can be summarized in the concept of "ravelization." Tzvi Medin developed this notion to account for the shaping of revolutionary consciousness in Cuba, which for him involved the "progressive establishment of a certain emotional atmosphere, a controlled terminological change, a hierarchic ascension in the source of the revolutionary message, the establishment of lexical and conceptual equivalences, the legitimization of exclusive connotations and so forth" (Medin 1990:167–168).

The powerful combination of a monumental space and ritualized performance served Fidel's shaping of social transformation, but it also reflected the power struggles of the time, wherein various competing groups within the Revolution contended for hegemony. Fidel employed the square to reiterate the idea of the guerrilla core as the sole forbearer of the Revolution against the increasingly powerful state bureaucracy and other revolutionary groups. While experts and professionals demanded the transformation of the Square according to Socialist and scientific urban planning, Fidel reclaimed the square as a commemorative space, a site of passionate and affective encounter with the masses. This move parallels Fernández' (2000:84) interpretation of the distinctiveness of revolutionary Cuba in terms of a dichotomy between rationalism and emotion. For him, if modern states need bureaucracies and instrumentalization to gain legitimacy in terms of economic performance and efficiency, the Revolution demanded passion and affective bonds.

The politics of passion pervaded the articulation of the official narrative and the way Fidel organized political socialization during the early years. Passion provided a personalist and epic political language that people understood, because it was based on collective norms, aspirations, and symbols that constituted the meaning of Cuban collective identity. Heritage is central to the articulation of passionate narratives because such narratives are essentially teleological, that is, oriented both to the past and to the future. The configuration of rituals and heritage in the early years shows that Fidel and the leadership largely preferred to be associated with idioms of national-revolutionary passion rather than with the state's bureaucratic rationality. This also explains both the unparalleled capacity of Fidel and his collaborators to outlast all kinds of crises and the longevity of the Revolution.

The Museum of the Revolution: History and
the Early Master-Narrative of Passion

Museums classify and order reality and knowledge within an institution-
ally controlled space. This makes them primary tools for historical production and political socialization that avoid contestation—if not during
their design and construction, then at least in the final representation
conveyed to the public. The problem Cuba faced was the lack of a developed historical narrative to represent in museum exhibitions. This in turn
explains the disordered evolution of museums during the Revolution's
early years and its emphasis on the spread of culture rather than on the
internalization of ideology.

During the 1960s, ensuring the control of history was fundamental for
the development of a distinctive revolutionary ideology. For Pérez, history functioned as a "handmaiden to the revolution, [serving] as a major
source of moral subsidy [and] conferring [. . .] a sense of continuity"
(Pérez 1980:83). The first history faculties opened with the Revolution,
and the revisiting of the national past triggered heated debates. Just after coming to power, the revolutionaries put the city historian of Havana
in charge of a commission for the reviewing of the texts on the History
of Cuba, following the indications of Antuña (2013[1959]). In a letter to
would-be minister of culture Hart Dávalos, de Leuchsenring writes that he
assumed the task because he considered it essential to carry out "a reform
of the discipline that shapes national consciousness" (de Leuchsenring
2013[1961]:516). At the time, national history had undergone a critical
appraisal and Marxist history was not unknown (see Rodríguez 1944).
However, there was a widespread general ignorance of Marxism-Leninism
among scholars and the public. Also, few history books were published after 1959 under the aegis of the underproductive Instituto de Historia (Institute of History), created by the Academy of Sciences (Moreno Fraginals
1995:12). This situation resulted in the massive importation and translation of Soviet history books. Soviet history gradually influenced some
sectors of Cuban politics and scholarship and, eventually, the decision on
what to represent in museums and how to do it.

Nonetheless, most historians continued the republican tradition
wherein history-culture and short-term historical understandings prevailed. The endurance of a positivist approach affected heritage policies,

and explains, for instance, Sánchez' constant attempts to collect objects and documents for display in the MR to "prove" the veracity and objectivity of the Revolution. Critics of the positivist simplification of history, such as Walterio Carbonell and Manuel Moreno Fraginals, demanded a new history for the new men. Carbonell (2005 [1961]) denounced the fact that revolutionary historians still explained the birth of the nation in culture-history terms by providing lists of great bourgeois figures. For him, a Marxist history should interpret the nation as the result of the class struggle and racial mixture between aristocrats and slaves. Similarly, Moreno Fraginals (1983) considered it unrealistic to live in a new society with old historic conceptions that emphasized anti-Hispanicism and avoided dealing with the role of black culture in Cuba.

Like many other intellectuals, Carbonell and Moreno Fraginals were "parameterized" and silenced during the repressive Quinquenio Gris (Grey Quinquennium) between 1971 and 1976. However, only after the 1970s would Cuban historiography become strongly influenced by Soviet ideology, banning authors and themes from publication and curtailing scholarly debate (Ibarra 1995). Official historiography started to describe the Republic as a pseudo-republic or neocolony, wherein sovereignty was mediated, corruption thrived, and the transition from colony to nation could not be realized in full. The republican experience was misrepresented as a period of vice, corruption, and subordination to U.S. rule, punctuated by some heroic deeds and revolts that anticipated the revolutionary redemption of 1959.

Gradually, Cuba tended to imitate the models of history production of other Socialist countries. Because historic narratives underpinned ideology, all Socialist states put history under strict control and created specialized institutions for its production and dissemination, with heritage and museums playing a central role. Socialist historiography was characterized by the attempt to combine nationalism with proletarian internationalism, the use of a vulgarized form of Marxism underscoring class struggle, the definition of a series of lineal historic periods, the doctrinaire use of reified concepts of struggle, rebelliousness, and sacrifice, and the establishment of connections between contemporary processes and protorevolutionary and nationalistic movements and social groups.

If Cuba could not produce the contents of a new history consistent with Marxism-Leninism during the 1960s, Soviet heritage forms and aesthetics had a certain influence in Cuban museums during the early days. Soviet influence was apparent in the museums created by MINFAR, while other museums dependent on the CNC embraced the values of the Enlightenment and humanism following UNESCO. On the one hand, this suggests that ex-PSP members of the CNC were not as orthodox in their implementation of Socialist ideas in terms of heritage as they traditionally have been portrayed in other fields of culture. Indeed, cultural production at the time cannot be explained as a simple conflict between freedom and PSP Stalinists. Rather, culture was a terrain of dispute between alternative cultural ideas and perspectives, the PSP not having a "monolithically restrictive approach to art" (Kapcia 2005:133).

On the other hand, the connection between MINFAR and the USSR is not surprising. They collaborated closely on military issues, as MINFAR started to support national liberation movements in Latin America and Africa and was among the few Cuban institutions with a solid structure at the time. Thus, understanding the birth of the MR in Cuba requires understanding museum policies in other Socialist states. During the first years after the October Revolution in the USSR, an avant-garde antimuseum discourse emerged that described museums as sites of contemplative and consumerist life reflecting bourgeois decadence (Groys 1994:145). A Soviet museology manual explained that bourgeois museums "could not unveil the essence of main historical periods, of socio-economical formations, of correlations between classes, of the class struggle" (Galkina et al. 1957:175). Despite the avant-garde critique of museums, the idea of creating a museum of the revolution in the USSR preceded the revolution, as also happened in Cuba. Then, a commission was set up only a few days after the Revolution that established the main aim of the museum: to reflect "the struggle and victories of the Soviet people in building the new life" (USSR 1977:71). There was a clear tension between the avant-gardes criticizing the museum concept, on the one hand, and the political leadership seeing museums as instruments of propaganda, on the other.

In Eastern Europe, museums of the revolution and Communist history appeared immediately after the region fell under the control of the USSR. These museums' adoption of the aesthetics of socialist realism and their rapid implementation suggest that they were replicas of the Soviet one. The subordination of museums to the propagation of ideology was common in Bulgaria, Czechoslovakia, Poland, and Romania and was pushed to the limit in North Korea. In China, the museum of the revolution followed the Soviet model and was responsible for keeping history under party control. However, its former curator, Su Donghai, has argued that Chinese museums were initially challenged and their quantitative development hampered because they "were considered to be the eulogies of the ruling classes of the old China" (Donghai 1995:66). Because prerevolutionary museums were seen as sites of bourgeois aesthetic contemplation, their revolutionary counterparts became utilitarian and served social functions, while objects functioned as proofs of historical materialism that should "teach lessons" (Varutti 2014:306).

The Cuban MR followed the patterns of other Socialist museums but presented some distinctive tenets. As seen at the start of this chapter, the revolutionaries planned the museum before the end of the war and then put it under direct control of Fidel through his secretary Sánchez and MINFAR. Sánchez' decade-long effort to collect objects and documents related to the Revolution resulted in the gathering of more than nine thousand items. In her letters to Fidel, Sánchez had spoken about creating a museum of the guerrillas, and it was only after Raúl took the lead of MINFAR that the museum was conceived from scratch as a museum of the revolution similar those of Socialist countries. The efforts to create the MR started in 1959 following Raúl's orders, and it was inaugurated in the Castillo de la Punta in 1961, as shown in figure 3.7. The decision to locate the MR in the Castillo was consistent with the larger plan to resignify key places of memory in Havana, because the Castillo was a symbol of Batista's resistance, being the last stronghold to fall in the war. The creation of the MR also revealed the close relationship between material culture, history, and the representation of national-revolutionary identity. To "purify" the Castillo de la Punta of its symbolic connection with Batista, every internal object was removed, including four machine guns that were replaced with weapons of the revolutionaries.

At the time, the press stated that the objective of the MR was to memorialize the seven years of heroic revolutionary struggle against Batista and to remind "future generations, as an example, what that fateful period of crimes, betrayals, robberies and mourning meant to Cuba" (Reyes Gavilán 1960:38). Furthermore, because "Cuba had quickly forgotten" the martyrs of the failed 1933 revolution, the revolutionary leaders did "not want to make the same mistake" (Reyes Gavilán 1960:38–40). In addition,

Figure 3.7. The first Museo de la Revolución in the Castillo de la Punta. Source: Reyes Gavilán (1960:38).

the youth had to know about "the years of harsh sacrifice that resulted in our new and gloriously reborn Cuba" (Reyes Gavilán 1960:40). The idea was to mark the republican period as undesirable heritage and provide the official interpretation of the so-called revolutionary patriotic deed (Reyes Gavilán 1960:80). Clearly, the MR had the double task of resignifying the place and exorcizing one part of the past while memorializing another. The aim was to emphasize martyrdom to generate among young people a sense of debt to the Revolution. To do so, the MR employed memory as a tool to construct a perception of the past as negative heritage and of the present as dominated by a future-oriented Revolution.

Soon after its opening, however, the MR was closed and transferred to the base of the monument to Martí in Revolution Square. Raúl inaugurated it with the Soviet ambassador Alexandr Alexeyev on the tenth anniversary of the *Moncada* assault, July 25, 1963. The exhibition, designed by architect Oliva, narrated the revolutionary events chronologically. It started with Batista's tyranny and the revolutionary martyrs and proceeded through the Moncada assault, the *desembarco del Yate Granma* (Granma Yacht landing), the war in Sierra Maestra, and Guevara's victory in Santa Clara, and concluded with an exhibition of the belongings of revolutionary martyr Cienfuegos. On display were clothes, Batista's police torture gadgets, prints and banners used by the revolutionaries, pictures, maps, and many documents, accompanied by a plane, a truck, and a tank. For Raúl, the MR represented "one more tribute of our people to its heroes and martyrs, and [a] source of educative and inspiring living example" (Museo de la Revolución ca. 1963). The MR highlighted the revolutionary myths of war experience and the worship of fallen soldiers, as did other military museums worldwide, but the central emphasis on the values of martyrdom and sacrifice brought it closer to museums in Socialist countries.

Then, Raúl (1966) created the section of history of MINFAR, which commissioned Jorge Ibarra to create a new handbook of Cuban history and developed an ambitious nationwide plan to heritagize revolutionary sites of memory. This project partially replicated the Soviet model whereby museums were under control of the Institute of Party History. Behind Raúl's project was the goal of expanding the scope of the historic narrative of the Revolution from the first ten years after the *Moncada* assault (1953–1963), as represented in the MR, to the War of Independence of the nineteenth century, in line with the myth of the "100 years of struggle." Following the successful process of educating the guerrillas of the Segundo Frente (Second Front) during the war, the troops now had to be educated in the Cuban long-standing tradition of struggle, and the sites where revolutionary events had taken place had to be marked and protected. The ambitious plan included the creation of provincial museums of the Revolution, the musealization of all the military fronts that had existed during the war, the construction of monuments and museums of the wars of independence of 1868 and 1895, and the collection of objects and documents of the *lucha contra bandidos* (fight against bandits) and against the United States. Although the plan was never fully accomplished, it influenced the large heritage production programs implemented after 1975.

Coinciding with the arrival of an itinerary exhibition of the Soviet Museum of the Revolution to Cuba, the MR at the base of the monument to Martí was dismantled in 1968. Unofficially, the exhibition was transferred to another site that was symbolically connected to Batista and the Republic: the Palacio Presidencial, where the MR remains. Over the course of six years, the history section of MINFAR reworked the exhibition, which reopened in 1974 with a completely different appearance.

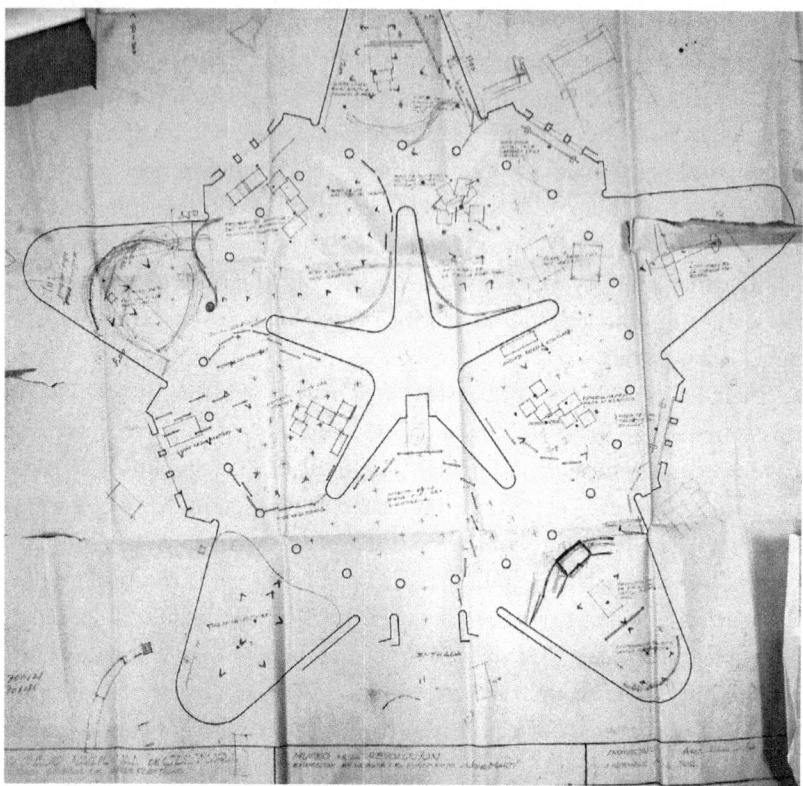

Figure 3.8. Plan of the *Museo de la Revolución* in the base of the monument to Martí in Revolution Square, by Raúl Oliva, 1962. Source: Centro Nacional de Patrimonio Cultural (CNPC) archive.

Throughout the early revolutionary years, the MR functioned as one of the central instruments for representing the ideology of the regime. It gave tangible form to the official reading of the past and passed a historical judgment that declared certain pasts illegitimate. Both the locations and the historic narrative of the MR were highly symbolic. The narrative was fundamentally Manichaean: it presented the republican past as something that could not come back and celebrated the Revolution as the ultimate redeemer of the nation in its transition toward Socialism. Manufacturing an official history was deemed essential in the exorcism of the republican past, whose negative aspects Cubans should not forget. The MR not only deployed a narrative to convey the ideological message but also used material culture to produce an affective atmosphere that created associations between negative emotions, the Republic, and certain objects. Torture implements and bloody clothes represented death and the maximum physical pain that could be inflected on humans. In turn, objects related to alcohol and tobacco, prostitution, elections, and politics were associated with corruption, vice, and sin. These negative features were opposed to the idea of the "good" embodied by the redeeming Revolution.

Cubans had to learn this message, for the truth of the Revolution was equated with the foundational myth of the nation—its so-called rebirth. The youth had to be educated in ideas of sacrifice, political consciousness, and the need to respect their elders for their heroic deeds, utmost sacrifice, and eventual martyrdom. This story can be described as the "early master-narrative of passion," for it presented a simplified version of the leadership's ideology but remained underdeveloped compared with that of subsequent periods. The narrative restrained the Revolution in its temporal scope, as it left aside a large part of the history of Cuba. But perhaps more importantly, it was a passionate narrative of heroism based on culture-history that was still far from the scientific objectivity and class struggle dialectics demanded by Soviet Marxism-Leninism.

Museums and the Humanist Redistribution of Culture

The national patrimony [. . .] was usufructed by small minorities that conceived it as exclusive heritage of the dominant classes, and only after the triumph of the Cuban Revolution in 1959 the collections of art, science, history and other cultural manifestations were put at the service of the people, not only for their aesthetic value and beauty, but also for their educative function, which aims to contribute to the deepening of the patriotic, political-ideological and cultural work of our people and, in particular, the younger generations, towards Socialist development.

(Ríos Marrero 1984:7)

The revolutionary government received vast collections and large buildings from the bourgeoisie. Some of these were transformed into museums exhibiting artworks to promote education and spread culture. This section analyses how the creation of museums served the revolutionary attempt to build up the new symbolic order and break with the past. In shedding light on the different logics actors followed during the early revolutionary years, I show that the CNC, responsible for the creation of most museums and controlled by ex-PSP members, embraced UNESCO values, which largely differed from MINFAR's alignment with Soviet ideas. This counters the idea that most CNC cultural politicians were orthodox regarding cultural affairs.

During this period, the regime was less interested in historic preservation and mostly attended to the creation of new museums. This relates to what many interviewees during my research defined as the "myth of the new" that equated everything "new" with modernity and progress (Segre 1994). The myth of the new conditioned both heritage and museum production in the early years of the Revolution. This is no surprise, as the Revolution identified itself with the new—the official calendar of the re-born Cuba starts counting years after 1959. Soviet Marxist-Leninist ideas of progress and modernization underpinned the myth of the new, as they considered that every stage of social development was intrinsically better than the last. Consequently, conservatism was equated conceptually with "the old," while social progress toward the construction of Socialism was considered analogous to "the new." As Baller put it,

> Progress is characterized by the incorporation of the lower (old) into the higher (new), and by the subordination of the former to the latter based on a rise of the organizational level of a whole. Regress, on the contrary, is tied with organizational degradation, with the transition to structurally lower levels and, therefore, with the subordination of the higher (old) to the lower (new). (Baller 1984:15)

Consequently, heritage preservation in museums or city centers could be justified only when it highlighted the heritage of subaltern groups or when it was framed as a symbol of modernity and progress. For instance, Baller argues that "by preserving valuable architectural buildings of the past epochs, the modern town, one may say, becomes 'more up-to-date'" (Baller 1984:187).

Unlike in other Socialist countries, however, the Cuban regime did not challenge or question museums as an idea. They were emphatically supported and accorded a central role in the promotion of nationalist and internationalist culture. The CNC was the main actor in the creation of new museums. CNC members embraced the values of Marxism-humanism and saw museums as social conquests and as devices of cultural promotion. This approach fulfilled the aspirations of left-wing intellectuals during the Republic: rescuing national culture while spreading the best of (Western) universal culture to the people. For instance, the National Museum opened galleries with reproductions of universal art and widely publicized them. Thus, there was no condemnation of bourgeois culture or classical art but rather their propagation in galleries and exhibitions throughout the country.

The revolutionary heritage authorities—mainly Arjona Pérez—created the unfounded but currently widespread narrative in Cuba affirming that the Republic had managed to create only five museums and that they were in deplorable condition. Because allegedly only five museums existed, the official view maintained that "the revolutionary government reconstructed these five museums and built others" (UNESCO Cuba 1969:16). Many museums already in existence, such as the Poey or the City Museum in Havana, were falsely described as original revolutionary creations. Certainly, however, many museums were opened, and by 1969 there were seventeen public museums and six more underway (Otero and Martínez Hinojosa 1972:27).

A document of the CNC from 1963 presented its list of priorities in terms of culture for the subsequent five years. The fifth priority was: "Opening new galleries and museums and readapting others, to bring different museum collections to the public" (quoted in Gordon-Nesbitt 2012:311). The aim was to transfer the former property of the elites into public hands and transform it into a national legacy enjoyed by all Cubans in museums for their education. The conversion of most iconic collections and museums of the republican bourgeoisie into public museums was permeated by Marxist-humanist and Enlightenment values and discourse. For instance, when the mansion of millionaire Julio Lobo became the Museo Napoleónico (Napoleonic Museum), the regime emphasized its commitment to UNESCO's call to make all collections public and free (UNESCO Cuba 1962b). The government lauded the opening of every museum in UNESCO bulletins as evidence of Socialist cultural and educational progress for the international community. The inauguration of the Hemingway Museum, for example, announced that the regime was attempting to celebrate universal values that could be learned and shared by everyone (UNESCO Cuba 1962a).

The creation of other museums, including the museums of Decorative Arts, Medical Sciences, and Colonial Art in Havana, the museum of Pharmacy in Matanzas, and the Cuban Ambience in Santiago, followed a similar logic. For instance, the stated aim of the museum of Natural Sciences in the Capitolio was to "educate and raise the cultural level of our people. This is why our museum emphasizes the dissemination of scientific knowledge to the masses at large. This is why we have made efforts to present knowledge in a didactic form" (UNESCO Cuba 1965:10). Thanks to the museum, Havana allegedly became "an enlightened city" (UNESCO Cuba 1965:9). The City Museum of the OHCH also promoted the propagation of culture and the eradication of inequalities between rural and urban areas, going beyond its walls to educate peasants and proletarians in the fields and factories. To justify this initiative, it argued that culture had to reach everyone everywhere and that museums had a central role to play in culture's dissemination (UNESCO Cuba 1971).

The promotion of museums as spearheads of civilization and culture was an extension of their promotion by progressive republican intellectuals, such as Bobadilla or Morey. Museums and other cultural institutions assumed the task of identifying the distinctive features of Cuban identity and tracing their historic development from a Marxist-humanist perspective. The aim was to emphasize continuity with these distinctive cultural features while inscribing them into the framework of universal culture. Cuban representatives of UNESCO considered museums useful devices for "ensur[ing] the continuation of universal civilization in the present and the future [. . .] being one of the most efficacious means to establish the historical character of a community" (UNESCO Cuba 1972:3). The obstinate humanist promotion of "universal values" in which Cubans had to be educated reflected the modernizing and colonial ethos of the Revolution. Museums were seen as functional instruments for incorporating popular culture into the universal culture promoted by the Revolution. For instance, the work of the Museum of Music was described as

> a stubborn attempt to identify our roots, reflect popular idiosyncrasy and to incorporate the collective heritage to the main trends of universal art [. . .] The new institution will intensify the studies on the relation between the height of national consciousness and the emergence of autochthonous values. (UNESCO Cuba 1973:6)

This emphasis was also apparent in the contradictions that emerged in attempts to fit Cuban popular culture with the so-called universal Western scheme of cultural progress. There were also difficulties in reconciling the birth of the Cuban nation and identity with the modern epistemology and racially white composition of the Revolution, due to the significance of Afro-Cuban traditions, people, and the overall transcultural character of Cubans. Although racial ideology was improvisational, the nationalist bent of the Revolution sought authentic Cuban traditions in the Afro-Cuban heritage to counter North American influence and eradicate ideas of white supremacy (Peters 2010:20). However, there was a constant tension between the celebration of Afro-Cuban mythology and heritage as symbols of national identity, on the one hand, and the growing scientificization of race derived from Soviet ideas, which aimed at researching, cataloguing, and exhibiting Afro-Cuban cultural traits from a scientific, atheist perspective, on the other.

Most ethnographers shifted from a wider understanding of popular culture to study and represent Afro-Cuban themes. Then, the creation of the Conjunto Folklórico Nacional (National Folkloric Group) in 1962 popularized the idea that folklore was almost exclusively related to African dances and music. As Peters argues, the parallel scientificization and folklorization of race as a national heritage to be celebrated "provoked indignation among those black Cubans for whom the religions served as a still-vital tradition connecting them to an original culture. For some believers, the modernist-atheist zeal to historicize and rationalize the sacred justifiably trailed disquieting whiffs of European imperialism's 'civilizing mission'" (Peters 2010:81). The studies of Miller (2000) have highlighted the ongoing tension in postcolonial Cuba between the negation and the incorporation of African heritage, especially as revealed in the ambiguous and continued use of civic and religious symbolism related to Afro-Cuban cults. The ambivalent use of political symbolism pervaded the public performances of revolutionary leaders, from Fidel to Juan Almeida and Celia Sánchez, but was also essential in the invocation of martyrs, in the use of public spaces such as Revolution Square, in the cooptation of key dates of the religious calendar, and in the tacit religious worship of Martí. For Miller, this was a clear sign of continuity with republican attitudes toward Afro-Cuban cults and people, which, for him, "clearly demonstrates that deeply rooted cultural practices are more resistant to change than are bureaucracies" (Miller 2000:36).

Another key symbolic move was the conversion of military barracks into schools and museums, following the example of the French Revolution.

This process symbolized the Revolution's replacement of barbarism with education through the creation of museums. It was considered that "among the elements that can most help us in improving the knowledge of our history are monuments and museums. We believe that there is no better means of education [. . .] than a museum" (UNESCO Cuba 1972:3). The most symbolic military site transformed into a museum-school was the Moncada Barracks. The museum narrated the story of the struggle against Batista with an emphasis on martyrdom, sacrifice, and military might and heroism (Limia 1978).

In Havana, the house of one of Batista's officials was transformed into the museum of the Campaña de Alfabetización (Literacy Campaign), reinstating the idea that the Revolution replaced violence with education. At the entrance, a plaque reminded the visitor of the martyrs fallen during the dictatorship (UNESCO Cuba 1967). The museum translated one of the most enduring myths of the Revolution, the Campaña de Alfabetización of 1964, into a heritage narrative of revolutionary triumph. The exhibition showed some pictures of the Campaña de Alfabetización and a striking number of documents to prove its veracity. Documentary evidence was always significant in Cuban museology, as a way of highlighting and "proving" the participation of the community in certain shared historical events. The hyperbolic use of documentary evidence was also characteristic of Socialist museology, which considered it a scientific proof of the narrative's authenticity and a way of ensuring that the visitor reached the "right" interpretation of the exhibition (Petkova-Campbell 2009:57–58).

The creation of new museums illustrated the revolutionary aim of spreading culture and creating a new consciousness. Museums served to recontextualize past Cuban identities and cultural features and to incorporate them as heritage into a discourse of modernity and universal values. Instead of criticizing or contesting museums, the Revolution officially celebrated and promoted them and used them as vehicles of political propaganda both internally and externally. Tellingly, only the inauguration of the museums created under the logic of Marxism-humanism, such as the Hemingway or Napoleónico, was aired in the UNESCO bulletins for a global audience as a proof of revolutionary progress. Contrarily, the inaugurations or transformations of museums that had been created during the Republic or of those developed by MINFAR, such as the MR, never appeared in UNESCO bulletins. These museums were concealed from the external audience, because they were intended to impose a dominant cultural model on the internal audience.

This apparently contradictory process can be understood through Herzfeld's notion of "cultural intimacy," which involves the recognition "of those aspects of a cultural identity that are considered a source of external embarrassment but that nevertheless provide insiders with their assurance of common sociality" (Herzfeld 2005:3). The dissonance between certain revolutionary uses of heritage and UNESCO-based norms can be interpreted as a response to a global hierarchy of cultural value, revealing that there was awareness about the fact that cultural policies tailored to local ideological needs did not adhere to the international norms rhetorically endorsed by the Revolution. Ultimately, however, the whole process suggests that the influence of the universal values embodied by UNESCO was significant among Cuban heritage institutions and professionals, which deviated from the Soviet-oriented tendencies of MINFAR heritage policies.

The museum policies of the CNC based on Enlightenment ideas considered that ideal human behavior had to be grounded in reason to ensure order, emancipation, and progress. The more reason guided individual behavior, the more powerful, autonomous, and free the people would be. The role of museums was no longer to present original or extraordinary artifacts, as during the Republic, but rather to exhibit elements that could be useful for education and pedagogy and for the propagation of revolutionary ideology. Museums were fundamental in the manufacturing of a shared national-revolutionary identity by promoting an ideal of homogeneity and providing a common ground for framing Cuban culture within world culture. Cuban museums therefore played a dual role: they symbolically expropriated the heritage from the former bourgeois expropriators and put it at the service of the people; and they attempted to reframe popular traditions in terms of universal culture. In other words, in identifying what was common in all of world culture, the redistribution of heritage was aimed at making Cubans believe that universal culture and values were also "theirs." This would ease the internalization of ideology for its familiar and "folk" appearance and the transformation of Cubans—mainly the youth—into new men, embracing the internationalist and universal values promoted by the Revolution. The Revolution aimed at breaking with the "negative" part of the past national culture and at establishing continuities with universal culture, and heritage policies were a fundamental means with which to achieve these aims.

Breaking with Monumental Representation

During the Republic, the standard procedure for constructing monuments involved civil associations creating commissions to collect money and lobby institutions. This practice ended soon after the start of the Revolution, as civic associations disappeared under the centralizing thrust of the government. For instance, the commission for the creation of a monument to "Eddy" Chibás publicly announced that it would give all the money collected to Fidel so he could promote its construction, which he never did. Besides this important shift, the main trends in terms of monuments during the early revolutionary years were the critique of republican monuments and changes in monument theory and practice. I analyze the tensions that emerged in both processes by exploring the development of three representative Cuban monuments and the larger trends of monumental production.

The centralization of monument construction made the state solely responsible for selecting the characters and events to commemorate in public space. The new standard procedure was to commemorate collectives rather than individuals while at the same time creating a sense of collective endeavor in the development of the monument. For instance, February 1960 was designated the "Month of the Collection for the Monument to the Martyrs of the Revolution." The monument was intended to commemorate "not only those fallen at the University of Havana, but all the fallen in Cuba in the freedom struggle, since Hatuey to the victims of 'La Coubre'" ("Mártires" 1960). Meanwhile, the Comisión Nacional de Monumentos was reconstituted and put under control of a guerrilla commander, Pedro Miret, and architect Oliva, designer of the MR (MINREX 1976). The focus of the Comisión shifted from the preservation of indigenous sites and colonial monuments to the declaration of revolutionary sites of memory as national monuments. For Oliva, in the attempt to find a balance between change and continuity, preservation and destruction, the *Comisión* intended to avoid underestimating the past as much as overestimating it, trying to find a fair relation between the past and our contemporary world, preserving what is permanent throughout every change. We will discover the new to emphasize the past, renovate the past to reinstate it, and enhance what we already possess. (Oliva 1963:3)

Reading between the lines, it is clear that "what was permanent" was the "good" national culture to be preserved: the radical, left-wing version of Cuban nationalism. The past was something "low" that needed to be resignified in order to be incorporated into the "high"—that is, into the new revolutionary culture.

The selection of the past and its projection in public space was to be achieved through the symbolic and material creation of new monuments. The symbolic production of monuments involved the transformation of places where certain historic events had taken place into sites of memory, while the material creation of monuments involved planning and building new structures and monumental areas. The Comisión led the first process, marking dozens of sites throughout the country with plaques, obelisks, and signs. Most of the first sites monumentalized were related to social revolts and revolutionary events, because the features related to the War of Independence and its heroes had been already declared heritage during the Republic. As a result, the country was filled with plaques marking sites like Abel Santamaría's apartment and the house where he was born, Playa Girón (Bay of Pigs) and the *desembarco del Yate Granma*, or the place where José Antonio Echeverría fell in combat.

A case study analysis limited to Sancti Spíritus Province reveals the revolutionary emphasis in commemorating military events and characters. Between 1959 and 1980, out of the seventy-two sites marked with plaques and banners, 45 percent of sites commemorated places where revolutionary martyrs fell in combat, 21 percent commemorated independence or revolutionary warriors, 15 percent commemorated the birthplaces of those warriors, and 12 percent commemorated military operations. Only the remaining 5 percent commemorated other characters and events. The Comisión declared some of these sites National Monuments, when they were crucial for the revolutionary ideology. Other features, such as the colonial historic centers, only started to be considered heritage to be protected and declared as national monuments from the 1980s onward.

The construction of new monuments mobilized more resources and caused more dissonance than the symbolic monumentalization of places carried out by the Comisión. As we have seen, Raúl and MINFAR had developed an ambitious plan, influenced by Soviet ideas, for the construction of monuments throughout the country. However, Cuba did not implement anything similar to the well-structured monumental plan put forward in the USSR. Lenin's plan had involved tearing down most previous monuments and the implementing sixty-eight monuments devoted to the intellectual and political forebears of the October Revolution. However, the poor quality of the monuments and their unenthusiastic public reception led to the suspension of the program in 1922 (Bowlt 1978).

In Cuba, the first task consisted of creating an official version of monuments of the Republic that passed judgment on them. This involved developing the idea that republican Cuba at the time was subordinated to foreign domination and, consequently, that republican monuments did not represent the true national identity. Various scholars maintained that monuments played a key role in the symbolic domination of Cubans by the bourgeois elite (U.P.01 Osvaldo Sánchez 1973:24–26). Or, as Cuban sculptor José Antonio Díaz Peláez put it, that republican monuments were "physically estranged from society" (Díaz Peláez 1979:135). The materiality of republican monuments was criticized for maintaining a "distancing" from society by being erected over giant pedestals at a considerable height above the street, square, or sidewalk.

Taking stock of republican monuments, Cuban architect Nelson Herrera Ysla considered that this alleged "distancing" resulted from an active republican "policy for the isolation and freezing of the revolutionary and anti-imperialist ideas" (Herrera Ysla 1980:6) of the leaders of the War of Independence. Cuban sculptor Enrique Moret further argued that republican monuments served to "enslave people and make them ignorant, superstitious, miserable and fearful," and although, he conceded, the Revolution has not generally changed the form of monuments, "what has changed is the addressee of the message [. . .] the monument now is at the service of the people and lauds them" (Moret 1975:19). In similar terms, Pereira affirmed that republican monuments functioned only as "vehicles of ideological manipulation, political demagogy, and instrumentalization for economic embezzlement" (Pereira 1994:18). Republican monuments were accused of drawing on the Greco-Roman universal cultural tradition in terms of content and form, and there was a call to put an end to the slavish imitation of European forms, which was considered a trace of material and epistemic colonialism (Rigol 2013:90–100).

If there was agreement about the critique of republican monuments, less clear was how a new monumental canon would be adapted to the requirements of the Revolution. The question of whether it was legitimate to construct monuments at all created a contradiction between the critical attitudes of scholars and professionals, on the one hand, and the needs of the leadership for symbolic legitimacy, on the other. This question was fundamental, because Socialist states considered that material infrastructure would determine consciousness. Or, as Caroline Humphrey put it after exploring Soviet policies on infrastructure, "Ideology is found not only in texts and speeches; it is a political practice that is also manifest in constructing material objects" (Humphrey 2005:39). The Marxist-Leninist concern for functionalism led to the rejection of beauty, which was considered a bourgeois value and thus ideologically corrupt. The consequence of embracing functionalism was that engineers and builders replaced architects, who were associated with bourgeois ideology (Segre 1998). After 1971, the state replaced Day of the Architect with Day of the Builder, transformed the Colegio de Arquitectos (College of Architects) into the Centro Técnico Superior de la Construcción (Higher Technical Center of Construction), and created the Faculty of Construction.

The first thing to note is that since the start of the Revolution there had been a series of key transformations in the conception of construction, architecture, and material culture broadly. To begin with, there was an increasing demand for interdisciplinarity in monument construction that was part of a process of depersonalization of artistic creation (Díaz Peláez 1979). This was paralleled by the gradual disappearance of the *firma,* the individual signature, which can indeed be considered as the sign that transforms art into a commodity in capitalist contexts (Baudrillard 1981:102). Both processes were part of a Socialist-inspired attempt to decimate architecture as a bourgeois discipline and to dominate and reorient individualistic impulses in monument production, recasting it as a collective rather than an individual endeavor. Consequently, what were once the individual works of artists, architects, and professionals became collective undertakings under state control, and building projects were often organized in collectives called Unidades Productivas (Productive

Units). To compensate for the exclusion of architecture and "aesthetic" concerns from the constructive endeavor, artists were called to join Productive Units. This was seen as a form of accomplishing the Socialist ideal of bringing together art and technique. Reflecting about this issue two decades after the start of the Revolution, Culture Minister Hart Dávalos rhetorically asked:

> Is it not necessary, perhaps, to consider that artists should play an important role in urban affairs? Are not the beautiful avenues an artistic expression of modern cities? Are not ancient cities preserved like artistic monuments? And, why should we not think that in the era of planning, artists should have a conscious participation and an increasing role in urban building? (Hart Dávalos 1977:3)

The Unidad Productiva 01 Osvaldo Sánchez was the most active in the theorization and building of monuments. The Unidad Productiva led the search for a new monumental paradigm. It criticized the assumption of foreign traditions in the construction of monuments by the republican bourgeoisie and affirmed that monuments served only to reinforce authority and to foster the "submissive acceptance of the dominant order" (U.P.01 Osvaldo Sánchez 1973:29). Classic monuments were defined as the visible embodiment of the state and its institutions, representing the fake "'ritual' of democracy, that is, the idealization of the temple of knowledge open to the whole community" (U.P.01 Osvaldo Sánchez 1973:29).

In this context, monuments would make sense only if they were both functional and embedded in quotidian social life. Indeed, according to Segre, "the ideological content of the Revolution should be identified with its 'functional' works" (Segre 1970:202–203), rather than with its aesthetic and formal creations. More profoundly, the idea that heritage served to reinforce hegemony and create social hierarchies led many revolutionaries in Cuba and other Socialist countries to the logical conclusion that an egalitarian society must avoid any form of monumentalization. Moreover, from the perspective of scientific atheism, the traditional monumental canon focusing on national heroes could be interpreted not only as the celebration of an individualistic and bourgeois ethos but also as the perpetuation of Catholic and religious forms of worship, which should be avoided under Socialism. Debates about monuments thus reflected a tension between a strict reading of scientific atheist conceptions and the sources of Cuban nationalism based on a sanctified view of heroes and martyrs that functioned under an apparent religious logic.

Radical architects also believed that monuments were contrary to the sense of dynamism and future-oriented progress that the revolutionary movement promoted. As Segre put it, if the Revolution espoused Marxist-Leninist dialectics and assumed the "continuous transformability of form and space in the dynamic changing functionalities of our society [. . .] the timelessness and eternity created by monuments should be rejected" (Segre 1970:200). For Segre, the solution to the tension between monumental representation and revolutionary ideology was balancing symbolism with functionality in every monument. Despite the fact that he criticized the monument concept in theory, Segre justified the continued use of monuments in practice. This was the case because, once in power, revolutions should "materialize symbols representing their vanguard action [. . .] based on the most advanced plastic and spatial manifestations of the time" (Segre 1970:202). The Cuban Revolution, however, had preferred to express ideology in what Segre defined as functional and "dynamic-educative-evocative" rather than monumental terms. Accordingly, for Segre there were only three ideologically valid monuments in the early revolutionary years: the monument-park to the University Martyrs (1965), the Demajagua (1968) and Playa Girón (1963).

These monuments were similar in terms of form and content. They commemorated collective actions of revolutionary struggle rather than individual heroes: the Cuban War of Independence, the participation of students in the Revolution, and the first U.S. defeat in Latin America, respectively. They also commemorated historical figures and events in their original locations, contrary to the republican tradition of placing monuments in the center of urban squares. Finally, they employed abstract art and avoided the simplistic realism that characterized previous Cuban monuments.

The commemoration of martyrs was a constant throughout the Revolution. In Santiago, the revolutionary authorities built the Pantheon to the Martyrs of the 26-J group and the monument to their local University Martyrs between 1959 and 1972. However, the most representative monument commemorating martyrs was built in Havana. The public call of the competition to create the monument to the University Martyrs envisioned it as a martyrology to the students who had died in different revolutionary struggles between 1871 and 1959. In this sense, it was in line with the narrative of the 100 years of struggle that characterized the early Revolution. The monument was placed in front of the University of Havana, which had been a hotspot of the struggle against Batista and where many students had been killed. The aim was to use heritage to transform the emotional atmosphere of the area, which was seen as a depository of negative heritage. The organizers of the competition justified the monument in these terms, arguing that such sites of memory forced Cubans to live "among undesired remains of previous generations" (Vergani 1963:19).

The winners of the competition declared their intention to break with the traditional conception of the monument placed on a pedestal and presiding over a square. Instead, their aim was to address the contradiction between aesthetics and functionalism by transforming the area into a "functional symbol" that could convey meaning while preserving the functionality of the square (Coyula Cowley 1963:13). The monument consisted of a series of curved walls that narrated through carvings and inscriptions episodes of Cuban martyrdom in the different historic struggles. The aim was to emphasize historic continuity and encapsulate it in the concept of sacrifice. As one of the architects of the winning team put it, "sacrifice— through death—provides coherence and continuity to the collection of martyrs (and why not, heroes?)" (Coyula Cowley 1963:14).

The designers also attempted to address the contradiction between revolutionary dynamism and the demarcations monuments created. They claimed that the monument had a pedagogic rather than aesthetic intention. Their aim was not to convey a sense of finitude but to explain the dialectics, the sets of causes and consequences, that underride historical development. In addition, they made the monument horizontal and avoided emphasizing any particular character, to avoid the sense of hierarchization and transcendence conveyed by traditional vertical monuments to an individual. Although the project clearly reflected the functionalism and antiaestheticism of the early revolutionary years, it was criticized for its excessive concern for beauty and its lack of functionality. For instance, Segre (1970) considered the monument-park to be flawed because it did not manage to create a symbol and convey meaning through functionalism only, and thus he found it similar to bourgeois monuments in its resorting to artful expression.

Segre equated functionalism with modernity and the new, and the ideas of the good and the high, while he considered aesthetic concern part of the bourgeois past, and connected to ideas of the bad and the low. This generated a tension between reality and ideology, as well as between past and present: because the monument did not make a functional contribution to social progress, it was not looking forward to the revolutionary future but rather commemorating the past using aesthetics. The architects of the winning team had anticipated this criticism. They humbly recognized that they had made some "ideological concessions" but justified themselves, arguing that it was understandable in the context of a "young Revolution" that still presented "moral and ethical attitudes proper of a liberal-bourgeois superstructure" (Coyula Cowley 1963:14).

Their self-criticism can be interpreted in the light of the complex debates about change and continuity and about artistic expression. The central question was about whether various forms of bourgeois artistic expression should coexist with purely Socialist cultural forms. For Mirta Aguirre and Edith García Buchaca, it was clear that bourgeois art and Socialist art were, in a truly Socialist society, mutually exclusive: one of the two different socioeconomic formations and their superstructures must cease to exist. In other words, they advocated for a break with the "bad" national tradition and for the imposition of socialist realism. Many Marxist-humanists rejected this view. Jorge Fraga (1963) argued that continuity with the bourgeois heritage was a necessary part of a process of proletarian reflection and critique that would give rise to the new Socialist form of expression. The monument of the University Martyrs revealed the difficulties faced by Cuban professionals and artists in resolving the tension between both theoretical positions in practice while fulfilling the state's need to project ideology through monuments.

Less tension surrounded the monument at the Demajagua, which commemorated the 100 years of struggle and the Cuban revolt against Spain. Like the monument of the University Martyrs, it employed a series of walls with inscriptions and reliefs to emphasize horizontality and represent historic progress. The monument represented the Cuban narrative of sacrifice and struggle as emerging from the earth in the natural environment of the Demajagua. Its symbolic aim was twofold: it represented the origins of the War of Independence as a struggle in and for the Cuban land, and it naturalized and reified the national-revolutionary narrative.

The case of the *Playa Girón* monument was different from the former two because it attracted international interest. Following the guidelines of a previous commission led by Fidel, the government launched an international competition to build a monument commemorating the Cuban victory over the United States (Castro 1961a). The organizers received dozens of monument proposals from all over the world (Pérez Beato 1964). Most of them were socialist realist Chinese and Soviet projects, but the international judges awarded the prize to an abstract monument designed by two Polish architects. This decision was in line with the rejection of socialist realism among intellectuals and artists and the dominant groups in government during the earliest years of the Revolution. The proposal by the Polish architects represented the U.S. defeat using large blocks of concrete emerging from the sea to symbolize the defense against an enemy that clashed with the beach and was repelled. A line of half-dug trenches would lead visitors inland toward a museum.

The winning project, however, was never implemented. Official sources justified this by arguing that the costs were too high and that its reading was ideologically problematic, for the monument emphasized the power of the invaders more than the heroic role of the defenders (Coyula Cowley 2007). Various interviewees argue, however, that the true reason the project was abandoned was that it was too abstract for the gradual turn of official Cuban architecture toward socialist realism, and mainly, because the Polish architects had "deserted to the enemy"—that is, they had fled to a capitalist country.

There is a tendency among scholars and architects to look at the most prominent monuments as representatives of a specific period. This perspective neglects the less spectacular monumental developments of the time that are often more revealing about the general patterns of heritage conceptualization and practice. According to Augusto Rivero Mas (interview, May 21, 2013), a Cuban sculptor with extensive experience in monument construction, the early revolutionary years were marked not so much by the most salient monumental projects than by the expansion of low-quality busts and monuments commemorating local heroes,

LOS MONUMENTOS
SON LAS CASAS
DE LOS HEROES
José Martí

PATRIA ó MUERTE

MONUMENTO
PLAYA
GIRON
HONOR
A LOS
HEROES
CAIDOS

VENCEREMOS

Figure 3.9. Announcement of the monument to the fallen heroes in Playa Girón, with a quotation from Martí stating, "Monuments are the homes of heroes." Source: Castro (1961a).

revolutionaries, and martyrs throughout the country. Most of these monuments were not the result of public competitions but were commissions given directly to specific sculptors by the politicians running mass organizations, public companies, ministries, and provincial governments (Veiga 1980:45).

As a rule, these monuments were realist and followed classic sculptural traditions of Italian origin. Because the best Cuban artists often rejected realism, politicians commissioned less skilled artists. Tellingly, when I asked various interviewees about this period, they described the monuments that resulted from official commissions as "realist" and "traditional" rather than as "socialist realist." Thus, instead of interpreting these monuments as a sign that socialist realism had been adopted as the official language of power, we can see them as reflecting a form of conservatism that promoted formal continuity with previous republican standards and with "tradition" broadly. Contrary to the republican period, however, these monuments were less luxurious and employed national materials from mines in Bayamo and Isla de Pinos, instead of Italian marbles, probably because of economic constraints and ideological requirements. In many ways, then, mainstream revolutionary monuments continued with previous monumental traditions in formal and aesthetic terms; what changed were the historical figures and events commemorated. As a Cuban sculptor put it when remembering that period, what "changed was the content, but the form endured" (J. Aguilera quoted in Rodríguez Joa 2009:31).

The difficulties involved in developing a new monumental canon consistent with the revolutionary ideology were articulated by one of the designers of the monument to the University Martyrs:

> In Cuba, due to the political contingencies, or maybe to a lack of concern for culture, the need to create a new figurative idea and a new expressive language coherent with the revolutionary and pedagogic function that monuments were supposed to fulfill became just a hope amidst the remembrances of those convulsive years of struggle. (Vergani 1963:21)

The early Revolution witnessed a debate between at least three understandings of heritage and, consequently, of how and whether to build monuments: First, heritage was seen as part of a bourgeois superstructure from the past to be suppressed and overcome, as seen in MINCONS plans to get rid of the monument to Martí. Second, heritage was seen as a form of collective self-representation of the body politic. This involved preserving the heritage idea but making it egalitarian in form and content, thereby symbolizing the union of the people and the leadership without hierarchies, as in the monuments to the University Martyrs in Havana or the Granjita Siboney. Third, heritage was seen as a form of celebrating the deeds of individual national heroes and martyrs, as in the low-profile monuments throughout the country. The tension between these three models was resolved in favor of the third, suggestive of the revolutionary will to preserve tradition and perpetuate previous models.

The institutionalization period would not deviate from this pattern, and the first and second forms of heritage production would be completely abandoned. Indeed, if the sculptural language and aesthetics employed by Soviet socialist realism were similar to that of Tsarist monuments (Lodder 1983:55), the same relationship can be established between most Cuban revolutionary monuments and their republican counterparts. This does not mean that Cuba adopted socialist realism but rather reflects the endurance of tradition and an aversion to making a radical break with the past in monumental forms.

The Revolution could not do without the monument form because, as elsewhere, monuments were useful for structuring ideology in space. Therefore, despite Segre's argument that Cuban architecture managed to express the ideological principles of the Revolution and to overcome the traditional and static conception of monuments, it is clear that experimentation was limited to a few projects under rigid state control. Revolutionary artists and professionals found it difficult to devise the adequate form with which to represent in monuments both the sense of emergence of the new and the break with the past. They failed to resolve the contradiction between monumental aesthetics and Socialist functionalism. This failure reflected a difficulty in establishing the necessary connections between political and artistic vanguards, a subject of heated debate in the early revolutionary years.

This failure notwithstanding, revolutionary Cuba underwent a complex process of formal and aesthetic reflection and experimentation that was innovative in many ways. The Cuban experience deviated from Soviet standards and also from those in Yugoslavia, Romania, or Bulgaria, where the party line was imposed in heritage production after the Communists came to power. Nonetheless, similar to the USSR of the 1920s, the Cuba of the 1960s exemplified what Janice Baker aptly described as "the difficulty of simultaneously developing critical modes of historical and aesthetic practice" (Baker 2010:47). A leadership determined to hold onto national tradition in order to ground the legitimacy of the Revolution restrained the attempts of cultural and artistic avant-gardes to break with the past.

In the words of a Cuban monument designer, the daunting questions that emerged during the early years were: "How can humanism [. . .] employ the same means of persuasion, communication and propaganda that were employed against them [proletarians]? [. . .] Has the new society the right to use the same technique to build the man of its time?" (Vergani 1963:27). Clearly, the leadership's answer to both questions was in the affirmative: forms could change, but the idea of the monument as such should remain unchallenged. Monuments fulfilled the double task of naturalizing and spreading the new master-narrative as a form of propaganda, as well as conveying the message of passion and affection demanded by a young Revolution aiming to create a new Socialist identity.

Conclusion

The early revolutionary years were characterized by a combination of pragmatic and experimental heritage policies. These policies reflected the complex and evolving social, political, and geostrategic dynamics of the time as the tiny island became a global point of focus for its key role in the Cold War. For the revolutionaries, heritage was secondary to geopolitics in the attempt to safeguard Cuba's sovereignty. Nonetheless, they saw culture and heritage as fundamental means with which to ensure internal support and legitimacy through the articulation of individual and collective experiences through a revolutionary ideology. With the means of production in the hands of the state—and with political contestation suppressed, coopted, or expelled to Miami—the inner circle around Fidel sought to acquire legitimacy and reinforce their position in the face of other power groups.

This initial period saw the fulfillment of many of the aspirations of republican left-wing nationalists. These included the creation of galleries with reproductions of universal artworks, the division of heritage collections according to their contents in well-funded cultural institutions, the creation of a fine arts museum according to international standards, and the active participation in global heritage institutions like UNESCO. Radical architects that had harshly criticized Martí's monument and the *Plaza Cívica* during the Republic were able to design experimental urban plans, while artists could challenge former monumental styles and traditions. Rather than a complete break with the past and a shift toward Soviet-style heritage policies, the early years involved a complex negotiation during which various autonomous groups promoted their agendas within the system. The leadership was concerned with satisfying the demands that legitimized the Revolution—the expansion of culture and education—and with providing a negative vision of the Republic to justify the break with the past and the historical need of the Revolution. However, the anti-institutionalism of the leadership and the lack of human and economic resources to build a strong institutional apparatus prevented a unifying and stable heritage policy from developing. Moreover, the heated debates about culture throughout the 1960s pushed heritage policies in different directions.

Despite the absence of clear guidelines of monument and museum creation, and the disorderly and continuous transferal of exhibitions between different locations, an analysis of the larger picture reveals the complex, but overall coherent, use of heritage during the early years. Because the nation had been symbolically reborn with the Revolution, the "prenational" past was represented as the "bad" and the "enemy." Consequently, its symbols had to be completely erased. Two main strategies for this goal were devised. The first operated in the short term, and its objective was to enact a break with the past. It involved the resignification of the main republican symbols and the use of history as a "testimony" to provide "proof" of the new symbolic order's veracity. This entailed the destruction, resignification, and transformation of symbolic republican buildings, mansions, and monuments. Museum exhibitions were rearranged to convey new historical meanings intended to spur disaffection for the republican past and allegiance to the revolutionary present and future.

The second strategy was geared toward the long term and focused on establishing continuity with the part of the national past and culture that had to be incorporated within the new symbolic order. This requirement subordinated heritage to the elaboration and representation of a coherent historical narrative that could grant meaning to the revolutionary ideology. For it to be successful, ideology had to be socialized through education and materialized in public space. This goal was partially accomplished by the placement of the production of history under state control, by the selection and sanitization of the "good" national culture, and by the development of new forms of heritage production.

Although artists, historians, and heritage professionals enjoyed a certain freedom of negotiation and debate in terms of form, the contents expressed via heritage could not be challenged. Briefly, the content of the

early master-narrative affirmed that there had been only one revolutionary process since 1868: the 100 years of struggle. According to this narrative, the U.S. intervention in Cuba and the establishment of a neocolonial
pseudo-republic that lacked sovereignty frustrated the prospects of full
independence. The narrative equated Fidel with Martí and praised both as
fathers of the *patria,* similarly equating the 26-J revolutionaries with the
mambises (the Cuban fighters of the War of Independence). All were heroes and martyrs who sacrificed themselves for the freedom of Cuba. Their
deeds had to be taught to younger generations, who could then follow
their example and thank them for the freedom they provided. The narrative aimed to maintain the sense of civil war in the collective memory,
which in turn legitimized the urgency of action that underpinned early
revolutionary politics.

The slow permeation of Soviet ideas resulted in a peculiar process of
nation-building whereby Cuban radical nationalist ideas gradually merged
with Marxism-Leninism. Whereas the first emphasized Martí's tradition,
charisma, anti-imperialism, and passion, the latter highlighted scientific
objectivity, historical materialism, solid institutionalization, and class
identity. As Anderson (2006:145) has pointed out, revolutionary nationalisms tend to emanate from the state and serve to consolidate its hegemony. However, although nation and Marxism-Leninism merged symbolically, Fidel actively used heritage to preserve the separation between
national-revolutionary identity and the state and to ensure his identification with the former. He satisfied the revolutionary demands for passion
that ensured legitimacy, leaving state technocracy and governmentality
to be associated with the bureaucratic ranks. Thus, although Fidel was
wholeheartedly committed to proletarian internationalism, he did believe
that the workers had national identities. The expansion of culture, heritage, and education was depicted as a triumph of *Cuban* Socialism aimed
at Cuban mastery of universal culture as the "raw material" of an authentic, folk culture.

Furthermore, because positivist history-culture could be easily reworked to fit Soviet Marxist-Leninist schemes, Cubans could refashion
their heritage production in terms coherent with Soviet ideas while preserving a certain degree of autonomy. Indeed, the Cuban relationship with
the USSR should not be interpreted in terms of neocolonialism but rather
as a form of crypto-colonialism. Herzfeld describes crypto-colonialism as

the curious alchemy whereby certain countries [. . .] were compelled to acquire their political independence at the expense of massive economic dependence, this relationship being articulated in the iconic guise of aggressively national culture fashioned to suit foreign models [. . .] Caught in the exclusionary logic of cold war oppositions [. . .] crypto-colonies were forced to play roles not of their own choosing. Within that larger geopolitical context, their civilizational discourses—pleas for recognition and respectability—followed the parallel dynamic of a global hierarchy of culture. (Herzfeld 2002:901)

Crypto-colonialism is closely related to the politics of representation, because it "insists on the glorification of a specifically national culture" in which "the rhetoric of 'heritage' is especially relevant" (Herzfeld 2012:216). The concept of crypto-colonialism proves useful for investigating the contradictory process whereby, in affirming its sovereignty and liberation from U.S. neocolonial domination, Cuba gradually reinstated its allegiance to and reinforced cultural and political bonds with the USSR. It might be argued that Cuban difficulties in escaping external pressures on its postcolonial cultural refashioning were similar to those experienced during the Republic, but the number of countries, traditions, and ideas influencing Cuban professionals and intellectuals was surely larger than in the post-1959 period. However, the gradual assumption of ideas from the Soviet Bloc should be understood as a contradictory tendency rather than a straightforward process, unfolding erratically between 1959 and 1990 and resulting in a peculiar blending of Soviet and Cuban heritage models.

Indeed, Cuba reversed the renowned Stalinist motto that established the limits of "deviancy" under Soviet rule to "national in form, Socialist in content." The paramount example was the dissolution of the National Museum and the creation of a MR emulating the Soviet model. The Cuban distinctiveness emerged in the content of the museum, which was far from Soviet ideology. The narrative emphasized radical nationalist ideas of collective identity grounded on struggle and sacrifice, with Cuban héroes, rather than economic classes, playing a central role. The MR was therefore Socialist in form but aggressively nationalist in content. The invocation of Socialist ideas was subordinated to the consolidation of national identity. In addition, the Cuban heritage field drew heavily from the humanist ideas of UNESCO, and some heritage professionals were trained in Paris rather than in the Eastern Bloc.

My interpretation suggests that rather than an all-encompassing national policy, the weak institutional structure of the early years allowed various groups and institutions to establish relatively autonomous relationships with each other and with foreign actors according to their ideology and background, with MINFAR being closer to the USSR and the state heritage institutions being closer to Paris, UNESCO, and the West broadly. Moreover, we must bear in mind that the most orthodox Communists from the PSP, such as Carlos Rafael Rodríguez or García Buchaca, differed in approach from their counterparts in other cultural institutions closer to Marxist-humanist ideas, such as Hart Dávalos. The question remains of whether, in affirming Cuban contents and Soviet forms, Fidel and his inner circle were sincerely committing to Soviet cultural and heritage ideas or just acting *as if* they were committing to them, for the sake of ensuring Soviet geopolitical and economic support. Probably, the answer stands halfway between both.

4

The Institutionalization of
the Cuban Heritage Field (1973–1990)

The 1970s and 1980s witnessed the institutionalization of the Cuban Revolution, which had important consequences for heritage theory and practice. The years of informality, discussion, utopianism, moral incentives, and experimentation gave way to rationality, pragmatism, economic incentives, and five-year plans. The priorities of the state were increasing productivity and popular obedience, rather than transforming Cuban culture, values, and people. A bureaucratic technocracy complemented the charismatic-personalistic centralism of the regime embodied by Fidel. The Thesis and Resolutions of the First Congress of the PCC of 1975, the Constitution of 1976, and the adoption of the System of Economic Management and Planning in 1975 formalized the institutionalization of the state.

The rapprochement with the USSR in terms of ideology and bureaucratic apparatus was significant, although Cuban-USSR relations were complex and their impact on internal structures and arguments contradictory. A bureaucratic apparatus started to emerge in the National Assembly, the Political Bureau and Secretariat of the PCC, the Central Committee, and Poder Popular (People's Power). This emergence was paralleled by the emergence of a multifaceted group of institutionalizers advocating rapprochement with Moscow and the establishment of an institutional framework based on the PCC. However, the power of the ex-guerrillas around Fidel counterbalanced the institutionalizers' actual agency. The maintenance of a clear separation between the leadership, state cadres, and organizations differentiated Cuba from other Socialist countries. The conflict between these two groups should be understood as a dynamic terrain of struggle with no clear boundaries. This underlying tension partially explains the sui generis and hybrid character of Cuban heritage and governmentality and shows that Cuba was no replica of Eastern Bloc countries (Kapcia 2014:120).

The institutionalization involved the end of the Quinquenio Gris, when those who did not commit explicitly to the revolutionary ideals were "parametrized," that is, repressed. Literary magazines were closed and ideological control concerning language, history, and the import of foreign and counter-revolutionary ideas in art was tightened. Soviet advisors dismantled the Department of Philosophy at the University of Havana and cleared libraries of "deviant" Marxist authors such as Louis Althusser, Herbert Marcuse, and Theodor Adorno. The now economically solvent and organized state was decentralized and authority redistributed to 14 provinces and 169 municipalities, most of which were new. The creation of new heritage and cultural institutions throughout the country generated a tension between the opening of new spaces for debate and practice, on the one hand, and the control over ideology, education, and culture, on the other.

A significant change for heritage policy and practice was the replacement of the CNC with the Ministry of Culture (MINCULT) in 1976. The new ministry ensured that ideology stayed coherent in the provincial and local institutions. MINCULT reported directly to the heads of the ruling national institutions and was responsible for providing nationwide guidance, technical support, and methodological advice. Although the commitment to Marxist-humanist values decreased during this period, Minister Hart Dávalos was no political orthodox. His appointment facilitated the rebuilding of relations of trust between artists and the leadership and gradually settled some of the most heated cultural and artistic debates.

These changes facilitated the debates about heritage that took place throughout the period and brought about significant consequences for heritage policies and for the understanding of Cubanness and national identity. The nation-building and revolutionary projects gradually converged, and national identification was reworked in terms of class identity. The representations of ideology and history increasingly mixed the passionate narrative of Cuban heroism and struggle with the scientific atheism behind the Marxist-Leninist narrative of class struggle. This chapter examines the role of heritage in the production, combination, and spread of both narratives. Exploring the dissonance involved in the creation of heritage reveals the underlying political tensions between artists and politicians, and between political institutionalizers and ex-guerrillas.

As the revolutionary focus shifted from revising the past to projecting a vision of the future Socialist state to be achieved, the construction of new heritage was emphasized while the reinterpretation and preservation of the past was downplayed. Accordingly, the plans for the construction of new monuments and museums are analyzed separately, as museums were closer to education and the spread of a historical master-narrative, while monuments were related to art, architecture, and spatial planning. This inquiry reveals the extent of the coloniality of power and the degree to which soviet Marxist-Leninist ideology was adopted in Cuba.

History as Ideology, Culture as Education: Conceptualizing Cuban Museums

The world we live in and the future we project demand an increasingly scientific teaching of history, that is, based on a Marxist-Leninist conceptual framework [. . .] History has to take over the hearts of the students if we intend to influence their patriotic and revolutionary education, which does not go against the constant presence of scientific reflections and demonstrations. The education of feelings must go hand in hand with scientific education.

(Díaz Pendás 1990:2)

The Cuban heritage field struggled to reconcile the revolutionary demands for passion and emotion with the scientific requirements of Marxism-Leninism. Nonetheless, the need to combine both became a priority, as history and heritage became central to the state's ideological agenda. Although state control over the intellectual and artistic field was never thorough in Cuba, the growing soviet influence led to a limitation of cultural experimentation and creativity for the sake of an overriding didacticism. This resulted in a blurring of the line between art, pedagogy, and propaganda and in the practical unification of education and culture. The

Congress of Education and Culture in 1971, held shortly after a bitter dispute between the leadership and European intellectuals, can be seen as the milestone that sanctioned the coupling between education and culture. As the Minister of Education Belarmino Castilla stated at the time, "Education and Culture form a homogeneous whole" (quoted in Abreu Arcia 2007:140).

Education gradually started to mean the inculcation of a Marxist-Leninist worldview among the "younger generations." Being educated implied acquiring "objective" knowledge of the laws of scientific Communism and political economy, which were underpinned by an explanation of historical development. History as a discipline was intrinsically linked with national-revolutionary identity, and Fidel (1968) emphasized its primary role as an endless source of inspiring sacrifice and struggle. This had important consequences for museums, which were seen as the second most important pedagogic institutions, after schools, and were required both to carry out historical research and to spread historical narratives. This approach is encapsulated by a museum director from the district of Centro Havana, who defined museums as "means of mass dissemination [. . .] where the history and the social values created by our ancestors can be learnt [. . .] including the scientific and artistic achievements that represent the evolution of human being" (Veila González ca. 1985:4).

Museums had to explain historical development according to Marxism-Leninism as a way of illustrating and reinforcing educative programs, especially those in fourth and tenth grades of school. Most methodological handbooks defining the procedures and techniques for teaching history in Cuba dedicated chapters to the role of museums as key complements to school lessons (Crego Fuentes 1973; Martínez Riera 1988). The museum was also considered by high-rank education official Horacio Díaz Pendás to be "a system of means for the teaching of history" (Díaz Pendás 1990:21). My visits to schools and my interviews with children and teachers confirmed that, to this day, the visit to the MR in Havana is a milestone in the educational journey. It was treated as either as a future experience that was considered important or as a remembrance of an exciting visit outside the school walls. Because museums targeted children, they were understood as conveyors of emotion. Accordingly, most handbooks highlighted the role of museums in inculcating the values of sacrifice, victimhood, and martyrdom by showing "real traces" of repression, struggle, and death.

Figure 4.1. Sculpture merging the figures of Martí and Lenin at the Instituto de Historia. The quote from Fidel reads "Two men from different historic periods and one single thought." Source: Author.

The MR exemplified the attempt to inculcate values through emotions: it exhibited the bloodstained clothes of revolutionaries and the picture of a man who wrote the word "Fidel" on a door with his own blood before dying.

A fundamental question is whether Cuban museology imitated soviet models. Most interviewees argued that soviet influence was feeble throughout the period and that Marta Arjona Pérez, the director of the state section of Patrimonio Cultural (Cultural Heritage) from the early revolutionary years until her death in 2006, was more influenced by UNESCO than by the USSR. This argument does not stand, however, in light of written documentation and actual museum practice at the time. In fact, this general opinion probably results from the prevailing attitude that emerged after the Proceso de Rectificación de Errores y Tendencias Negativas (Process of Rectification of Errors and Negative Tendencies) in 1986, which encouraged Cubans to both reject and forget the soviet-influenced past. Indeed, Cuban intellectual Navarro (2002:120) has shown how the Proceso de Rectificación involved the reconversion of hard-liners through the rewriting of biographies and ideological shifts. In reality, a significant number of Cuban museum professionals were trained in Socialist countries, the only available museological guides were those translated from Russian, and Marxist-Leninist ideology and aesthetics pervaded museum content and form. Moreover, quantitative obsession, rigid methodological procedures, and soviet-style aesthetics became intrinsic components of Cuban museum practice. Cuban museums became places of initiation and ritual for schoolchildren, war veterans, members of the pioneer movement swearing oath, and university graduates, a function that Western museums seldom have and that probably derived from soviet museology.

Marta Arjona Pérez played a central role in the conceptualization and implementation of museums in Cuba. She overtly considered museums as instruments of ideological propagation: "Some bourgeois scholars oppose this view arguing that, if we do not proceed with caution, history museums can cease to be instruments of education to become devices of propaganda" (Arjona Pérez 2003:96). Because she defined propaganda as the "effort to propagate an idea," she considered it legitimate for museums to concentrate on "the dissemination of the Marxist conception of history, art or science, depending on each specific museum" (Arjona Pérez 2003:96). She conceived history museums as devices for the resolution of social problems and as transformative tools that could articulate the lives of Cubans as part of a Marxist-Leninist narrative (Arjona Pérez 2004 [1986]:24). Her views did not differ much from those of Eastern Bloc museologists, who considered museums as instruments of both pedagogy and propaganda (e.g., Anoschenko 1977:63; Klausewitz 1988:17). Even Arjona Pérez's definition of museums was close to that in a soviet museology handbook: "Soviet Museums are an efficient propaganda tool for communist ideas, for the communist conception of the world and thus for communist education" (Galkina et al. 1957:3). Similarly, for Baller, museums "do not only promote the dissemination of knowledge of the country's past and do not only develop aesthetic tastes in people, but also actively disseminate the scientific, Marxist-Leninist world outlook; they assist in educating young people in the revolutionary traditions of the communist party" (Baller 1984:193). The Escuela de Museología (School of Museology) that functioned in Havana under the aegis of the Centro Nacional de Conservación, Restauración y Museología (National Center of Preservation, Restoration and Museology, CENCREM) between 1980 and 1984 was in charge of transforming these theoretical principles into practical methodologies. Its aim was to educate the hundreds of museum ranks required for the implementation of a large museum network. The ideas of Cuban museographers like Teresa Crego Fuentes (1973), trained in Czechoslovakia, underpinned the theory and practice of the Escuela. But it was Héctor Montenegro (1982), head of the Escuela, who produced a handbook of "methodological instructions" in which he partially adapted soviet museology to the Cuban context, including the technique of "methodical recollection" of heritage objects, rigidly regulated museum structures, objectives, and functions. In our interview, Montenegro recognized that he had to include soviet ideas in his handbook, despite having been trained in Paris and being more supportive of UNESCO guidelines. When Montenegro fled to the United States, the Escuela fell into oblivion and his more critical writings were erased. Indeed, these writings were retrieved only thanks to the collaboration of Montenegro and some of his former students. Nonetheless, many museum procedures and structures are still influenced by Montenegro's methodological instructions.

Because museum contents were determined by ideology, the handbook of the Escuela focused on technical issues and provided detailed accounts of all kinds of methodological procedures. It defined museums as producers of ideologically informed cultural history for educative purposes as well as spreaders of history, art, and science. Museography and museum aesthetics were deemed useful only when they could facilitate the "correct assimilation of the message intended for transmission" (Montenegro 1982:3). Museums were defined as instruments for transmitting ideological messages aimed at transforming consciousness to shape a specific national-revolutionary Cuban identity. But the carriers of these messages were not the museums themselves; nor did museums hold transformative potential as such. It was the heritage features they preserved, exhibited, and assembled into meaningful representations of historical development that fulfilled those tasks.

As Arjona Pérez put it, the function of museums was to position heritage as the historical underpinning of identity that allowed the masses "to identify themselves in the true essence of their historic-cultural roots" (Arjona Pérez 2004 [1986]:34). She defined heritage as "the cultural inheritance and the crucial basis of museology": "Heritage assets are the materials from which museology draws; hence their importance, for without them we could not reconstruct the development of society" (Arjona Pérez 2004 [1986]:35). Accordingly, museums were conceived as places where "heritage features and historic narrative should be presented in a specific context in dialectic relation [. . .] following scientific philosophical conceptions according to an objective, a thesis to be demonstrated—every museum is also a proved thesis" (Arjona Pérez 2004 [1986]:36). Furthermore, Arjona Pérez posited a causal determinism between a community's metacultural selection of heritage assets and that community's identity. Accordingly, "cultural identity is produced through heritage [. . .] Heritage is initially passive, it exists as an object [. . .] and it is the community [. . .] that selects it as an element to be preserved" (Arjona Pérez 2004[1986]:13).

This is a key move for legitimizing ideology, for it ensures that present identities do not result from the pre-Socialist past but from the active appropriation of specific heritage features as "raw material" from the past. It is only in the process of selecting specific heritage from the past that collective identity emerges and is "proved," heritage being a passive repository until it is activated by society. In other words, identity is not conceived as an unmediated inheritance from the past but rather as a social construction derived from present-day action. Arjona Pérez' views were in line with soviet conceptions of heritage as a present-centered instrument for human transformation. For instance, for Baller, heritage should have a normative and regulative function, in tune with the establishment of "new norms and patterns of behavior, a new morality, new traditions and customs [. . .] on the principles of collectivism, internationalism and communist humanism" (Baller 1984:265).

Arjona Pérez's understanding of heritage also shows that the importance of museums derived from Cuban education's emphasis on material culture. Objects were seen as part of the economic infrastructure that could spark public interest in the past, thus facilitating the internalization of the ideological message. The reason for this emphasis was expressed in a museology handbook widely distributed in Cuban museums. In it, Wolfgan Klausewitz, the renowned curator from the German Democratic Republic, emphasized that without objects

> scientific knowledge cannot advance, and the appropriation of the objective reality in the process of social reproduction is precluded. Historic objects *are the appropriation of the past*, they give the measure of the political, economic and cultural development of a period and a society in a specific territory [which is] essential for understanding the phases of social evolution, and to document and demonstrate the material progress accumulated hitherto. (Klausewitz 1988:5; emphasis mine)

Objects contributed to the development of the new man, who had to appropriate all past achievements of humanity to develop a fully formed consciousness. But objects were not supposed to *represent* the past. They provided the scientific evidence to *demonstrate* the current state of socioeconomic development according to the scientific laws of Marxism-Leninism.

Arjona Pérez's definition of heritage was in line with the new Cuban Constitution. The charter established a direct relation between cultural identity and heritage: "The state preserves the cultural identity of Cuban culture and ensures the conservation of the cultural heritage and the artistic and historical wealth of the nation" (G. C. 1976a). Interestingly, the first law dictated by the newly constituted Poder Popular addressed heritage. Law 1 of Protección al Patrimonio Cultural (Cultural Heritage Protection) accorded a central role to museums in heritage management and effectively blurred the boundaries between public and private memories and heritage (G. C. 1977). It required individuals to register personal possessions as cultural objects, including family heirlooms, gifts, and biographical objects that could be requested for museum collections and public exhibition. The law accorded increased powers to museums, which could now resignify private histories and memories in their own terms by requesting objects belonging to individuals and families.

As producers and disseminators of an officially sanctioned history, museums embodied state power and expressed it at various levels: the architecture and organization of buildings, their collections, objects and narratives, and their aesthetics. My analysis of new museums and the re-arrangement of republican and early revolutionary museums will focus on two main groups. The first comprises the municipal and provincial muse-ums created under Law 23 of Museos Municipales (Municipal Museums) (G. C. 1976b). These museums were homogeneous in form and content and served to produce and propagate the simplified ideology of the re-gime—the master-narrative—and to create specific links between mean-ings and objects that underpinned the narrative, or symbols. The second group includes museums designed for marking, reifying, and reproducing specific myths of the master-narrative: the birth of Cuba, the advent of the Revolution, the building of Socialism, and the struggle against inter-nal and external enemies.

Municipal Museums: The Nationwide Materialization of a Master-Narrative

As the ideological coherence of the regime increased, the government intensified its commitment to forming a new identity that would allow Cubans to imagine their own national community in terms of plurality, simultaneity, and a homogeneous empty time, in line with Anderson's (2006) account of the emergence of national identities. Different initia-tives resulted from this endeavor, such as the attempt to combine cul-tural and economic production through the creation of "history halls" in workplaces (PCC Holguín 1978). However, the largest initiative by far was the creation of the municipal museum network, which provided for the establishment of a museum in each of the 169 new municipalities. This was an effort of such dimensions that it was equated at the time with the Campaña de Alfabetización of the 1960s (Arjona Pérez 2004 [1986]:96).

The quantitative expansion of museums was largely due to the creation of the municipal museums. From 28 museums in 1969, the number had grown to 235 in 1983. Of these, 163 were municipal and provincial, 49 spe-cialized, and 23 memorials. The mission of municipal museums was to "bring to the remotest parts of the country the image of their history and identity" (Arjona Pérez 2004 [1986]:31–32). And it was quite literally so: the centralized bureaucratic heritage logic was "dispersed" to create a nationwide homogeneous narrative through museum display. Accord-ing to Law 23, these museums were required to align local histories with the national master-narrative through the creation of an object-based exhibition in a building. Thus, museums enacted a top-down "localization" of national history, instead of opening a path for local histories to make the national from the ground up. Most early revolutionary museums had been created after the donation or expropriation of bourgeois properties. However, the collection of objects in municipal museums was carried out based on the requirements of the master-narrative to be represented, and also taking into account the pedagogic needs of schools. To do so, museum workers used the "methodological recollection" system developed by Montenegro in the Escuela de Museología. Drawing on the powers accorded them by Law 1 on Cultural Heritage Protection, museum professionals and local historians collected objects from abandoned bourgeois houses and by "suggesting" to people that they donate family heirlooms considered of heritage value to the museum. The word "suggesting" was emphatically used by different interviewees, implying a narrow boundary between coercion and consent.

Municipal museums were informally called "polyvalent" by workers because they did not specialize in specific collections or themes, as the "specialized" museums did. There were specific methodological instructions for the creation of the museums, including Preparatory Tasks, Scientific Conception, Thematic Plan, and Exhibition Thematic Plan, which replicated soviet models (Galalova 1987). Those were in line with the nationwide transformation of architecture into construction under Socialist premises, whereby MINCONS created systemic projects with ready-made templates for hospitals, factories, and houses. Similarly, a team in Havana was devoted to the mass production of museums. The director was architect José Linares Ferrera, educated in museology in Czechoslovakia, and current president of the International Council of Museums (ICOM) in Cuba. The team developed two basic templates for municipal and provincial museums and then designed the museology and museography of each museum exhibition. They installed most museums in brand-new buildings, which had to be painted white to highlight the materials on display. The contents of the museum plan were provided by a team of historians in Havana and, sometimes, by museum workers and historians in the provinces. The pictures, panels, and historic texts produced by this team were then sent to each museum. The commitment to incorporating "the best" of all previous historical developments in the formation of the new man

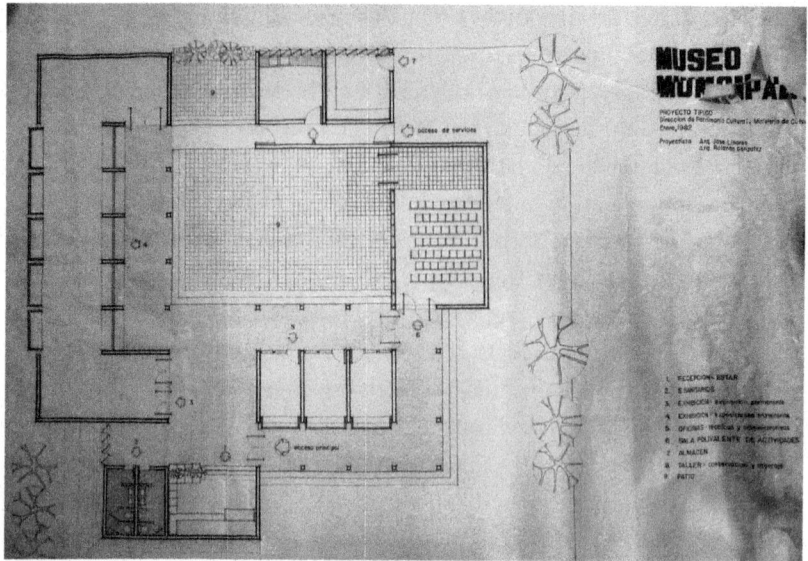

Figure 4.2. Standard project of municipal and provincial museums, by architect José Linares. These projects include the indicative contents to be exhibited in each room. Source: CNPC archive.

meant that all museums had to create a gallery of universal art with eighty reproductions of master artworks.

The mechanical reproduction of a museum template throughout the country reflected the transformation of architects into builders that produced standardized spaces through standardized means. As Linares Ferrera now acknowledges, the saturation of historical information contained in these museums made them resemble "books hanging in walls" (interview, March 20, 2013). Indeed, soviet museology handbooks recommended surrounding objects with words and explanations to prevent deviations in the interpretation of the exhibition: "In order to help the visitor examine the exhibits in a correct manner and to draw the correct conclusions, quotations and texts by the curators are introduced into the exhibition" (Galkina et al. 1957:177). The emphasis on documentary evidence similarly reflected the will to turn visitors into eyewitnesses to a past that justified the present: "In the exhibition, the visitor will see the concrete materials that he would have seen were he the eye witness of the strikes at the beginning of the 20th century" (Galkina et al. 1957:176).

The size and reach of the museum network, however, could not conceal the fact that most museums were poorly made due to overwhelming bureaucratism, quantitative fixation, and *maratonismo* (the rush to fulfill five-year-plan deadlines rather than do things properly). Consequently, hundreds of heritage items deteriorated or were lost or damaged. Most museums were not appropriately equipped to preserve collections, remained partially finished, or had to close soon after they were inaugurated. Nonetheless, the authorities considered the campaign a success (Marrero Oliva 2004).

The municipalities and provincial capitals that already possessed museums were forced to reorganize their collections to fit the new paradigm established by Law 23. This process generated some controversies. Most curators I interviewed in the provinces, including Camagüey, Holguín, and Santiago, interpreted this imposition as the introduction of soviet museology in Cuba. In Holguín, the whole exhibition of the museum La Periquera was rearranged, because the new procedures required the display to progress in a clockwise direction from right to left, symbolically equating the historical evolution from political "right" to "left." The relevance of the shift was clear in the historic museum Oscar María de Rojas in Cárdenas. Although the museum had already undergone transformations during the early revolutionary years, according to the museum staff it had to be reworked again. The new exhibition had to prove a series of theses: that the republican bourgeoisie had created it to reproduce its hegemonic power, that the museum trust was composed of rich people, and that the Revolution had put it at the service of the masses (Torres et al. 1984).

In Ciego de Ávila, the conversion of a Spanish barracks into a provincial museum motivated a long-lasting controversy regarding the display of two sculptures of Spanish soldiers at the front door. While the local PCC historian and Havana authorities wanted to replace them with sculptures of Cuban *mambises*, the provincial director of Cultural Heritage Norma Pérez Trujillo insisted in keeping them as testimonies to "real history" (N. Pérez Trujillo, interview, April 1, 2013). However, "real history" did not fit the standard master-narrative that had to be displayed on municipal museums. Consequently, Pérez Trujillo was accused by the local PCC historian of "national betrayal" and "apology of colonialism" and was ultimately threatened with losing her job and benefits. After 1990, ideological pressure diminished, and the contested soldiers have remained in place, but controversy about them is ongoing in Ciego de Ávila.

The narratives of municipal museums were standardized by establishing a common methodological, aesthetic, and discursive framework. This is illustrated by the documentation from the Centro Nacional de Patrimonio Cultural (National Council of Cultural Heritage, CNPC) in Havana. This documentation sheds light on the functioning of the bureaucratic heritage logic and reveals the close relationship between material culture and history in heritage processes. In the few cases when local commissions managed to carry out historical research and plan their own museum display, heritage authorities in Havana required them to create a museum script including a historical plot and the objects that would be associated with each historic period in the exhibition. The scripts had then to be sent to Havana, where their ideological and methodological suitability was checked by reviewers at MINCULT's Department of Cultural Heritage (Montenegro 1982:22). Museum scripts were documents that combined text and images to provide the grammar of museum exhibition under carefully patterned and controlled procedures. The exhibitions created meaningful narratives in which every historical period was represented by a standardized set of objects. Each set of objects had to show how different subaltern classes had revolted against the dominant classes in each historic era, exemplifying the rebellious Cuban spirit.

This was consistent with the Marxist-Leninist ideas that became dominant within the master-narrative. The master-narrative promoted by the regime posited various stages in terms of the subaltern and exploited social classes. Historic continuities were interpreted in terms of class, connecting prehistoric "primitive communism," slaves in antiquity, medieval serfs, and contemporary proletarians. This model, widely applied in European Socialist countries, was gradually adopted in Cuba as awareness of Marxism-Leninism and soviet influence increased but had to be adapted to Cuban history. Accordingly, the narrative started with the first subaltern group that existed in Cuba: the indigenous. Against most historical evidence, museum scripts had to highlight the supposedly natural indigenous inclination to rebel against Spanish invaders. In terms of Cuban distinctiveness, the Marxist-Leninist class-based interpretation was combined with traditional Cuban culture-history: archetypal heroes such as Hatuey or Guamá, who were supposed to embody the Cuban rebel spirit, eventually represented the indigenous peoples in museums.

The fact that some Cuban territories lacked archaeological or historical evidence of an indigenous presence did not affect the master-narrative, which had to remain homogenous throughout the country. The consequence of this ideological commitment was that museum narratives enacted a form of symbolic deterritorialization. This means that historical discourses were disconnected from concrete local geographies and social groups and universalized in the atemporal essence of the nation. For instance, the reviewers in Havana of the script for the "29 of April" museum in San Luis commented that the new plot should "demonstrate" the indigenous presence in the area (CNPC 2008). If there was no evidence of indigenous presence in the territory, or museum staff had no indigenous objects to put on display, these had to be imported from other areas. This happened, for instance, in the provincial museum of Las Tunas, where indigenous objects were brought in from Holguín. Similarly, the shackles, chains, and cauldrons that constituted the set of objects meant to represent African slaves and demonstrate their rebelliousness were brought in from Matanzas. An interesting omission is that when the scripts accounted for the development of villages and cities, they usually avoided mentioning the fact that the settlers were Spanish with different cultural and linguistic backgrounds. Positing an abstract idea of Cuban identity based on class entailed neglecting complex historical dynamics and the different ethnic, racial, and cultural affiliations of Cubans.

After representing the indigenous past, the era of slavery during the colonial period was presented as a struggle between landowners and a stereotyped class of Afro-Cuban slaves. This image of the colonial era was related to overall changes in the understanding of Afro-Cuban culture due to growing soviet influence. The scientific atheism underpinning the work of ethnographers and anthropologists led to a separation of the spiritual and religious from the material and performative aspects in representations of Africanness. Historic representations similarly subsumed cultural and ethnic aspects under a class component. Slaves were presented in idealized *palenques* (independent settlements created by Maroons) in close association with the land and nature, and *cimarrones* (Maroons) were celebrated and identified with the transhistoric Cuban spirit of rebelliousness and struggle.

Miller (2000:41) has rightly argued that Castro often invoked the names of Cuban martyrs to invoke their power and to provide historical grounds to the Revolution. The emphasis on martyrdom and slave resistance connects with the sanctification of death among African slaves in Cuba, for whom ancestors provided a form of continuity between past, present, and future. As Peters argues, "The image of the slave in post-revolutionary discourse in the early 1970s served as a rhetorical tool to mark connections between a subjugated past riddled with inequalities and the revolutionary promise of social justice for all Cubans" (2010:57). Thus, the sacrificial tradition and emphasis on "martyrcentrism" and moral obligations within national-revolutionary ideology cannot be understood solely as the transformation of an underlying catholic faith into a civic religion of the Revolution but as another form of combining Marxism-Leninism with specifically Cuban national traits.

In this way, Afro-Cuban culture was inscribed into the national imaginary to serve political needs without accounting for its endurance and role in contemporary Cuban life. This nationwide tendency to elide the Afro-Cuban strand in the national cultural experience was mitigated in predominantly black areas of eastern Cuba and especially in Santiago. Here, Afro-Cuban culture and life were more visible and present in museums and cultural exhibitions, such as Casa del Caribe (House of the Caribbean) or Casa de las Religiones Populares (House of Popular Religions). In predominantly white areas like Havana, African references were, and remain, less visible, as shown by Tisdel Flikke's (2006) analysis of Afro-Cuban museums in Cuba.

Following the period of slavery, the narrative focused on the War of Independence and their heroes. In this period, the new master-narrative influenced by Marxism-Leninism converged with the previous template of the 100 years of struggle, which emphasized the idea that the War of Independence and the Revolution were the same historic process. Museums were also required to demonstrate the presence of heroes and especially of Martí in their territories. The set of objects representing this period included all kinds of belongings of the heroes, with an emphasis on weapons and specifically the machete. The symbolism of the machete—a blade used by slaves on sugarcane plantations that turned into a weapon during the war—is obvious. It therefore combined the revolutionary myths of struggle and sacrifice, war and work.

The representation of the republican period changed little when compared with early revolutionary museums: municipal museums had to denigrate the pseudo-republic by showing torture gadgets and other objects symbolizing vice, corruption, and the U.S. presence. Frequently, the abandoned furniture of emigrated bourgeois families became part of the museum display as a representation of republican vices and inequality. Any idea or event that could convey positive values about the pseudo-republic had to be erased. For instance, the original script of the municipal museum of Morón, in Ciego de Ávila Province, included a list of local intellectuals and artists and stated that they "contributed to the formation of a whole generation of people from Morón during the republican era" (Museo de Morón 1981:21). When the script was sent to MINCULT in Havana, the reviewer crossed out "formation" and added "deformation" as the word that should appear in the museum exhibition, asking the museum workers to rethink the part of the script covering the republican period. Clearly, the republican past had become a repository of negative heritage.

This narrative emphasized the revolutionary break with the Republic and created a sense of continuity between the War of Independence and the Revolution. This twofold task required museum scripts to highlight the clandestine revolts and struggles of proletarians and students during the republican era. For instance, the original 1982 script of the "29 of April" museum in San Luis, in Santiago de Cuba Province, was required to "prove the strength reached by the workers' movement during the neo-colonial period" and "the participation of the people from San Luis in the clandestine and insurrectional struggle" (CNPC 2008). Museum exhibitions underscored the role of the PCC in these rebellions, celebrating Communist leaders such as Antonio Mella and Antonio Guiteras and overlooking the agency of other groups. This emphasis on the PCC's role can be interpreted as the consequence of its greater power during the period of institutionalization, as it had been previously overshadowed by the higher profile of 26-J guerrillas. Along with documentary evidence, the most common objects symbolizing the period of revolutionary underground struggle during the Republic were banners, leaflets, ribbons, medals, party licenses, weapons, and clandestine prints.

After the struggles of the republican era, museum narratives continued with the 26-J movement and the Moncada attack. Then, as the 29 of April museum was requested to do, museums had to "show the martyrs fallen in the different phases of the national liberation and internationalist struggle" (CNPC 2008). The period of guerrilla war during the 1950s was represented by weapons, maps, pictures, and clothes. The last narrative stage was the Accomplishments of the Revolution, wherein museums were required to prove the socioeconomic achievements of the Revolution in every village and to highlight agricultural, industrial, or infrastructural improvements in the area. The revolutionary achievements could not show or even suggest the possibility of negative consequences of the changes brought about by the Revolution. For instance, the Morón script affirmed that some indigenous archaeological sites had been destroyed due to the revolutionary expansion of agriculture land. The reviewer in Havana added a note blaming the cultural authorities of the municipality and the museum for not protecting these sites and for attributing it to the socioeconomic development caused by the Revolution (Museo de Morón 1981).

Because history was highly ideological, any deviation from the master-narrative could be considered an "ideological concession" or even a "betrayal" and cause museum workers to lose their job and benefits. When the history of a certain village did not match the master-narrative, the reviewers emphasized the need to divide the plot into historical stages. For instance, a reviewer suggested to museum workers in Morón that they divide the region's history into the following stages: "indigenous, colony, War of Independence, intervention and American economic penetration, pseudo-republic, struggles after the *Moncada* and Revolution" (Museo de Morón 1981). This chronological division of history also mirrored the school programs of Cuban history. According to David Gómez Iglesias (ca. 1985), director of the provincial museum of Holguín, museum workers had to make the museum a material illustration of history handbooks.

Museography was responsible for the articulation of the historical narratives in books and of museum scripts into a visual and material representation. During the institutionalization era, museography acquired a greater role because museum design and aesthetics were considered fundamental for the correct transmission of ideology. In this area, the influence of Cuban architects who had studied in Socialist countries was clear. The initial municipal museums deployed their narratives in three visual rows or levels. The upper row indicated the historical period—colony, pseudo-republic, Revolution—with a color or a similar set of images. The central row focused on specific events of the period, and the lower level displayed objects that demonstrated the veracity of the event and the period as a whole.

Figure 4.3. The three levels of museum display in four museum exhibitions from a similar period. The upper part of the exhibition portrays images that indicate the historic period. In the middle, large banners explain facts or characters with text and image. Below, objects representing facts specific to the historic period are displayed in showcases. Provincial museum of Villa Clara. Source: Compiled by the author from CNPC archive.

The quantitative analysis I carried out in different museums throughout the country revealed that most objects collected and displayed were historical. The most numerous artifacts on display were weapons, followed by clothes, documents, and personal belongings. This finding illustrates the significance of history and military events in the symbolic imaginary of the Revolution. Every assemblage of objects fulfilled a specific role in reinforcing certain aspects of the narrative. For instance, weapons were the signifiers of "struggle" and "rebelliousness." Bloodstained clothes and personal belongings made humans present by manifesting their absence, thus signifying "martyrdom." The ubiquitous shackles and chains representing slavery in the colonial period materialized the idea of "injustice," namely, that which triggers struggle and rebellion.

Museums presented *gigantografías* (large banners) and exhibition panels that completely covered their walls. The objects were exposed below or in front of the panels, usually filled with text. The idea was to surround the visitors with the display so that they would focus exclusively on the ideological message and its presentation. Cuba replicated the profusion of written documents that characterized Eastern Bloc museology, which considered that written documents constituted the main data with which to illustrate historical progress. Towns often used documents to prove their involvement in the Communist and revolutionary past and thereby increase their significance and the funds allocated to them (Petkova-Campbell 2011:75). In Cuba, this happened, for instance, in the museum-house of the II Congress of the Marxist-Leninist Party in Caimito, where the script proudly emphasized the local role in the organization of the first underground Marxist congress, in 1934 (CNPC ca. 1985). Similarly, the script of the municipal museum of Manzanillo stressed that a revolutionary club had existed in the town since 1875 (Consejo de Estado 1979). These museographic patterns evolved, although their underlying philosophy remained the same, until the late 2000s, when minimalism became fashionable.

Beyond museology and museography, museums were key producers of historic and scientific research. The investigations by municipal museums reveal their central role in the production of history, in the education and inculcation of values in children, and in the overall conception of museum education. As for museum scripts, investigations had to be sent to the Department of Cultural Heritage in Havana for review. These investigations show that history was not conceived as an explanation of social dynamics or, as in culture-history, as a linear narration of facts. Rather, history functioned as a mixture of culture-history with vulgar Marxism-Leninism that attempted to reconcile a class-based narrative focusing on the exploited classes, with the nationalist narrative of struggles and revolutionary heroes. Museums used history as a pedagogic instrument to inculcate key beliefs and concepts such as imperialism and rebelliousness. To ensure

Figures 4.4, 4.5, and 4.6. The changing aesthetics of museums in Cuba. There is a tendency to abandon the Soviet style, overburdened with information, and move toward minimalist aesthetics. *From top to bottom*, the provincial museum of Villa Clara in the 1980s, the municipal museum of Caibarién in the 2000s, and the museum of Morón in the 2010s. Source: CNPC archive (*top and middle*), author (*bottom*).

that children understood the determinist plot of the master-narrative, they had to learn the mechanisms of cause and effect that triggered the change from one historic phase to the next. In one experiment in the museum of Manatí, children were shown pictures and objects of indigenous Cubans and then were asked to explain the reasons why they "constantly revolted" against the Spanish colonizers. As the museum curators proudly claimed, after the activity the children could

> perfectly explain why the Guamá rebellion occurred [. . .] The activity also provides a good example of the formation of their future convictions, because the students understood that it is necessary to rebel against injustices, as Guamá did against the conquerors. In parallel, the children developed a strong emulative behavior. (Avila Mariño and Rodriguez Peña ca. 1985)

Marxist-Leninist pedagogy considered that belief influenced behavior and that, consequently, a proper understanding of historical development could transform consciousness. The more children internalized revolutionary beliefs and developed emulative behaviors, the more their attitudes would be replicated in society.

Educational experimentation using heritage for the inculcation of ideology was common throughout the country. This included soviet-style strategies of psycho-transformation for the inculcation of patriotic, anti-imperialist, and collectivist values in children. Without going into detail, the main activities were those organized by the *círculos de amigos del museo* (circles of museum friends) and the *tertulia cultural* (cultural gatherings), all intended to bring the community together and to transform its aesthetic and cultural tastes. Another common experimental initiative was the *museo móvil* (portable museum), which consisted of a big case containing representative heritage objects of each stage of historical development and a panel for their display. Museum curators took it to peasant, military, and workers' communities far from the municipal centers to raise ideological and cultural awareness. Furthermore, Cuban museums developed the *museoterapia* (museum-therapy) following soviet ideas of the transformation of personality through art. According to workers of the provincial museum of Cienfuegos, the aim of *museoterapia* was to heal the sick and the elderly in hospitals "using the potential that museum objects hold" (Benet León et al. 1989:n.p.). Thus, the effort of museum workers to reach the population at large and spread the master-narrative was substantial and innovative in many ways.

Specialized Museums: Combining Nationalistic
and Revolutionary Narratives

The specialized and memorial museums that emerged with the process of institutionalization responded to slightly different logics than municipal museums did for a number of reasons. They addressed specific topics and therefore could not be completely standardized, some were reworkings

Figures 4.7 and 4.8. *Left*: gallery of reproductions of universal art. *Below*: mobile museum toolkit. Source: Arjona Pérez (1984).

of previous museums rather than new creations, and they resulted from the agency of different power groups. This does not mean that they went against the prevailing master-narrative but rather that they complemented it and reinforced some of its specific building blocks: the myths and their symbols.

While the Cultural Heritage section of MINCULT implemented municipal museums, MINFAR and Celia Sánchez in the Council of State led the creation of most of the specialized and memorial museums. Other museums responded to the will of specific institutions to rearrange their displays in line with the new visual and aesthetic canon, as exemplified by the Museum of Natural Sciences and Havana's City Museum. As shown in the previous chapter, when the Academia de las Ciencias opened the Museum of Natural Sciences in the Capitolio during the 1960s, it had received the collections of Cuban archaeology and anthropology and exhibited them as part of Cuban "nature." After 1975, the Marxist-Leninist narrative accorded the indigenous a place in history as one of the subaltern classes struggling against domination. Thus, they had to be rescued from the natural realm and incorporated into the Marxist-Leninist master-narrative.

To do so and to update the museum narrative, Linares Ferrera set out a substantial plan to rearrange the whole exhibition and transform it into the Museo del Hombre (Museum of Humankind) (CNPC ca. 1980). The project envisaged a series of rooms explaining human evolution from the oldest species to contemporary humans, with a focus on the anthropization of Latin America and Cuba. Two rooms explained the "disintegration of the primitive community" and "the birth of the class society." The symbolism of the museum was apparent: it equated the primitive community with "primitive Communism" and considered it part of the natural state of things. This reality was disrupted by colonialism and capitalism, and thus the Revolution had to restore it through the establishment of a classless society. The project, however, was never implemented. According to Linares Ferrera (interview, March 20, 2013), the reasons for this were both its large scale and the advent of the 1990s crisis.

The City Museum, the heart of a renewed OHCH under the direction of Eusebio Leal Spengler, adapted its collections to reflect contemporary Cuba during the 1970s. The photographic documentation held by the OHCH shows that the transformation of the museum from its republican to its current form was striking. Contradictions emerge between archival data and the interviews with current museum curators, who argue that the museum has been unchanged since its reinstallation after 1968. Certainly, the narrative of the exhibition remained essentially close to culture-history, but the museography wholeheartedly adopted soviet aesthetics and forms for at least two decades. The walls of the Capitanes Generales, the utmost symbol of Spanish colonialism, were covered with large billboards overloaded with texts and images. The museum displayed objects on white pedestals and plaques and actively celebrated commemorations of relevant dates in the international calendar of Socialist countries.

These two examples pale compared with the largest musealization plans on a national scale, set out by the MINFAR and Sánchez at the Council of State. These plans had been ongoing since the 1960s but were intensified during the early 1970s, reflecting the agency and autonomy of the ex-guerrillas in terms of their conceptions of history, heritage, and museum practice. The first defining trait of these museums was their focus on specific characters or events that highlight the narrative of the 100 years of struggle rather than on the evolution of social classes throughout history, as in Marxism-Leninism. The plans envisaged the commemoration of the War of Independence and revolutionary heroes through the creation of museums in the houses where they were born.[1] The proindependence heroes were represented as the direct predecessors of the revolutionaries, who were the legitimate heirs of the ideas of these heroes, just as Martí preceded Fidel, his legitimate heir.

House-museums articulated official narratives by giving coherence to the past, concealing historic contradictions, and providing a sense of continuity. Each house-museum celebrated a specific historical figure and connected it to previous and subsequent events and characters to guarantee historic continuity. The museum script of the house-museum of revolutionary martyr Abel Santamaría, for instance, presented four rooms dedicated to the assault on the Moncada Barracks (CNPC ca. 2012). However, the fifth room focused on issues only indirectly related to Santamaría or the Moncada. This room projected the museum backward and

---

1   House-museums were built for the War of Independence heroes Carlos Manuel de Céspedes (1968), Ignacio Agramonte (1973), Calixto García (1976), and Antonio Maceo (1974); and to revolutionary heroes José Antonio Echeverría (1973), Abel Santamaría (1973), Rubén Martínez Villena (1976), Jesús Montané (1983), Celia Sánchez (1983), Juan Manuel Márquez (1989), Camilo Cienfuegos (1989), and Serafín Sánchez (1990).

forward temporally, by denigrating the pseudo-republican past and high-lighting the U.S. threat while celebrating the liberation brought by Fidel's ideas and the progress toward a Socialist future. Therefore, although house-museums were self-contained in spatial and temporal terms, they highlighted every possible connection with other historic events. The aim was to generate a tightly woven web of interconnected symbols and myths that underscored historic continuity between the prerevolutionary tradition of struggle and sacrifice and the revolutionary present, thus reinstating the myth of the Cuban rebellious spirit.

The documentation at the CNCP shows that mass organizations created tiny museums following similar patterns, but at a secondary, local level, commemorating local martyrs of the historic struggles. These museums highlighted the internationalist martyrs, especially as the conflict between Cuba and South Africa reached its peak in Angola during the 1980s. Other museums reinforced the foundational myth of the Revolution: participation in the guerrilla war. For instance, the aim of the house-museum for Celia Sánchez in Manzanillo was to posit Sánchez as the female Cuban revolutionary model. To do so, the museum explicitly focused on the relationship between Sánchez and the three weapons she used during the guerrilla war. The museums of Abel Santamaría and Celia Sánchez both proudly participated in the myth of the assault on the Moncada or the guerrilla war as symbols of belonging to the ex-guerrillas. This display illustrates a broader point about museums created by MINFAR: they always highlight the relationship between the leadership and guerrilla myths, while the class struggle and the Marxist-Leninist narrative is almost always absent.

Another series of museums served as relays to link historical periods with specific heroes, while reinstating the myth of external and internal threat to the Revolution. For instance, the architectural plan of the museum of the Lucha contra Bandidos (Fight against Bandits) in Trinidad narrated the fight against CIA-supported guerrillas within Cuba, displaying U.S. weapons and objects from these "bandits" (Linares Ferrera and MINCULT 1984). Surprisingly, however, the museum devoted a room to the Brigadas Universitarias (University Brigades) commanded by José Antonio Echeverría during the republican period, because, according to museum workers, these were "predecessors of the struggle against bandits" (Gutiérrez González and Morales Fuentes ca. 1985). Thus, two apparently unrelated events with no historical connection were symbolically linked to reinstate historic continuity.

The Museum of the Lucha Obrera (Workers' Struggles), inaugurated in 1982 in Manzanillo, performed a similar role. The museum intended to establish a connection between Communist leaders and the Communist Party during the republican period and the PCC as it was refounded after 1965. The aim was to suppress the dissonance associated with Fidel's turning former Communists away from power for more than a decade. Again, historical continuity was created through the decontextualization of historic actors and processes. Similarly, the creation of the museum of Clandestine Struggle in 1976 aimed to establish a symbolic link between the subversive actions of different political groups during the republican period and the revolutionary clandestine activities of the 26-J movement. The museum script focused on the figures of Frank País and Celia Sánchez and avoided addressing the complex amalgam of groups involved in that revolts and their relations with the 26-J (CNPC 2009a; Martínez Riera 1988). These are just a few examples of how museums helped to establish a dense network of symbolic relations between myths and historic events that underpinned the master-narrative.

An analysis of MINFAR museum policies reveals the shifts in heritage production in relation to the previous period and illustrates the relative autonomy and contradictory ideological stance of MINFAR within the regime and in relation to Marxism-Leninism. After 1973, MINFAR reinvigorated its program of heritagization following the plan originally devised by Raúl in 1966, which avoided references to Marxism-Leninism and focused on the celebration of significant events associated with the ex-guerrillas and their deeds. This plan can be interpreted as an attempt by the ex-guerrillas to preserve their symbolic legitimacy against alternative groups of power. The underlying tension between both groups was confirmed by a letter by Celia Sánchez (1978a), in which she reprimanded the regional PCC leader of Santiago when he tried to monumentalize some sites related to the war in the Sierra Maestra: revolutionary deeds were a matter for the ex-guerrillas.

MINFAR used anniversaries to inaugurate monuments and museums as a key symbolic strategy. The Museum of the Revolution (MR) and the museum-school Moncada had been inaugurated on July 26 on the tenth and twentieth anniversaries of the *Moncada* assault. MINFAR devoted the thirtieth anniversary to the Second Military Front during the guerrilla war. A large Museum of the Second Military Front and a mausoleum were inaugurated on July 25, 1973, and in 1978, respectively, as part of a huge commemorative historic complex that is still under construction. Following the patterns of other specialized museums, the first room was dedicated to the antecedents to the war and to the Cuban people's tradition of struggle as represented by the heroes of the War of Independence (CNPC ca. 2010). Again, this pattern reveals that, by 1978, MINFAR self-identified with the narrative of the 100 years of struggle that was characteristic of the ex-guerrillas, without including Marxist-Leninist features, such as indigenous people or slaves. The Museum Girón articulated a similar narrative commemorating the Cuban victory at Playa Girón. Two rooms of the museum were expanded in 1976 with the similar aim of enlarging the historic scope of the narrative, accounting for the historical periods both previous and subsequent to the U.S. invasion.

Meanwhile, MINFAR put architect Raúl Oliva in charge of the reworking of the museum-school Moncada at the Moncada Barracks. The Moncada July 26 in Santiago was the twin of Havana's MR. It was, and probably still is, the second most ideologically significant museum in Cuba. It was inaugurated in 1960, but from 1964 onward it had only four rooms, representing the assault on the *Moncada*, open for display (CNPC 2009b). Its refurbishment in 1973 emphasized its pedagogic orientation and included some Marxist-Leninist features in the narrative, with the aim of expanding its chronological and thematic scope. According to the museum guide, "all our history appears in the museum [. . .] as a didactic synthesis for future generations" (Limia 1978:17). Each historic phase was represented with a color: blue represented the emergence of Cuban national consciousness during the War of Independence, black was equated with the "dark" republican period, green signified the rebirth of Cuba during the revolutionary war, and red indicated the emergence of Socialism. This pedagogic structure was designed to affirm historic continuity. For instance, the museum guide underscored the historic continuity of the narrative by considering the slaves the "substitutes of the Indians [. . .] that foreshadowed [. . .] the appearance of the father of the patria, Carlos Manuel de Céspedes" (Limia 1978:11).

Similarly, the MR underwent significant changes during this period. Whereas the Ministry of Culture controlled the Museum of the Revolution in the USSR, MINFAR kept control of it even after the creation of MIN-CULT in Cuba. As we have seen, the MR had been dismantled in the base of the monument to Martí in Revolution Square. It reopened in the Palacio Presidencial on the symbolic date of January 2, 1974, which commemorated the victory over Batista. In 1976, MINFAR inaugurated the Memorial Granma next to the MR to exhibit the Granma yacht used by the 26-J revolutionaries to land in Cuba and start the war. According to the pictures at the MR archive, the exhibition of 1974 presented twelve rooms, in which the history of the Revolution was limited to the narrative of the 100 years of struggle. However, MINFAR completely transformed the MR in 1988 with soviet assessment and technical support, and its appearance remained largely unchanged until its refurbishment in 2012.

The huge exhibition of 1988 abandoned the narrative of the 100 years of struggle and aligned itself with the Marxist-Leninist elements within the dominant master-narrative. It comprised thirty-eight large rooms narrating Cuban history from the pre-Hispanic past until the Accomplishments of the Revolution of the 1980s. Four rooms were dedicated to the colonial period, twenty-one to the pseudo-republic and clandestine struggle, and eighteen to the Revolution. The museum resembled municipal and provincial museums, but its scope was universal rather than local: it encompassed the entire master-narrative and incorporated every myth and symbol into the exhibition. As the museum director affirmed, the aim was to "associate each period of Cuban history with specific revolutionary traditions, telling the indigenous and slave rebellions [. . .] accounting for the transformation of the Spanish into creoles, and the formation of the Cuban nationality [. . .] The museum is for history classes what laboratories are for science classes" (J.A. Pérez Quintana, interview, March 17, 2013). In other words, the museum served to scientifically and factually demonstrate the Marxist-Leninist historical narrative.

Thus the MR started to resemble other museums managed by MIN-CULT, employing similar texts, images, and material culture to represent specific events or periods—weapons, torture instruments, and so on. Similar to the Museum Moncada 26 July in Santiago, the MR became didactic and represented each period with colors. The major novelty in the exhibition was the emphasis on the role of the PCC and Marxism-Leninism in the revolutionary process—a role not often granted to the PCC by the leadership. Many display cases in the rooms of the pseudo-republican period were devoted to Communist leaders and clandestine activities. According to the conceptual framework of anthropologist Ana Alonso (1988:33), the MR enacted a departicularization of historic processes, emptying them of meanings that tied them to specific contexts and places. Thus, it was possible to suppress the fact that ex-guerrillas and ex-members of the Communist Party were conflicted and instead present them as unified and nationalized as part of the Revolution and the "tradition of struggle."

The rooms dedicated to the Accomplishments of the Revolution highlighted the fraternity between Socialist nations and the committed internationalism of the Cuban Revolution. One large banner read: "The figures that symbolize our ideology preside over the area where the three congresses of the PCC and the whole political system of our country are represented" (Museo de la Revolución ca. 1988). A sign for the first congress of the PCC with the Cuban and red flags in it was surrounded by the figures of Marx, Engels, and Lenin on the left, Independence War heroes Céspedes, Maceo, and Martí on the right, and revolutionary heroes Cienfuegos, Guevara, and Mella below. The banner represented the Cuban nationalist and Marxist-Leninist ideologies as one reality. The inclusion of Mella, cofounder of the PCC during the Republic, in the pantheon of mythical heroes, along with Cienfuegos and Guevara, was a clear sign of the prominent role accorded to the PCC.

My analysis of MINFAR heritage policies therefore reveals that the former differential character of MINFAR museums and their symbolic association with the ex-guerrillas blurred gradually. By 1988, MINCULT and MINFAR museums were largely similar, a further sign of the convergence of national-revolutionary and Marxist-Leninist aesthetics and narratives. This also illustrates the significant extent to which soviet heritage criteria and values had penetrated MINFAR, the Council of State, and various Cuban institutions by 1988, precisely when the Cuban leadership had started the Rectificación de Errores and the USSR had started to crumble.

The Conflict over Monumental Representation

Based on the documentation in the archive of the Consejo Asesor para el Desarrollo de la Escultura Monumentaria y Ambiental (Advisory Board for the Development of Monumental Sculpture, CODEMA) and various interviews, this section traces the main shifts in the creation of monuments during the period of institutionalization and the controversy their implementation produced. Unlike museums, monuments were conceived as artistic creations, and aesthetic appeal was considered necessary for improving the public reception of the ideological message. Therefore, their didactic and propagandistic aims had to be balanced with a certain degree of freedom for artistic expression. Monuments reconciled the will of politicians with artistic freedom and required the involvement of different groups of professionals in their design and construction, from architects to sculptors and spatial planners. This resulted in a distinctively Cuban form of designing and constructing monuments.

If, as Kapcia notes, during the early years of the Revolution there was a "lack of institutions, spaces and a perceived academy against which a dissident vanguard might form publicly" (Kapcia 2005:167), at this time artists could unite against an official academy and its cadres. Nonetheless, the limits of artistic freedom were severely curtailed throughout the period following the orthodoxy of the Quinquenio Gris, whose influence loomed large until the early 1980s. Shifts in the USSR influenced Cuban heritage policies and partially explain why the PCC strongly supported heritage production after 1975. Between 1964 and 1982, Leonid Brezhnev curtailed Nikita Khrushchev's liberal reforms and reinvigorated socialist realism in culture and art. The USSR also started to accord a primary role to cultural and artistic diplomacy, shifting from a disregard of cultural heritage and a promotion of modernist images of the USSR toward a willingness to spread the riches of Russia's presoviet cultural heritage to serve foreign policy (Gould-Davies 2003:208). The Cuban lobby still held sway on power positions in the USSR, and Soviet Union–trained technocrats and personnel occupied prominent positions in Cuba, influencing policies in different fields.

In Cuba, the official ideas on culture and art at the time conditioned the construction of monuments. The First PCC Congress in 1975 highlighted the central role of culture and art in the demonstration of continuity with previous cultures, the consolidation of the Revolution, and the impulse toward the future Socialist reality (PCC 1976). The Congress had reaffirmed the artistic formal freedom proclaimed by Fidel's "Words to the Intellectuals." However, it would be analytically naïve to disconnect artistic forms from content and from the institutional and sociopolitical framework of their production, which favored culturally orthodox positions at the time. Abstract art was not at the center of debate, because it had become marginal and deviated from the mainstream art promoted by the Revolution, which was characterized by its nationalist content and its social commitment to including the masses in culture.

Scholars and intellectuals denounced abstract art as bourgeois and as a burden of the past that must be overcome for truly revolutionary art to emerge (Fernández Mayo and Nuiry Sánchez 1986; Portuondo 1979). Even after the development of a more discursive atmosphere in the intellectual and cultural spheres in the 1980s, abstract art was questioned for its lack of commitment to social issues and the Revolution, and it was harshly criticized in art history handbooks (Jubrías 1989:26–30, 62–63). This opening during the 1980s was more restricted in the field of monumental art, due to its public character and representational power. This situation resulted in the emergence of a hybrid monumental canon, thanks to artist's resistance to the imposition of realism. Because neither the PCC nor the state assumed socialist realism as the official aesthetic language, it is necessary to explore whether this was also the case in practice and its implications for heritage theory and practice.

A Monumental Plan for the Revolution

The Cuban historian Mariela Rodríguez Joa defined Cuban monumental art during the period of institutionalization as "an expression of the system of ideological values [of the] new society, whose aim is to contribute to the political and aesthetic education of our people" (Rodríguez Joa 2009:30). Monuments were conceived as artistic creations that responded to the "necessity of evoking, remembering and dignifying relevant episodes and names of our history" (Rodríguez Joa 2009:30). It was considered that national identity and history had been insufficiently or imperfectly represented in the public space, and significant investments were channeled to monumental production after 1973. This entailed the institutionalization and standardization of monument production and the end of avant-garde experimentation that existed during the early revolutionary years.

The institutionalization of heritage was a contradictory process whereby dialogue about monuments was encouraged while experimentation and creativity were limited. During our interviews, different professionals and academics agreed that the turning point in monumental art was the inauguration of a successful project during the July 26 celebrations in Santiago in 1973. This was the monumental complex on the road to the Granjita Siboney, where 26-J revolutionaries had gathered before the assault on the Moncada. As usual, most of the ex-guerrillas, politicians, and regional party leaders were present at the inauguration, and afterward many of them started monumental programs in their regions and institutions. This move calls into question the view of a sovietized cultural policy in Cuba during the Quinquenio Gris, at least in the heritage field, because the monument was openly abstract and far removed from socialist realism.

The monument was built by a group of fourteen architects who designed it with the aim of commemorating the martyrs of the assault on the *Moncada*. In total, twenty-six monuments, employing abstract forms, minimalism, and land art, were positioned along the road, to represent each martyr in groups of two or three. Volunteers constructed the monuments using cheap local materials. Each monument had the name and profession of the martyr inscribed on it. Some of the projects fulfilled the Marxist requirement to combine functional and expressive features that had previously troubled Cuban heritage professionals, such as a bus-stop memorial. For these reasons, the Granjita Siboney monument fulfilled many of the aspirations of avant-garde monumental art of the early revolutionary years, namely, the importance of functionalism, the minimization of realist representation and sumptuousness, the use of local materials and voluntary work, and the symbolic connection between class, martyrdom, and struggle. The monument illustrated the potential to develop abstract and high quality monumental art in Cuba and contrasted with the figurative canon that would become mainstream shortly afterward.

Some monuments planned during the period of institutionalization, such as the mausoleum to the Mártires de Artemisa (Martyrs of Artemisa) or the Desembarco del Yate Granma, followed similar ideas and abstract forms. However, these lacked the popular character of the *Granjita Siboney* and employed luxurious materials. In Artemisa, for instance, ex-guerrilla commander Ramiro Valdés described the mausoleum as a material reminder of the fact that "the Revolution is a process in which men and different generations come and go, and if Cubans sacrificed themselves in the past, other Cubans must do it today and tomorrow" (quoted in Herrera Ysla 1980:5). The mausoleum guide shows that every detail was designed to play a symbolic role, from the "purity" of the form of the cube associated with the Revolution to the didacticism of the internal friezes (Herrera Ysla 1980).

Of course, all monuments are intrinsically symbolic signifiers; what changes are what they signify. Contrary to the Granjita Siboney, which granted full representational status to individual biographies and history in an intrinsic relationship with the monuments, the mausoleum to the Mártires de Artemisa posited the Revolution as a transcendent essence in which specific individuals played no significant role. The ideology of the Revolution was the framework of reference, described as standing out-side and above the lives of the people that die for the Revolution and the monument that commemorates them.

After the increase in monument construction that followed the inau-guration of the *Granjita Siboney*, a group of intellectuals and professionals led by Celia Sánchez, Fernando Salinas, and Rita Longa pushed Minister Hart Dávalos to institutionalize and centralize monument production and instill some order in the field. This resulted in the creation of the Con-sejo Asesor para el Desarrollo de la Escultura Monumentaria y Ambiental (CODEMA) in 1980. As CODEMA's ex-director and sculptor Rita Longa recalled in a 1993 report, the origins of CODEMA date back to 1975, when the PCC brought together a group of artists and asked them to produce "criteria to promote the construction of commemorative sculptures as weapons of ideological strengthening through the creation of monuments that tell our history and that of our heroes" (Longa 1993:n.p.).

CODEMA replaced the Taller Guamá (Guamá Workshop), which gath-ered many sculptors under the Unión Nacional de Escritores y Artistas (National Union of Writers and Artists), and the Instituto Nacional de la Industria Turística (National Institute of Tourism Industry), which su-pervised the aesthetics of tourism installations. In 1978, MINCULT cre-ated the Fondo Cubano de Bienes Culturales (Cuban Fund of Cultural As-sets), which ensured economic support for the monumental plans that CODEMA started to monitor and assess officially after 1980. The official objective of CODEMA was to "promote, develop, dictate and assess [. . .] the aesthetic qualities of the monuments [. . .] in coordination with the Instituto de Historia del Movimiento Comunista [Institute of History of the Communist Movement] and the history sections of the MINFAR, MININT [Home Office] and MICONS" (G. C. 1985:n.p.).

These changes granted the PCC direct control of monument production in forthcoming years. In similar terms to soviet legislation (USSR 1977:5), the Second PCC Congress in 1980 concluded that "special emphasis must be given to the development of sculpture, monumental and muralist works that perpetuate our history and commemorate the leaders, heroes and martyrs of the nation" (PCC 1987:71). The official definition of monuments was provided by CODEMA: "Every sculpture and monumental complex or work meant to be permanent that is coherently integrated in an environment, aimed at the commemoration of events or characters of historical, political, cultural or social significance" (CODEMA 1985:Ch. 3). Ultimately, CODEMA was in charge only of the technical and formal aspects of monuments, because content could not be negotiated. The scientific character attributed to the master-narrative provided so-called objective content, leaving room for discussion only on technical and formal alternatives.

One role of CODEMA was to contribute to the shaping of the population's aesthetic criteria through the establishment of a nationwide homogeneous pattern of visual representation. This was in line with MINCULT's broader aim to educate Cubans in aesthetics and culture (Hart Dávalos 1983). In a letter to MINCULT vice minister Marcia Leiseca, Longa (ca. 1985) explained at length the complexity of the tasks assigned to CODEMA. For Longa, Cuba lacked, almost entirely, expertise in constructing monuments. Consequently, she considered it necessary to draw on the experience of other Socialist countries. Many Cuban experts had visited and studied in these countries and written reports about their experiences that could be adapted to the Cuban context. Furthermore, specialists had to be educated in the field of monumental works because Cuban sculptors were not used to the huge size of the monuments the PCC plans demanded.

Most Cuban artists studied at the Instituto Superior de Arte (Higher Institute of the Arts, ISA), created in 1976, but the ISA did not train sculptors in large-scale works like monuments. This was so despite the presence of various soviet professors who taught at the ISA until the late 1980s. The ISA taught art and aesthetics from a Marxist-Leninist point of view, but soviet professors did not impose socialist realism or a narrow aesthetics. As Luis Camnitzer argues, "The use of these Marxist-Leninist approaches by instructors is far from homogenous or guided by unifying directives. Instructors study in different places and use different sources as references, mostly gathered through individual research" (Camnitzer 1994:124). This relatively liberal artistic education partially explains the disputes between artists and commissioners throughout the period.

My analysis of internal correspondence and reports in the CODEMA archive reveals the institution's internal functioning. CODEMA members met monthly to discuss the suitability of projects proposed by the different commissioners, to monitor the progress of monumental Works, and to launch new monument projects. They maintained intense personal and written contact with the most active promoters of monuments: Fidel, Raúl, Sánchez, and other ex-guerrillas, regional and local governments, state institutions and companies, the PCC, the Council of State, MINCULT, and MINFAR. CODEMA had provincial branches, which gathered annually to check the progress of the monumental program. It was responsible for carrying out Cuba's first nationwide monumental program. The program was unprecedented in scope, although its implementation remained partial, subject to vicissitudes and a lack of coordination between different provinces. The program established six main typologies:

Monuments to commemorate historical events considered positive and useful for the enhancement, consolidation, or defense of the Cuban nation. A PCC report officially requested that these monuments should clearly differentiate between the colonial, the pseudo-republican, and the revolutionary periods (Hart Dávalos 1981).

Monuments without positive values for the Cuban nation that had to be marked, analyzed, and used didactically to reveal their real character for the future generations—that is, those that had to be resignified.

Monumental complexes located in the future city centers of provincial capitals commemorating a significant local patriot—for example, Revolution squares.

Monuments commemorating patriotic figures in large parks and areas of leisure.

Monuments commemorating patriots or Cuban and international revolutionaries in economic, social, or cultural buildings.
Monuments commemorating Cuban internationalist warriors.

CODEMA and the PCC drew up lists of monuments according to the program guidelines and highlighted monuments with positive values for the nation and Revolution squares. The PCC proposed twelve affirmative monuments, the resignification of one negative monument, five Revolution squares, one monument in a productive area, and two parks and monuments commemorating internationalist warriors. Almost all of these monuments were related to military deeds and historic characters. CODEMA, focusing on the same topics as the PCC, went further, proposing forty-three monuments for the colonial period, eight for the pseudo-republic, and twenty-one for the Revolution. The aforementioned monumental plan put forward by Raúl and MINFAR in the 1960s significantly influenced both programs, establishing continuity between the pre- and postinstitutionalization processes.

The different drafts of the program in the CODEMA archive show that CODEMA and the PCC agreed on the fate of the most contested Cuban places of memory. Both considered that the polemical and abstract project that had won the international monument competition to commemorate the fallen at *Playa Girón* in 1963 should be discarded for ideological deviation. The only negative monument the PCC considered worthy of resignification for didactic purposes was the San Juan Hill in Santiago, as the U.S. army had turned it into a symbol of the victory over Spain and Cuba. CODEMA also recommended resignifying the monument commemorating the *Maine* in Havana and displaying the fragments of the broken U.S. bald eagle in the monument. However, none of these resignifications were performed. The regime's focus on the future led to a greater interest in producing and spreading new representations of ideology, which stood in marked contrast to the Revolution's early years, when emphasis was given to the resignification of a preexisting heritage.

The projects described in the program as "affirmative monuments" were aimed at the materialization and spread of the official narrative and the reorganization of the visual landscape of most Cuban cities. The list of monuments proposed by CODEMA included twelve memorializing rebellions by various groups, including the indigenous, peasants, slaves, students, workers, and women, and a series of battles, campaigns, struggles, and martyrdoms in the different historical periods. Only the proposals to commemorate the various Cuban constitutions deviated from the military pattern. There was no questioning of this military symbolic hegemony, but it was only Jesús Montané Oropesa, ex-guerrilla commander and PCC central committee member, who pointed this out. In a letter to Hart Dávalos, he suggested that it might be good to "include in the plans of sculpture, monument and muralist works the relevant figures and events of Cuban culture" (Montané Oropesa 1982:n.p.). However, Hart Dávalos did not answer and Oropesa's request was never satisfied.

As with museums, the program's central aim was highlighting the "continuity of struggles" throughout history. The monuments representing the colonial period underlined the War of Independence and the role of Martí, while those addressing the pseudo-republican period represented it as a series of struggles. The main deviations from the Marxist-Leninist and class-based patterns were the prominence of nationalist themes—War of Independence and Revolution—and the emphasis on the unity of workers, peasants, and students rather than on one of them as the "vanguard" revolutionary class, like soviet proletarians or Chinese peasants.

The monuments of the revolutionary period represented this period as a struggle against illiteracy, imperialism, and internal dissent. The two largest monumental complexes would represent two key revolutionary foundational myths: Desembarco del Yate Granma, planned since the early 1970s, and the war in the Sierra Maestra. Both had to be built in seven phases, and in the case of Granma, each phase had to be inaugurated annually during the anniversary of the landing. The projects aimed to inscribe revolutionary myths into the visual landscape not only through the creation of material symbols but also through ritual performance. Accordingly, the Granma project envisioned a big square next to the landing area where Fidel would deliver the inaugural speech and other regional leaders could commemorate the landing each year.

My analysis of monumental construction reveals not only the primary role the leadership accorded to heritage but also the fragmentary character of Cuban governmentality, even during the institutionalization period. The objectives of the program were only partially accomplished, and most monuments have remained unfinished for decades, including those considered key by the leadership, such as the aforementioned monumental complexes to the Desembarco del Yate Granma and to the war in the Sierra Maestra. However, it is difficult to retrace the evolution of each monument, as the 1990s crisis had a significant impact on the preservation of archival material and many personal stories were lost due to emigration. The artists I interviewed recall how, for instance, the *Desembarco del Yate Granma* underwent constant changes for years before finally being abandoned. In turn, the original plan of the war in the Sierra Maestra was only partially accomplished (CODEMA 1975).

A series of reports at CODEMA and the Council of State between 1978 and 1988 regarding both projects reflected the overall lack of coordination and an underlying conflict between the ex-guerrillas and the political ranks. Provincial PCC leaders constantly requested funding to carry out their own heritage works and transform the original projects (CODEMA 1986; González Quintana 1978). To these requests, Sánchez aggressively replied that these monuments were the concern of the Council of State, where she ran the section of historic affairs in close connection with Fidel. In the case of *Sierra Maestra,* Sánchez argued:

> One of the essential prerequisites to ensure the coherence and quality of all the works implemented in the *Sierra Maestra* is their harmony. We think that the independent construction of monuments without the necessary harmony and coherent criteria would negatively affect the outcome of the works, which we must bequeath to the future generations of our fatherland. (Sánchez 1978b)

Because of the erratic organization of the project, only isolated parts of the large monumental complex were implemented. The actions and claims by regional PCC authorities were both the result of a lack of knowledge of the central plans in Havana and a reaction to the inactivity of the central institutions. Similar complications took place with most monument projects throughout Cuba. The monument dedicated to slave rebelliousness and the Afro-Cuban rebel Carlota, the Triunvirato, was meant for inauguration in 1983 but remained only partially built when it was inaugurated in 1991. Also, the state and its institutions commissioned many projects illegally, dealing directly with sculptors who would not oppose the will of the authorities and who followed socialist realist standards. This went against the state's own legislation, which provided that only CODEMA could launch competitions. But CODEMA also launched and awarded many monument competitions that it never implemented.

The documentation retrieved in the CODEMA archive allowed me to reconstruct the disorderly but more or less standard procedure for the implementation of monuments. However disorderly the implementation, CODEMA built many monuments following a similar pattern. Normally, local or regional institutions, state companies, or organizations contacted CODEMA to commission a monument. Then, CODEMA launched and announced a competition in the national media. Briefing leaflets that included the rationale of the project in evocative and highly symbolic terms, setting the spatial context, the content to be expressed, and the expected results, were distributed among interested people. A program summed up what artists were expected to include in their projects, which sometimes involved carrying out historic research to contextualize the monument and presenting architectural and sculptural plans and models. For instance, the competition to commemorate Sánchez in Manzanillo after her death required the monumentalization of a street with allegoric references to her personality, tastes, and life (CODEMA 1984a). The project had to include a representation of her favorite flowers and create spaces for cultural activity and leisure. The technical procedures were set out specifying the expected date of inauguration in 1985.

Because the content was set, discussions usually revolved around the forms and aesthetics of monumental representation. For instance, ex-guerrillas complained about the program of the competition, arguing that Sánchez should be represented as the 26-J warrior she had been, implying that she should be portrayed in military uniform and armed, as she was in the local museum dedicated to her. Artists, however, pushed toward more abstract representations. CODEMA members tried to reconcile the positions, arguing that Sánchez was being represented as she was perceived in her childhood town. To lessen the pressure from ex-guerrillas, CODEMA (1984a) suggested that, at the very least, the project should present a realist representation of Sánchez. When the monument-street was finally inaugurated—four years later than expected, in 1989—it was a hybrid between realist and abstract art. It combined a plaque with an abstract design of Sanchez's favorite flowers, white ginger lilies that symbolically evoked her presence, and a realist bas-relief representing her face. The year after, an entirely realist representation of Sánchez was inaugurated in the nearby city of Media Luna to satisfy the official demands for a completely realist representation of Sánchez.

The hybrid articulation of abstract and realist aesthetics in Cuban monuments resulted from the power negotiations between artistic expressive freedom, some commissioners' attempts to impose realism, and ex-guerrillas' desire to commemorate their deeds in their own terms. The monument to Sánchez is, however, the exception rather than the rule. She was a representative of the cultural field, and artists were given more room for employing abstract forms in that competition. In general, Cuban monuments represented Socialist contents and were realist in form. This became clear in CODEMA'S first monument after its legal constitution. El Che y los Niños (Che and the Children), inaugurated in 1981, was a typically socialist realist representation of Guevara, although, according to a CODEMA member, its technical quality was greater than that of most revolutionary monuments hitherto made.

Similar aesthetics were employed in the monument to Echeverría in Cárdenas, the five-meter-high Cienfuegos in Yaguajay, and the monument to Rafaél Orejón in Moa. The authorities gave the commission for a monument to Rafaél Orejón directly to a trusted official artist, Thelvia Marín, without letting CODEMA intervene in the process. This drew critiques from CODEMA, which affirmed that the resulting sculpture was amorphous and poorly made. Although illegal in theory, this became the usual procedure when commissioners intended to implement a project without delay and debate. Monuments avoiding CODEMA supervision employed highly simplistic aesthetics to establish connections between different symbols of the narrative, as usually happened in monuments promoted by MINFAR. For instance, the monument commemorating the Cuban Missile Crisis in Banes displayed Communist and Cuban symbols along with Soviet Union missiles, symbolizing their "attack power" and the alliance between Cuban and Soviet Union forces.

The fourth point of the monumental program consisted of creating large spaces of popular leisure commemorating heroes in Santiago and Havana. In Santiago, a large park was dedicated to Frank País, a revolutionary leader and 26-J member killed by Batista forces in 1957. CODEMA members rejected the project that would preside over the park, because of its large size and its blatant realism. They criticized not only the form but also the content of the monument. They argued that País never wore the military clothes with which he was to be represented and that consequently the monument would become just an idealized figure of an unspecified 26-J warrior that would be unfaithful to País' personality. This is, however, precisely what the commissioners wanted: the homogenization and departicularization of the narrative and the erasure of every potential dissonance in the events and characters it represented.

Heritage also served to perform and negotiate international relations. The most significant case was the project to create a monument to Lenin in Havana's Parque Lenin (Lenin's Park). The monument was central to the increasing attentiveness of soviet foreign diplomacy to cultural and artistic issues but also reflected underlying Cuban–Soviet Union tensions. Since 1980, soviet bureaucrats, architects, and artists, especially the famous Lev Kerbel, had been in contact with their Cuban counterparts to promote the creation of a huge socialist realist statue dedicated to Lenin, offering their own materials and workers. CODEMA's frequent meetings to discuss the matter and the number of people involved reflected the leadership's sense of urgency to make the project a success, but delays could not be avoided. Various soviet vice presidents and ministers of culture insisted on its inauguration in November 1982 to commemorate the sixty-fifth anniversary of the October Revolution. Cubans, however, wanted to inaugurate the project on the 26 July and to use local materials to avoid a public interpretation of the monument as subordination to soviet command. In a clever reordering of soviet symbolism, the Cuban representatives meeting the soviet delegation also astutely sidestepped the soviet determination to add a large red flag to the monument, by affirming that "they considered Lenin's face as their own flag" (Quintana and Cabrera 1982).

The largest and heaviest monument in the country was inaugurated on January 8, 1984. The inauguration commemorated the twenty-fifth anniversary of the Cuban Revolution, making it seem a Cuban rather than soviet accomplishment. The media and the authorities proudly announced that it was the first monument to Lenin in America, when actually the oldest one, dating from 1924, is just a few kilometers away from Havana, on Lenin Hill. The inauguration highlighted the friendship and collaboration between the USSR and Cuba and involved the performance of rituals

Figure 4.9. Inauguration of the monument to Lenin at Parque Lenin in Havana.
Source: CODEMA archive.

by pioneer children. Pioneers always played a fundamental role in monument and museum inaugurations, as a way of symbolizing their responsibility for the preservation of the revolutionary heritage for the future.

The process showed the key role heritage played in geopolitics and Cuba's diplomatic relations with the USSR and other Socialist countries. The symbolic ceremony of Cuban–Soviet Union friendship could not conceal their political differences and the coloniality of the Cuban heritage field. Although Cubans attempted to make the monument appear to be a manifestation of the regime's ideology, soviet heritage criteria and values informed the contents and the terms of the debate, as reflected in the discussion about the dates of the inauguration, the origin of the materials to be employed, and the insistence on socialist realist aesthetics.

The Revolution Squares as the New Socialist City Centers

The original CODEMA plan to create "monumental complexes located in the centre of provincial capitals and named after a significant local patriot" (CODEMA 1981:n.p.) eventually manifested as the replication of Havana's Revolution Square in the provincial capitals. The influence of Stalinist and post-Stalinist urban planning and monumental programs in Cuba became apparent in this field. For historian Heather DeHaan, under Stalin,

> "visionary planning" gave way to a Socialist Realist "iconographic" approach to urban planning whereby iconographers (i.e., planners) copied sacralized models articulated elsewhere (i.e., in the Moscow city plan) onto their own palette [. . .] so Moscow became the new icon, the aesthetic model to which all cities and villages in the Soviet Union had to conform [. . .] Architectural mimicry of the capital signaled provincial success, even as it affirmed the provinces' subordinate position in the socio-geographic hierarchy. (DeHaan 2013:Ch.4)

The main characteristics of Stalinist urbanism endured in the USSR. The central districts of cities were designed to stage events enacting soviet collective identity and state power, developing spacious boulevards and public squares to serve as marching grounds and hubs for the proletariat (DeHaan 2013). These ideas underpinned the Cuban plans, as the provinces had to imitate Havana's model. Cuba deviated from soviet standards only in its emphasis on the commemoration of nationalist themes and figures in the new city centers.

In Havana, Revolution Square continued to operate as the central place of symbolic power and political performance for Fidel, where he celebrated the 26-J and May Day in front of thousands of Cubans. In the provinces, however, the squares were intended to fulfill manifold functions according to the new ideological and socioeconomic status quo. Cuban urbanists assumed that Socialist urban development would differ from bourgeois urbanism, and thus openly challenge previous colonial and republican city centers. Far greater investments were made in building new squares than in restoring traditional city centers, which were actively despised.

The squares represented the utmost attempt to bring together, in terms consistent with Marxism-Leninism, all the spheres of production of space and heritage. According to Socialist architect Hans Meyer, this implied the "materialization of the commingling of the most diverse artistic proletarian expressions: mass cinema, theatre, sport, mass demonstrations" (Meyer 1972:72). He argued that Socialist "buildings are not artworks. Their quality must be sought in their size and their functions" (Meyer 1972:72). The new squares epitomized the Marxist-Leninist myth of the new. Marxist-Leninist ideas considered that new Socialist urban space would transform the behavior, social identity, and subjectivity of the masses. One of their key promoters, Fernando Salinas, encapsulated this in his characterization of Revolution squares as "the highest symbolic expression of the revolutionary culture of each town [. . .] Rather than a public space, a Square is a meaningful environment. Human beings create these meanings with their historic memories and their imagination of the future. They do so by living their quotidian socio-economic, ideological and cultural relations in close connection with these spaces" (Salinas 1985:n.p.).

The squares were large-scale commemorative landscapes that assembled a set of elements into a meaningful heritage representation. Spatial planners saw them as the new city centers of the Socialist city and as spaces for displaying political power. The intention was for Poder Popular, the PCC, and other key institutions to have their buildings there, in front of the monumental sculptures that presided over the square and from where leaders delivered speeches to the masses. The squares thus also functioned as places of encounter between the political leaders and the masses, in a ritual of performance of power and popular subordination to it. The aim was to draw a symbolic connection between the state institutions and the meanings expressed in the monumental area.

Planners regarded the squares as future areas for leisure and social life and surrounded them with large prefabricated buildings for popular housing, sports stadiums, theaters, and *casas de la cultura* (houses of culture). Soundtracks with patriotic themes and lyrics were composed ad hoc and played constantly. Large esplanades were conceived for mass rallies and military parades, especially for the 26 July celebrations. Most squares were inaugurated on July 26 to establish a symbolic link between the revolutionary past and its projection into the future. Symbolically, the squares aimed to represent local patriots and histories as part of the national narrative. This concern for local memories attempted not to highlight local identities but to demonstrate, in a top-down manner, that every person in Cuba was consistently part of the same master-narrative. The squares materialized the symbolic content of the master-narrative through different representational dispositives, including sculptures, art, billboards, flags, friezes, plaques, music, and a museum. Administrative teams were appointed to run the museum and the different activities held in the squares, including pioneers and students' visits and oaths, graduations and tours for workers, conferences, and conventions.

The large amount of resources and time invested in the squares turned them into contested spaces and made them the focus of public interest, prompting heated debate among the cultural workers and artists and between them and different political actors. This debate derived from the new and distinctively Cuban monumental typology. Although other Socialist countries emphasized the construction of new civic centers, these centers lacked the heritage and commemorative component of Cuban squares. Unsurprisingly, the leadership wanted to secure strict control over the construction of the new squares to guarantee ideological coherence with the official narrative. As was common with other monumental typologies, they first gave square commissions to low-profile artists who were ideologically unproblematic, without launching a public competition or letting CODEMA intervene in the process. This contravened state legislation and was a blow to CODEMA, which had been planning the squares for a long time. The squares of Holguín (1979), Bayamo (1982), and Santa Clara (1988) were commissioned to José Delarra, and the Square of Sancti Spíritus (1982) to Thelvia Marín. Both orthodox artists had affinities with the ex-guerrillas, and their history of struggle against Batista made them part of the inner circle of trust, but they were scarcely respected by their fellow sculptors.

The politics of art in Socialist countries with centralized means of production like Cuba highly conditioned the role of artists and, indirectly, of heritage production. If profit making and public or institutional recognition determine the cultural and economic capital of artists in capitalist societies, then Socialist societies framed cultural politics in terms of political status and cultural authority (Verdery 1995:93). The freedom of artists was curtailed further in Cuba as it was compulsory for them to work for a public institution. They were able to become self-employed workers only after 1988, when the weakness of the state and the need to let artists earn currency abroad led to a decrease in constraints. Before then, however, artists had to compete with each other to maximize their bargaining power with bureaucrats higher up who could fund their projects: they had to find a balance between proposing avant-garde projects that would never be implemented and totally subordinating themselves to political demands. Project commissioners judged artistic performance in terms of ideological compliance, not in relation to public satisfaction or profit making. For them, it was crucial to employ monumental figurative forms that did not leave open the interpretation of the past, as abstract art would do. And this required the collaboration of trusted artists like Delarra and Marín.

The procedures and controversies surrounding the revolution squares can be reconstructed through the documentation in the CODEMA archive, including the reports, correspondence, designs, and media coverage that each project elicited. The squares of Holguín and Bayamo were built following similar patterns. The artist Delarra designed both monumental areas without freestanding sculptures and with an imposing frieze—sixty-one meters long in Holguín and twenty-five in Bayamo—with an attached podium below it, where the authorities stood during rallies, parades, and speeches. The friezes represented the historical evolution of Cuba according to the master-narrative and included quotations from Fidel and other patriotic and revolutionary leaders. The aim was to emphasize historic continuity and make the present appear as the inevitable outcome of historic development. The Bayamo case was an exception, because there was a colonial square in the city that had been renamed the Square of the Revolution by Carlos Manuel de Céspedes in 1898. This square had been devoted to a local figure, Perucho Figuerero. In a sign of respect for local traditions, the new square of 1982 was called Plaza de la Patria (Square of the Fatherland), rather than Square of the Revolution.

In the Calixto García Square in Holguín a broken star in the center of the frieze split history in two. At the left stood the prerevolutionary past and at the right the revolutionary past and present. The frieze represented the master-narrative through scenes of simple visual recognition and interpretation, emphasizing notions of class struggle, rebelliousness, and heroism. History started with a colonizer subduing the natives with a cross and ended with Martí and Fidel. According to the media at the time, their appearance at the end of the narrative was an attempt to create "a representation of historical continuity" (Eliseo August 5, 1979:56). The square in Bayamo had similar characteristics, with its monument housing a museum and administrative offices underneath it. The museum displayed pictures and objects of the revolutionary leaders, but documents and pictures of the time show that square museums were conceived generally less as spaces of representation than of ritual, where commemorations, awards, oaths, and events with pioneers took place.

The Serafín Sánchez Square in Sancti Spíritus (1982) was the first to include a huge freestanding socialist realist sculpture in the monumental area. The artist Marín created a sculpture that was five meters high and weighed seven tons and was designed to represent the humanist side of independence warrior Serafín Sánchez, depicted teaching a slave to read. At the time, different social actors considered the quality of the artworks in the squares of Holguín, Sancti Spíritus, and Bayamo, as well in as the squares of minor cities such as Ciego de Ávila and Matanzas, some of which were never completed, to be rather low. Indeed, CODEMA reports contain continuous complaints about the poor quality of monuments since the early 1980s. Beyond CODEMA, the issue became a public embarrassment that the government wanted to address. Some years after the construction of the square of Bayamo, Cuban art historian Pereira considered that the monument to Serafín Álvarez presented:

a pretentious symbolic representation of a chaotic narrative of national patriotic heroes, with unequal expressive languages and an overall poor quality in most figures [. . .] with errors of perspective and disproportionate forms that affect the aesthetic and conceptual results of the artwork. (Pereira 1994:145)

From 1983 onward, heritage policy shifted and public competitions supervised by CODEMA preceded the construction of Revolution squares. This did not ensure artistic freedom, as those commissioning monuments forced changes in all the projects, but there was room for debate and artistic experimentation. Even after a decree was passed in 1985 guaranteeing CODEMA total control over monumental works, CODEMA's members kept denouncing regional branches of the PCC and some ex-guerrillas' illegal commissioning of works, by artists such as Delarra and Marín. Specifically, CODEMA denounced the commissioning of Delarra to create the 5 of September Square in Cienfuegos, the monuments to the Tren Blindado (Armored Train) in Santa Clara, to Tania and Camilo in Pinar del Río, fifteen monuments in the Villa Clara Province and different monuments in Japan, Spain, and Mexico. This circumstance reflected the weaknesses and tensions underlying Cuban governmentality, even at the height of the institutionalizing period.

The Mariana Grajales Square in Guantánamo was the first square resulting from a CODEMA competition, in 1985. The competition required participants to carry out historical research about the martyrs and heroes of Guantánamo, specifically the historical continuity of Cuban struggles, the blend of the independence and revolutionary wars, and the role of Guantánamo in the Space Race as hometown of the first Cuban astronaut (CODEMA 1984b). The team that won the competition included some of the most renowned Cuban artists at the time. Although the competition stated that artistic expression would be free, the team leader, sculptor José Villa Soberón, had designed a project that would satisfy the authorities' preference for realist representation. Therefore, although abstract forms prevailed, Villa Soberón preferred to include the figurative representation of Mariana Grajales and a symbolic cavalry charge in the project (interview, May 15, 2013).

When Villa Soberón and his team won the competition, they learned that the regional PCC and sculptor Delarra had secretly agreed to make some changes to the project, including the addition of a large socialist realist sculpture of Frank País. The resulting monument combined abstract and socialist realist features designed and built by different artists. This hybrid aesthetics was a material reflection of the underlying contestation around the symbols represented in the square. Another element of dissonance was the public reception of realism. According to ex-CODEMA secretary and ex-president of the CNPC Margarita Ruiz Brandi (interview, April 23, 2013), it was a common argument among bureaucrats that socialist realism was not an ideological decision made to please the USSR but a choice based on the tastes of the people, who did not understand abstract art. The competition in Guantánamo refuted this argument, as the public polls carried out showed a preference for the most abstract projects.

The CODEMA competition for the Ignacio Agramonte Square in Camagüey, inaugurated in 1989, attracted national interest. The project envisioned the replacement of the colonial and republican city centers with a new Socialist city center surrounding the square, although it was never fully implemented. The winning project was predominantly abstract, but political pressures forced the inclusion of a socialist realist sculpture

Figures 4.10, 4.11, 4.12, and 4.13. *Top left*: original model of the Mariana Grajales square in Guantánamo. *Above right*: inauguration of the square by Castro. *Top right*: realist representation of Mariana Grajales. *Right*: realist figure of Frank País added to the project. Source: CODEMA archive.

of local independence hero Ignacio Agramonte. Because the traditional square in the city center of Camagüey was also named after Agramonte and presided over by a mounted statue of him, the sculptors of the revolutionary square underscored the difference with the traditional representational pattern by dismounting Agramonte and presenting him walking "out of time" (CODEMA 1988).

Different interviewees in the provinces signal a tension between the national and the local representations of history and identity displayed in the squares. The local challenge to the revolutionary attempt to establish a metonymic relationship between Havana and the provinces surfaced most clearly in Camagüey, a city with a strong local identity. Fernando Crespo Baró, former director of the development of Camagüey's square, recalls

Figure 4.14. Abstract projects presented to the CODEMA competition of the revolution square in Guantánamo, which the people from Guantánamo enjoyed. Source: Compiled by the author from CODEMA archive.

Figure 4.15. Collages of the monumental friezes of the revolution square Ignacio Agramonte, in Camagüey. Source: Author.

that narrating local stories and praising local heroes could cause political problems (interview, April 10, 2013). Events of national relevance like the Moncada and the Desembarco del Yate Granma had to be included in the frieze of Camagüey, and the national relevance of the local hero Agramonte had to be underscored. Similarly, the Marxist-Leninist concern with materiality required that monuments be built with materials from different parts of the nation. The revolutionary nation had to be not only symbolically represented but also physically constructed with national materials. Accordingly, the square in Camagüey was built with stones from Bayamo and marble from Villa Clara.

If the location of sites where the past is remembered actively conditions the process of commemoration and has symbolical connotations, then the construction of the new city centers in urban peripheries to the neglect of historic city centers had a clear meaning: the new city centers would reconcile the best of national traditions with the future-oriented prophecy of Socialism. The Cuban Dirección General de Planificación Física (General Direction of Physical Planning) was the main institution promoting the creation of new city centers. This process usually involved both a passive neglect of colonial and traditional urban centers and their active denigration. For instance, the project to create the Juan Gualberto Gómez Square in Matanzas explained at length the reasons the colonial city center was outdated and worthless. It was described as "congested with traffic and pedestrians, polluted by noise and dust, lacking green areas, parking lots and urban functions generally" (CODEMA 1990a:n.p.). This description justified the construction of the new square and city center and the abandonment of the old city center. Similarly, in the Mariana Grajales Square, the competition required bidding teams to carry out spatial studies, because, as Longa put it, the square would become the new "urban heart of Guantánamo" (Longa 1984:n.p.).

The Ernesto Guevara Square in Villa Clara, built in 1988, was without doubt the most controversial of all. The analysis of the troubled process leading to its construction reveals the underlying political conflict between artists and the ex-guerrillas. Guevara had come to symbolize the humanist values of the Revolution: sacrifice, consciousness, anti-imperialism, solidarity, and patriotism. Profiting from Guevara's myth, however, the Revolution fostered his image but not his ideas and values. When the square's commission was given directly to Delarra and the design for

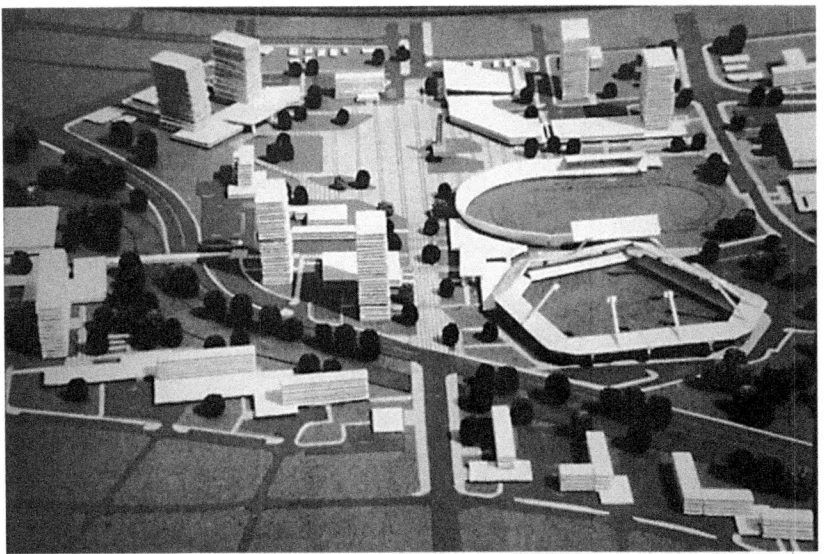

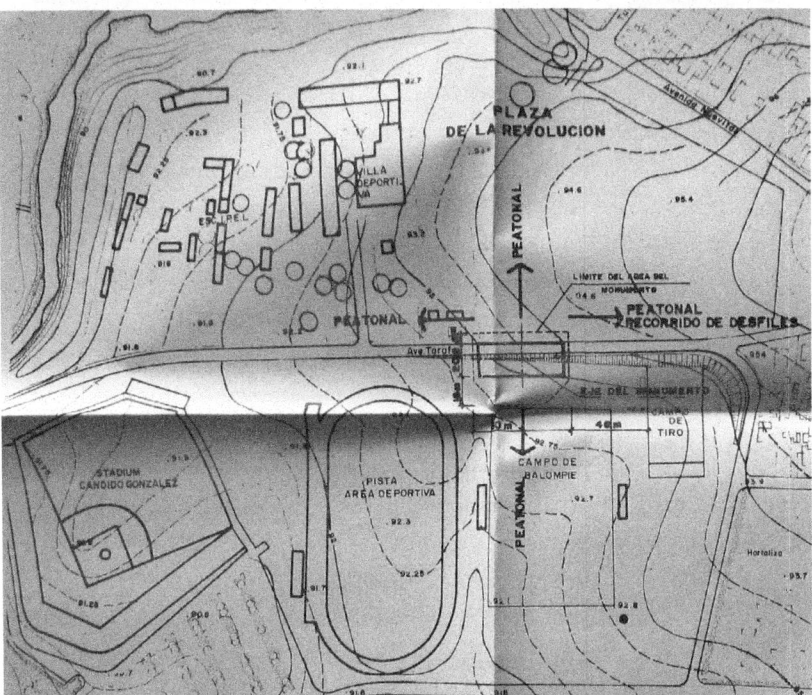

Figures 4.16 and 4.17. *Top*: model of the revolution square Ignacio Agramonte in Camagüey, and *bottom*: original plans for the square and new city center. Source: CODEMA archive.

Figure 4.18. The square today. Source: Author.

Guevara's monument made public, artists and CODEMA declared the project an attack on freedom of expression and on Guevara's figure. The project envisioned the square as the future city center of Santa Clara. It also planned a monumental representation of Guevara, with a twenty-five-meter-high socialist realist bronze statue and a huge frieze and museum below the monument narrating his war deeds.

Guevara's ex-wife Aleida March, fellow guerrilla Víctor Bordón, and MINFAR commander Juan Almeida Bosque, known for his fondness in cultural projects, wholeheartedly supported the project. Nonetheless, CODEMA launched a public campaign against the project and tried to gain the support of different personalities and to force MINCULT to enforce the law and open the competition to the public. MINCULT, however, remained silent. In turn, Almeida Bosque (1983) sent a letter to Longa to justify MINFAR's commitment to the project. He argued that it would go against Guevara's ideas to organize a competition with a cash prize, and consequently that it would be better to continue employing volunteers. Among these volunteers, of course, was the sculptor Delarra.

In a letter to CODEMA, monument expert and architect Mario Coyula Cowley (1983) strongly rejected the project. He argued that it was not enough to reduce the size of the sculpture, as CODEMA had requested. For him, the problem was not formal but conceptual: the idea ran against Guevara's most intimate beliefs. Following Coyula Cowley, CODEMA members claimed that the project should follow Guevara's values: "Non-conventionality, lack of rhetoric, simplicity, austerity, human values and heterogeneity of perspectives. The monument, however, is conventional, rhetorical, grandiose, imposing, superhuman and static. It is, in short, a monument of the nineteenth century for a man of the twenty-first century" (CODEMA 1984c). Clearly, the conflict between parties played out through competing interpretations of Guevara's heritage. Eventually, CODEMA arranged a meeting with MINFAR and PCC representatives. In the meeting, Arjona Pérez supported CODEMA's position, arguing that Guevara destroyed the monuments erected in his honor while he was alive. Then, in the middle of the heated debate, sculptor Villa Soberón left the room and went home to find Guevara's *Man and Socialism in Cuba*. He returned to the meeting to read an excerpt wherein Guevara criticized socialist realism:

> What is sought then is simplification, something everyone can understand, something functionaries understand. True artistic experimentation ends, and the problem of general culture is reduced to assimilating the Socialist present and the dead (therefore, not dangerous) past. Thus socialist realism arises [. . .] But why try to find the only valid prescription in the frozen forms of socialist realism? [. . .] We must not, from the pontifical throne of realism-at-all-costs, condemn all art forms. (Guevara 2005:162)

Ultimately, however, the project was implemented as proposed. CODEMA managed to reduce Guevara's realist sculpture from twenty-five to seven meters in height, but it was then put on an eighteen-meter-high pedestal, thereby creating a similarly imposing spatial and aesthetic effect as the original format. The square has not become the new center as anticipated by its promoters and stands in the periphery of Villa Clara devoid of social life. Nonetheless, the commoditization of the myth of Guevara attracts thousands of tourists to the monument every year, especially after the opening of a memorial with his remains, brought over from Bolivia in 1997. The whole process revealed that heritage was a contested terrain and that its symbolic power did not escape anyone. Ex-guerrillas, in this case

Figure 4.19. Monumental area of the revolution square Ernesto Guevara, in Villa Clara. Source: Author.

led by Almeida, did not hesitate to reassert their power and bypass state legislation and institutions when necessary. In turn, the official silence of MINCULT throughout the process reflected the leadership's lack of real delegation of powers to state institutions.

The last of the squares to be completed was the Antonio Maceo square in Santiago, between 1983 and 1991. It was the largest monument in terms of size, investment, and symbolic significance. Conceptual and technical problems delayed the project, as no factory in Cuba had ever produced materials of such dimensions. The project encapsulated most of the contradictions of Cuban monumental representation. The project was largely an initiative of Santiago's PCC branch, and CODEMA participated only by writing some reports and checking its nine-year evolution. The guidelines for the square's design provided for the construction of a central monument to represent the local hero Maceo, of which two competing teams presented opposing conceptualizations. The team of Alberto Lescay portrayed a large realist and figurative mounted Maceo, while the team led by Guarionex Ferrer and José Antonio Choy López presented a completely abstract project, in which Maceo was represented as thirty-one metal machetes rising from the earth, symbolizing a cavalry charge and the start of the war against Spain.

However, dissatisfied PCC commissioners in Santiago asked both teams to get together and rethink the whole project. The twenty-five artists, designers, architects, historians, and musicians that comprised the new team delivered a report to the provincial PCC arguing that "Maceo could be represented symbolically without the need to resort exclusively to a realist representation" (quoted in Rodríguez Joa 2009:78). However, the PCC rejected this view and unanimously decided that "the realist figure of General Antonio Maceo must appear in the Square, preferably on horseback" (quoted in Bazán de Huerta 1994:65). Sculptor Lescay was sent to Leningrad and Moscow to learn from the Russian models of large realist sculpture, and specifically to draw inspiration from the statue of Peter the Great. Paradoxically, the revolutionary leaders wanted to replicate the formal expression of the Tsarist regime overthrown by the Russian Revolution to emulate a soviet style that had become the representational language of power in Cuba.

The square was eventually inaugurated in 1991, reconciling the demands of artists and commissioners by including both abstract and realist art. Lescay's realist sculpture of Maceo stripped him of the traditional Cuban symbols and forms of representation of War of Independence heroes. A socialist realist Maceo appears on horseback, without the mambí hat and the machete, his open hand calling the Cubans to war. The sculpture stands in total spatial and symbolic disconnection from the huge abstract machetes. The elements differ in typology, style, material, and color. The stark division between the two forms of representation reflected the underlying political tensions between artists and commissioners. This can be perceived indirectly in writings published after the inauguration of the monument, which have tried to conceal these tensions and provide the "ideologically correct" interpretation by insisting on the monument's formal coherence. For instance, Cos Causse affirmed that the machetes could be interpreted as symbolizing the "consolidation of the Cuban nation throughout the Ten Year War. Starting from a horizontal position and from scratch, there are ups and downs until it becomes vertical as an irreversible reality" (Causse 1991:54; see also Parra Donet 2008).

The project revealed that artistic freedom was severely limited in various ways. Choy López, designer of the machetes, wanted the monument

Figure 4.20. Realist sculpture of Antonio Maceo, by Antonio Lescay. Source: Author.

to be completely abstract. But, as he argues, "we knew that those in power would not allow us to build an abstract square [. . .] They always understood the machetes as an artistic hoax; what mattered for them was Maceo's sculpture" (interview, May 17, 2013). Asked about the project, current CODEMA president and sculptor Tomás Lara Franquis said: "Artists never wholeheartedly accepted socialist realism. Fundamentally, our strategy was to work the symbolic elements with figurative forms in combination with other abstract or expressionist forms. Artists always pushed to the limits of their freedom, but with a clear understanding that the figurative elements had to appear" (interview, March 29, 2013). Thus, for critical artists and architects, socialist realism was not an ideological construct but a real material imposition by powerful actors—which they rejected formally and, ultimately, politically. Its power to assemble history and materiality in the service of legitimacy made heritage a unique case in Cuba, as monumental production was one of the few fields where socialist realism became a more or less stable and identifiable expressive language of power in public art and monuments—however contested and hybridized it was. Monuments during the institutionalizing period served as key conveyors of ideology while constituting a terrain of dissonance. The variety of themes was narrowed down and the experimentation of the early years was abandoned. A focus on national heroic individuals and idealized social classes replaced the earlier focus on the memorialization of historically contextualized collectives such as students or workers. As happened with museums, policies shifted from resignifiying past monuments to building new ones to propagate the new ideology. This reflected the self-confidence and future-orientation of the regime.

The new squares expanded the model of Havana's Revolution Square to the provinces, with the aim of providing the symbolic and physical environment for public ritual and massive popular participation. Nonetheless, when the transformative thrust of the early years became institutionalized, and more bureaucratic than popular, revolutionary rituals became sclerotic. The moderate republican cultural elites had conceived the Plaza Cívica in Havana as a symbol to be observed, while the revolutionaries reworked the square as the stage for Fidel's performative ritual. Instead, the provincial squares were commemorative spaces conceived as metaphors of the organization of the state and its institutions, which were physically present in them.

Based on Marxist-Leninist ideas of progress and modernization, the squares attempted to combine infrastructural and social transformation. What made Cuba distinct from other Socialist countries was its insistence on including commemorative monuments in the new Socialist city centers. Those monuments intended to uproot Cubans from their traditional ways of life and physical spaces and to incorporate them into Socialist city centers representing the official ideology through museums, friezes, and monuments. The commemorative function was an attempt to assuage the contradictions between nationalist and Socialist identity, tradition and modernity, exacerbated by new city centers.

The shift in heritage policies was also apparent in the form in which the symbolism of the new squares was articulated. The narrative displayed in

Havana's Revolution Square during the early years suggested a symbolic and even allegorical relation between Fidel and Martí, as expressed in the connection between the revolutionary leader and the ideal of nation embodied by Martí. The link between nation and Revolution had gradually become a symbol by virtue of the creation of a public interpretive habit through rituals performed on key dates of the revolutionary calendar. Physical or contextual resemblances were nearly nonexistent between Fidel and the denoted object, that is, the revolutionary nation represented by Martí's monument. The socialist realist characteristic of the new squares established an iconic, rather than symbolic, connection between the leader and the material expression of the narrative. The speech, the clothes, and the attitudes of those performing revolutionary ritual on the stage of the squares resembled the material and sculptural representations surrounding them, the music, the banners, and the monuments.

The transition from symbolism to iconicity is not random. Herzfeld (1992:68–69) has shown that icons are often employed by totalizing ideologies because they look natural or can be naturalized, contrary to symbols, which are arbitrary signs that require interpretation. This iconic grammar both reflected and helped to develop the combination of revolutionary nationalism and Marxism-Leninism. Fidel and the Revolution had to be represented as the historical redeemers, in terms of myth and passion, but also as the necessary outcome of the scientific historical laws of Marxism-Leninism. The provinces required unambiguous socialist realist icons rather than symbols, because there, unlike in Havana, Fidel could not perform rituals habitually and thus create interpretive habits. As in the porticoes of medieval cathedrals, ideology had to be constantly and publicly displayed, even when the ritual of mass was not being held. Since the completion of Santiago's square, only the Vicente García Square in Las Tunas has been built, in 1997. The desovietization process after 1986 and the economic and ideological crisis of the 1990s marked the decline of the revolution squares, which were doomed to decay in the peripheries of Cuban cities until the present day.

Conclusion

The institutionalization of the Revolution transformed heritage into a central instrument of governmentality. The regime dispersed central power to local and regional centers without letting communities intervene in the more important decisions concerning history or heritage in their areas. Different groups within the state and its ranks of politicians and professionals decided what, when, and how something or someone was classed as heritage. The articulation of perceptions of time and history in the public sphere through heritage was fundamental, because the meaning of ideology rested in the cultivation of a sense of historical development. Education, art, museums, and monuments were deemed crucial for building legitimacy and for producing a sense of estrangement from a certain national culture and a sense of continuity with another. This explains the emphasis on the break with the past and the embracing of the new man, the new city centers, and the new society.

The institutionalizing period attempted to achieve coherence between real social processes and the theoretical roles accorded to heritage in Socialist society. This process can be interpreted in the light of Baller's (1984) conceptualization of the stages of Socialist heritage management. For him, during the early revolutionary years, heritage policies should aim at the quantitative redistribution of culture and at the resignification of features to be incorporated into the new society. In a more mature phase, the roles of heritage shift to emphasizing the internalization of ideology and the construction of new, future-oriented meanings and symbols. The institutionalization period in Cuba aligns with Baller's second phase, as the regime used heritage to inculcate ideology among Cubans. The construction of new monuments and museums overshadowed the resignification of past features and heritage preservation efforts—in colonial city centers, for instance.

The highly ideological use of history envisioned an unchanging society endowed with a homogenous identity. The convergence between an increasingly artificial heritage production and a reified living past, and the expansion of museums and monuments, has been connected by different authors with the decline of engagement with "real history" (Appadurai and Breckenridge 1992; Maleuvre 1999). The combination of different discursive styles and practices resulted in a characteristically hybrid Cuban narrative. This narrative did not account for the development of a cultural form through time but posited an essential identity outside time: the revolutionary nation in its different manifestations. The plot reconciled the culture-history narrative of the national heroes, elite and aristocratic in their social origins, on the one hand, and a Marxist-Leninist narrative portraying a series of subordinated classes struggling against injustice, on the other. Ultimately, what provided coherence to the narrative was not reason but belief in a metaphysical substance—"the rebellious people"— that functioned as a historical subject present throughout all phases of historical development. The historical continuity of the people's struggle against injustice and its culmination in revolutionary triumph is what the narrative strove to prove.

Assuming that histories are ideologically constituted, the particularity of Cuban and other Socialist narrative constructions was their grounding in a reified master-narrative that was accorded a scientific and rational status. The master-narrative expanded to include the previously disregarded indigenous and Afro-Cuban pasts in terms of rebel subaltern classes, thereby overlooking issues of race and ethnicity. The pasts of the indigenous people and slaves could be safely incorporated into a heritage narrative because they were "dead." However, the living cultures of Afro-Cubans were more challenging, because their practices and beliefs could be classified by the scientific rationality of Marxism-Leninism only as "ethnic" and "superstitious." The symbolic outcome of this process was the collapse of ethnic and racial difference with nation, nation with class, and class with Revolution. This involved a process of naturalization and departicularization of the narrative. Through it, the state presented social and historical actors and processes as unmediated essences, curtailing the meanings connecting them to real contexts, places, and groups and incorporating them into the dominant master-narrative.

The representation of this master-narrative via heritage was nonetheless contentious. The tacit rejection of socialist realism by artists led commissioners to provide some room—probably more than they wanted to—for creative freedom. Thus, the politics of heritage was a multilayered reality and a field of tension wherein different factions competed for power. This shows that the Cuban state was never monolithic and questions the extent and solidity of the institutionalization process, which foreign scholars and commentators have probably overemphasized. Nonetheless, those in power always firmly controlled cultural politics and often resorted to trusted artists when they needed to, especially those among the ex-guerrillas.

If, as Kapcia (2014) has argued, the Cuban system is constituted by

different circles of power, then there were at least two clearly differentiated circles in the field of heritage. The ex-guerrillas controlled the contents of monuments and museums and emphasized nationalistic themes.
The soviet-leaning individuals, with different positions in the state and
ranks of the PCC, supported socialist realist forms and a greater role of institutions. They tried to impose socialist realism by influencing key institutions such as MINCULT or CODEMA, but they never fully achieved this,
as many directors of secondary institutions, artists, and cultural workers were either not entirely committed to soviet ideas or openly rejected
them. State institutions served as sites for encounter and debate between
different views, but the ex-guerrillas bypassed them when needed. Both
groups, however, encountered the subtle but constant resistance of certain artists to their aesthetic and political agendas. Artists were also a
highly complex and heterogeneous group. Some were complicit with the
establishment and others were openly critical. Nonetheless, they were
fundamental to the definition and transformation of heritage politics and
policies throughout the period.

The ambivalence of MINFAR heritage policies revealed the complexity of the Cuban–Soviet Union relationships. MINFAR played a contradictory role in the commemoration, preservation, and heritagization of
the foundational myths of the ex-guerrillas and in combining those with
the emerging Marxist-Leninist narrative developed by the new institutions, including the PCC. Although the ex-guerrillas strove to preserve a
narrative predicated on heroism, charisma, and sacrifice, they gradually
embraced the Marxist-Leninist logic, which emphasized institutional solidity and party rule. The question remains as to why ex-guerrillas—or at
least some of them—adopted socialist realism as their preferred method
of heritage expression, as became clear in the case of Guevara's monument
and the increasing influence of soviet ideas on the MR.

This observation has three potential explanations. First, it could be related to MINFAR's leader Raúl. He was politically close to the USSR and
could have functioned as the ideological bridge between nationalism and
soviet Marxism-Leninism. Second, socialist realism did not differ significantly from the traditional figurative style of prerevolutionary periods.
This similarity made it a very suitable form for representing the symbols
of power, because it was familiar to Cubans. Third, socialist realism was
able to provide a firm representational language to symbolize power and

to convey ideology via heritage. This official language was lacking after the inconclusive cultural debates of the 1960s over the "correct" revolutionary form of expression. The fact that realism remains the official representational regime decades after the soviet collapse supports the latter assertion.

From the perspective of heritage, the attitude of the Cuban leadership can be interpreted as the adoption of a more pragmatic and less ideologically driven position in its relationship with the USSR. Cuba did not simply import socialist realism but adapted its contents and forms to the Cuban context—realism connected well with the prerevolutionary ideas of cultural modernism and neoclassical aesthetics. The regime combined the contents of the Marxist-Leninist narrative with nationalist-revolutionary themes, while socialist realist forms were at times hybridized with the abstract art promoted by Cuban artists. This was so especially after the opening in artistic expression during the 1980s. Thus, far from seeing a slavish imitation of soviet models, the institutionalization period involved the continuation of the crypto-colonial relationship that was already hinted at in the previous period. Cubans adapted soviet forms of expression for pragmatic reasons rather than wholeheartedly adopting them or believing in their ideological appropriateness for the Cuban context. Indeed, the process of absorbing soviet domination was mixed and erratic in its effects, which fits the crypto-colonial model well: emulation and resentment often go together in such cases.

This again distinguishes Cuba from Eastern European countries and brings it closer to countries like Vietnam, Laos, and China. These countries probably provide a better comparative framework for Cuba, because their revolutions intimately connected the postcolonial experience of national liberation with the modernization project of Marxism-Leninism (Long 2012). As in Cuba, these countries projected a master-narrative based on a vulgarized form of Marxism-Leninism predicated upon the themes of martyrdom and national humiliation, with the Communist Party playing a central role in redeeming the nation through struggle and sacrifice. The Cuban trajectory after the collapse of the Soviet Union, however, would again reinstate the distinctiveness of the Revolution among other Socialist countries.

The Reification of Ideology as Heritage and the Return of the Nation between 1990 and 2014

It is not surprising that Cubans grant culture a place of pre-eminence in the middle of such hard times. To defend culture is to defend what we are. What we were. And what we will be

(Sánchez, October 20, 1992:22)

The previous chapter showed that Cuba had imitated soviet heritage ideas to a significant extent. Consequently, the blow inflicted by the collapse of the Soviet Union, in 1991, cannot be overstated. The initial implementation of mild reforms in the Proceso de Rectificación in Cuba as a reaction to Gorbachev's *perestroika* gave way to a devastating economic crisis known as the Periodo Especial en Tiempos de Paz (Special Period in Times of Peace), which started in 1991. The country had to reduce expenditure and build a self-sufficient economy based on tourism and foreign investment, which made Cuba dependent on the interests of foreign capital and visitors. The main discursive lines in Cuba shifted from Marxism-Leninism to trying to reformulate an ideology based on a sense of Cubanness as opposed to Socialist internationalism. The Revolution—still a strong national signifier—changed the content and the form used to tell the national narrative. References to a utopian Socialist future shifted to an emphasis on cultural heritage and national identity, now understood as a heterogeneous blend of cultures rather than as a class-based

Marxist-Leninist new man. This led to the increased reliance on "heritage" and to revision of the national narrative, with its supporting monumental and museum structures.

This period also witnessed the important reemergence of the OHCH and its leading role in the restoration of Old Havana. However, this chapter focuses only on state-sanctioned heritage to contextualize the heritage work of the OHCH, which will be analyzed in the next chapter. This chapter explores the consequences of the collapse of the USSR for heritage theory and practice while shedding light on the main tenets of the Cuban context after 1990. What new uses of heritage emerged in a context of rapid ideological, social, and political transformations? Did continuities and ruptures with the previous heritage politics and policies represent a significant shift in representations of national identity and in ideological rhetoric?

Answering these questions can help us to understand the ambiguous period that started with the collapse of the Soviet Union, which is fundamental for contextualizing current developments in Cuba. The key shift in official attitudes toward the past involved abandoning the future-oriented revolutionary emphasis on creating a new man and society and embracing a form of cultural nationalism reminiscent of the early revolutionary years and its myths—the unfinished revolution, Martí, and the War of Independence. This shift was sanctioned by the new constitution passed in 1992, which underscored Martí's ideas and suppressed references to Marxism-Leninism. This also meant that culture and the master-narrative started to be considered as two separate entities. Economic collapse forced the regime to change many of its policies in order to encourage economic growth. The use of dollars was decriminalized, economic performance and profitability started to be a concern for state companies—including museums and heritage institutions—and foreign investment and tourism were allowed. Indeed, the number of tourists increased from 300,000 in 1990 to three million in 2014, with tourism representing 50 percent of the national income throughout the 1990s.

The sense that the sovietizing master-narrative brought with it universalizing and abstract tendencies led to an interest in embedding personal identity in space and time and to a revalorization of the sense of place, the local, and the particular. This involved an association of revolutionary values with the ideology of the *campesino* (peasant) lifestyle and its associated qualities of frugality and altruism. Sociologist Mike Featherstone (1996) has described this phenomenon as "cultural localism," a neoromantic re-enchantment of tradition and the vernacular. Cultural localism was an issue for the Cuban regime that significantly affected restoration policies for heritage processes. Indeed, Cuba started to reassess its colonial and republican heritage and to look to the past rather than focus exclusively on a utopian Socialist future.

Apart from cultural localism, a key element was the reawakening of a banal form of revolutionary cultural nationalism. National heritage became the stage for a conflict over the definition of the Cuban self-image and national narrative and over the features of Cuban culture that should be preserved and represented for Cubans and foreign visitors. The regime launched a series of campaigns, from the Batalla de Ideas to the Campaña por la Libertad para los Cinco (Campaign for Freedom for the Five) to promote a symbolic war over memory and heritage with the United States and the exile community in Miami.

Different authors have interpreted the post-1990 period in Cuba as a form of late Socialism associated with the end of Communism, as the emergence of a nationalist, state capitalist system, and as another form of postsoviet transition to democracy (Chávez 2005:1). It has also been described as an awkward reinvention of the system that blends capitalist reforms with Socialist development strategies, still self-defined as Socialist and not necessarily on its way to capitalism (Frederik 2012:13). The PCC claims its legitimacy now from its self-presentation as the defender of national traditions and heritage. The party is still as firmly in power as it is in China, Laos, and Vietnam but has not yet implemented free market reforms to the extent it has in these countries. Following the interpretation of the Cuban system as a form of state capitalism, the significant shift was that the end of Soviet Union subsidies meant that Cuba had to compete in real terms in the global economy. This required a structural change in economic planning focusing on tourism revenues, and, consequently, a new ideology to generate consensual hegemony about the new status quo.

The OHCH restoration project in Old Havana is one of the first and most visible market-oriented experiments based on heritage tourism in Cuba. The OHCH has focused academic and public debate after 1990 on heritage and political significance, becoming an institutional actor with the potential to ease the process of reconciliation with the exiled community.

This chapter will therefore examine the broader context within which the OHCH operates in order to appreciate how it departs from the state discourse. It thereby reveals the multisided character of the Cuban heritage field after 1990 as the outcome of the different logics and tensions of the time.

The Return of the Nation and Identity

Despising our heritage, or using it for commercial purposes, is something that has nothing to do with the true scientific attitude in the exploitation of cultural features [. . .] The use of heritage for commercial purposes [. . .] erases the profile of cultural identity because of a mediatized and thoughtless touristification. Unlike this situation of cultural wreckage in the capitalist world, Socialism has been a staunch advocate of the cultural heritage of the past.

(Arjona Pérez 2004 [1986]:38)

The requirements of the times forced Cultural Heritage Director Arjona Pérez to readapt her discourse to the new ideology. In the 1990s, she moved from a definition of museums as vehicles of ideological propaganda to considering them as "representatives of the personality of our people, its projection in artworks and its evolution until present [. . .] The local spirit, and the nation, are the crucial raison d'être of these institutions" (Arjona Pérez, February 2, 1990:86). This change encapsulates the shift of state heritage discourse toward nationalism and cultural localism, incorporating ideas of ecology, quality of life, cultural identity, and tourism as a way of preserving heritage.

Between 1990 and 2014, heritage was part of the attempt to disentangle the idea of nation from Marxism-Leninism and to rearticulate notions of national identity. The regime reworked previous heritage narratives and symbols to incorporate local and personal identities into the new nationalist doctrine through reframing education, history, memory, and museums. This tendency stemmed from the need to adapt heritage policies to the rapidly changing socioeconomic and political context affecting Cubans—from the unfeasibility of traveling to the increasing individual identification with state companies demanded by new labor policies. This process was not devoid of contradictions, as the economic reforms undermined much of the original values of the Revolution. Consequently, the cultural authorities responsible for heritage policies faced the dilemma of making the history and values of the Revolution appear relevant to an individualistic society that in reality was far removed from these ideals—and all without encouraging critical ideas that could turn against the system.

Cultural authorities had to address this challenge at a time when most heritage institutions were crumbling and decision-making returned to the inner circle of power, making the transmission of ideological messages a more direct process and less conditioned by other actors. CODEMA continued to exist on paper, but its agency was severely curtailed and its provincial branches disappeared. It became a sculpture studio providing support to artists working for the new tourism industry, and opportunities to develop monumental public art almost disappeared. The Cultural Heritage section of MINCULT became the aforementioned Centro Nacional de Patrimonio Cultural (CNPC) after 1995. The objective of the CNPC was to enhance and rationalize heritage production and to establish branches in all provinces. However, shortly after its creation, the central CNPC building in Havana partially collapsed and its performance deteriorated. The activities of the CNPC increased only gradually during the 2000s, especially under the directorship of Gladys Collazo in the 2010s. Her appointment as CNPC director marked a turning point in Cuban heritage management. She was not a PCC, MINCULT, or state bureaucrat but a close collaborator with OHCH director Leal Spengler, who had appointed her to the post.

The fact that Leal Spengler, an openly Catholic and non-Marxist historian, has reached such a high level of power and influence in this period reflects the deep changes that have taken place in the heritage field. Indeed, until the 2010s, many heritage workers saw the CNPC as the bulwark of the most orthodox professionals opposing the economic exploitation of heritage, its opening to tourism, and the abandonment of Marxism-Leninism. After the death of the powerful Arjona Pérez in 2006, however, Leal Spengler and his OHCH were left free to gradually take over the CNPC and other state institutions such as CENCREM and in 2012 the UNESCO-Cuba chair. Similarly, the Comisión Nacional de Monumentos and the headquarters of the International Council of Monuments and Sites (ICOMOS) and ICOM, unified since 2009, fell under the aegis of the OHCH despite the fact that Arjona Pérez had previously controlled them. In other words, a heritage entity restricted to Old Havana was taking over state institutions with a national scope.

The OHCH has also been the main representative of a larger tendency that has also affected state institutions: a return of culture-history and the gradual volatilization of the sense of teleology implied by Marxist-Leninist historiography. This also involved a reassessment and nostalgia for the colonial and republican periods that the Revolution had openly denigrated until 1990. Cuban scholars and professionals started to study and celebrate republican buildings, as well as republican intellectuals and artists such as Lydia Cabrera, Fernando Ortiz, Jorge Mañach, and Mario Carreño. This did not imply a complete break with previous forms of heritage production but rather a shift in the ways representations of national identity in monuments and museums were aligned with the reinterpretation of history and education and reworked according to the scant economic resources of the period.

The revolutionary regime had used Marxism-Leninism to articulate Cuban identity based on a homogeneous conception of class that neglected personal identities and individual creations. However, this ideological influence was gradually weakened in favor of a new vision of the country's heritage. The result was a combination of the old ideas and practices with those that emerged from the new situation, something highly ambivalent and difficult for museums and heritage professionals to transmit. Although all interviewees in the heritage field agreed that identity was emphasized after 1990, the content of that identity remained unclear. Political campaigns such as the Proyecto Identidad (Identity Project) and the Batalla de Ideas pointed to a renewed attempt to "massify" culture and education in a way reminiscent of the "politics of passion" of the early years. According to a member of the Instituto de Historia, Yoel Cordoví Núñez (interview, May 23, 2013), these initiatives celebrated Martí and local relevant characters, who for the first time since the Revolution were not necessarily martyrs or warriors.

The reassessment of national identity was paralleled by an in-depth revisiting of history. The thriving academic revisionism mainly expressed in the journals *Temas* and *Contracorriente*, starting in 1995, challenged the dominant view that equated the Republic with evil and negated the idea that Marxism-Leninism or the Revolution had a history. Most traditional themes of revolutionary historiography were questioned, including the ahistorical narrative of the 100 years of struggle, the historic analysis based on class struggles between specific heroes and groups (students, slaves, etc.), and the generalization of Marxist-Leninist theory at the expense of archival work. In our interview, Díaz Pendás considered that the 1990s

> did away with dogmatic conceptions imported from the USSR [. . .] and now we are trying to turn towards identity, drawing on culture for the understanding and forging of a historic memory. There is an effort to use history to reconcile people with their identity as a nation, with their cultural essences, integrating them with the locality, seeking approaches closer to social history [. . .] to find the elements of integration between nation and nationality, these elements that Fernando Ortiz had called *ajiaco*. (Interview, February 15, 2012)[1]

He recognized, however, that despite the collapse of the USSR, "the Soviet handbooks, the materialist approach to history, and the Marxist-Leninist vision of reality still influence the teaching of history" (interview, February 15, 2012). His words encapsulate the tension of the period between the reformist agenda based on nationalism and cultural localism, on the one hand, and the Marxist-Leninist tradition that pervaded heritage policies, on the other. This contradiction emerged most clearly in the contrast between our interview, in which Díaz Pendás conveyed a sense of political opening and change, and his books, which are charged with empty ideological rhetoric and citations of soviet authors (Díaz Pendás 2008, 2010). In fact, while a small sector of critical scholars has begun to adopt a different approach toward history, the history taught to children remains mostly unchanged.

In rhetorical fashion, Cuban intellectual Fernando Martínez Heredia has emphasized the difficulty of extricating history as master-narrative from real history as such: "History, understood as the history of Cuba (always the difficulty of separating name from content)" (Martínez Heredia 2005:294). Indeed, the new educational recommendations for history classes in schools stressed the need "to employ as much time as required to disclose the truth about the United States [and to] link the national and local histories organically" (Díaz Pendás 2010:6). At the same time, official

---

1   *Ajiaco* is a kind of soup that, according to Ortiz, represents the transculturation, or mixing, of Spanish, Afro-Cuban, and indigenous cultures.

history sanctioned the production of cultural localism. Various interviewees acknowledge that the emphasis on local identity was the result of PCC provisions in the early 1990s, which resulted in the creation of a master's degree in regional history at the national Instituto de Historia.

According to ex-director of CENCREM and UNESCO Chair Mercedes García Santana, there were consequences of this emphasis on local history in terms of heritage. "Museums," she observed, "had to start working hand in hand with local historians, carrying out a serious research of the republican period and including in the museum the history of the Revolution" (interview with M. García Santana, April 2, 2013). In other words, museums were required to respond to real historic dynamics, at least to a certain extent, rather than to merely represent an abstract master-narrative. The creator of the dozens of municipal museums in Havana Province during the period of institutionalization, Lelis Marrero Oliva, summed up the change in museum work derived from academic revisionism:

> Previously, it was impossible to display traitors to the fatherland in the museum, but now it is possible to talk about them and to show their legacy, along with that of other intellectuals and professionals who left Cuba [. . .] Museum scripts must adapt to the current times. Before, all museums had a room of martyrs, they were extremely boring [. . .] and they all resembled each other, from one side of the island to the other. (Interview, April 2, 2013)

Nevertheless, the extent to which museums were adapted to the new context cannot be overestimated. First, although the inclusion of new themes and objects in museums became possible in theory, major economic constraints prevented many institutions from changing their exhibitions and scripts. Second, museums responded to developments based on both academic and institutional logic and have been subject to tensions between the former and the new ideology throughout the period.

Interestingly, the recategorization records of museums at the CNPC archive show how, after 1990, museums have incorporated new narratives and aesthetics without completely relinquishing the Marxist-Leninist tradition. Accordingly, museums have not suppressed the martyrs' rooms or radically altered the aesthetics of exhibitions but rather have created new rooms dedicated to ethnography or to relevant local intellectuals, artists, and musicians. Instead of replacing one heritage discourse with another, new heritage features relating to the new multicultural ideology and concerns for local identities have been added in a sort of palimpsest. In some cases, a spatial rearrangement of the exhibition complemented this thematic overlapping. For instance, in my interview with the director of the Museum of Guanabacoa, Lourdes Millet Ramos, she explained the recent rearticulation of the functions of the museum in three different buildings. The traditional exhibition was reworked with an emphasis on Afro-Cuban folklore intended for tourism, another building was devoted to the martyrs, and a new house was designated for local artists (interview, March 12, 2013).

It is interesting to compare the Museum of Guanabacoa, created in 1964, and the Municipal Museum of Regla, created in 1982 under the aegis of Law 23 of Municipal Museums. In both museums, Afro-Cuban material culture plays a significant role. The exhibition in Guanabacoa is more context-specific and has been quick to adapt to the new ideological requirements and tourism expectations. However, the collection in Regla still presents the characteristic assemblage of objects of the period of slavery sanctioned by the master-narrative of the institutionalization period, that is, shackles, chains, and so on. This shows that museums created during the early revolutionary years had more freedom in terms of content and form, probably due to their own institutional inertia and to their difficult fitting within the post-1975 standardized museum procedures.

In terms of museography, the aesthetic conception of museums has gradually shifted toward minimalism and the exhibition of unmediated objects. For museum designer Enrique Hernández Castillo (interview, May 5, 2013), minimalism was a reaction to soviet flamboyance, didacticism, and gigantism. As he told me, the adoption of minimalism by architects and designers was limited because it could be interpreted as a deviation from the official orthodoxy with political connotations. Nonetheless, there has been an increasing concern for aesthetic appeal in Cuban museums that has also been documented in post–Soviet Union Eastern Europe and China (Bădică 2014; Varutti 2014).Young architects have attempted to create museum designs in tune with contemporary international trends. This has typically involved a decrease in the density of texts, keeping information panels and features on display to a minimum, and leaving the walls uncovered to highlight the architectural environments.

The intervention of the OHCH in 2010 in the flagship state museum of Frank País, in Santiago, is evidence of this tendency toward minimalism, which reveals a gradual loosening of soviet-influenced museography. An analysis of the different museum scripts preserved at the Frank País Museum archive testified to three main rearrangements throughout its history, showing that the OHCH intervention did not radically alter its narrative content. However, the OHCH has implemented an aesthetic reworking of the museum that conveys a more humanist and sociocultural understanding of the revolutionary leader Frank País, in contrast to the military tone and grey atmosphere that previously had prevailed. Young museum designers have perceived this intervention as a sign of the potential that aesthetic concerns have to effect change in the interpretation of museum content, and thus in its political reading. However, this so-called aesthetization of museums aimed at public consumption and making museums more tourist-friendly has been regarded by orthodox cultural workers as a betrayal of the real function of the museum, which is to convey ideologically informed messages. As Hernández Castillo argued, this has been the case despite the fact that young architects have generally been forbidden from making the slightest changes in content and narrative in the state museum network.

A close look at the transformations in the emblematic MR after 1990 encapsulates this shift in heritage discourse and practice. Although because of its national scope the MR has not incorporated references to local identity, it has cleansed its exhibition of references to the soviet period. The MR has removed pictures and banners of Marx, Engels, and Lenin and Communist symbols, as well as references to a shared past with other Socialist countries. In one of the interviews with the director, he proudly affirmed that there was only one reference to Lenin and Marx in the sixty-five-page-long, 2013 version of the script that the museum plans to implement in 2016 (Museo de la Revolución 2013). Moreover, the script envisaged that the new exhibition would rework its aesthetics to make it more palatable to a wider public.

The ideology of cultural localism emerged more clearly in the analysis of the state network of municipal museums, which replicated the transformations adopted by the MR at a national scale. Interestingly, the documentation at the CNPC archive shows that the scripts of municipal museums were reworked in terms of narrative content according to instructions provided by the CNPC in Havana, principally after the 2000s.

Official provisions from Havana demanded that municipal museums comply with the requirement to include local identities in their exhibitions. The shift from chronological to thematic approaches went hand in hand with an emphasis on local identities and figures. Similarly, attention was paid to the particularities that made localities different from each other, while references to Marxism-Leninism and the PCC were kept to a minimum.

A survey of municipal museums throughout the country suggested that the new ideology of cultural localism did not entail an increased autonomy for museum workers in terms of the narratives and aesthetics museums adopted. Indeed, as had previously occurred with museum scripts during the period of institutionalization, CNPC workers in Havana made corrections and suggestions to the scripts sent by museums from different parts of the country. In the case of the municipal museum of Banes, museum workers sent a renewed script proposal similar to the former Marxist-Leninist master-narrative but leaving out references to cultural localism. CNPC reviewers were not happy with the proposal and suggested the following changes:

> Identify the historical evolution of Banes as an organized and individualized community [. . .] demonstrate that cultural identity is a coherent system throughout each of the historical phases in Banes [. . .] frame the relationship between museum and public taking into consideration both the local community and foreign tourism. (CNPC 2012a)

Reviewers in Havana forced museum workers to adopt cultural localism to emphasize via heritage the historic continuity of the community's identity. This situation indicates the confusion that reigned in the provinces regarding the new plans set out in Havana. Indeed, Cuban provinces tended to be delayed in their implementation of new plans and ideas, and heritage policies were no exception. This was the result not only of practical problems related to economic shortages and provincial workers' avoidance of change but also of the difficulties in interpreting the political connotations of the new instructions coming from Havana.

The CNPC now forced new local narratives to converge with a nationwide narrative underpinned by Fernando Ortiz's (1987) concept of transculturation, which posits that the distinctiveness of Cuban identity derives from the mixing of Spanish, Afro-Cuban, and indigenous cultures. Although Ortiz had fled the country and the authorities considered him a traitor, his ideas about culture became mainstream after 1990. For instance, the new script developed in the municipal museum of San Luis attempted to combine revolutionary and transculturation ideas, with the novelty of including references to different sociocultural groups: "The convergence of indigenous and Spanish cultures in the natural territory of Cauto Cristo underpinned our socioeconomic development based on agriculture and livestock, which are symbols of our identity and the backdrop of our rich cultural traditions and revolutionary struggles" (CNPC 2008). Similarly, in the municipal museum of Pilón, the new script proposal developed by museum workers set out nine central objectives for the exhibition. While most of the nine objectives emphasized cultural history and local identity, none of them referred to struggles, heroes, or class identity (CNPC 2012c). Furthermore, cultural localism permeated museum work, and museum investigations started to focus on how to relate with local communities and how to implement the pedagogic interpretation of local heritage. Museum investigations emphasized the need to use local culture and identity, rather than the abstract master-narrative, as the main interpretive framework. These changes all reflect a new way of articulating the relationship between the national and the local via heritage. The local was no longer officially interpreted as a particular realization of a master-narrative and its historic phases but, as the recategorization record of the municipal museum of Pilón stated, as "a crucial actor in shaping national culture" (CNPC 2012c). Along these lines, Manzanillo, the hometown of Sánchez, was no longer conceived as the result of a dialectical succession of sociopolitical struggles resulting in a "rebellious" town—as the original script had it—but rather as "the symbiotic outcome of cultural traditions, multiple ideas and aesthetics, local facts, events and characters and specific identity building processes" (CNPC 2012b).

The new rhetorical discourse of museums emphasizes a reified form of local identity related to imaginaries of cultural localism. Although these changes might seem compelling, a closer look reveals their continuity with old ways of thinking about history and conceiving the nation. The new museum scripts simply replace the previous Marxist-Leninist jargon with idioms of culture and local identity. However, they still understand history and identity in a deterministic fashion that is partially derived from the mixture of culture-history and the vulgarized version of Marxism-Leninism that became dominant in the previous period.

Museum discourses reflected the deterministic approach to history and culture. In them, the portrayal of a Cuban nation born from transculturation replaced the representation of a Cuba forged through revolutionary struggle. In other words, the language of cultural anthropology gradually replaced Marxism-Leninism as the official discourse. Furthermore, if under the sovietizing master-narrative personal identity had faded into class identity, personal identity was now blurred under broad ethnic categories (indigenous, Afro-Cuban, or Spanish). Thus, Cuban museums have not become epistemologically reflexive or postmodern in the sense of providing multiple interpretations or questioning the notion of representation inherited from soviet museum theory and practice.

This situation is reflected in policies about folklore. From the beginning of the Revolution, the eagerness of the predominantly white leadership to raise awareness of color differences often entailed the folklorization of blackness, and folklore increasingly became synonymous with Afro-Cuban culture during the 1970s and 1980s. This process involved promoting the appreciation of Afro-Cuban music, dance, or dress and the study of Afro-Cubans by anthropologists and historians in institutions such as the Instituto de Etnología y Folklore. Soviet Union–trained anthropologists such as Jesús Guanche or Rafael López Valdés had striven for decades to continue Ortiz's work and decide which elements of Afro-Cuban culture were fit for national identity. However, as Peters shows, "during periods of diminished Soviet influence, the Revolution's insistence on a purely class-based analysis of race would cede to a more balanced view that took into account the myriad ways that color prejudice operated within society" (Peters 2010:86). One of these periods in which African culture gained significance as a repository of Cuban identity was the 1980s. But the interesting shift after 1990 was that the former process of folklorization converged with the ideology of cultural localism, resulting in a higher visibility of Afro-Cuban culture within the wider culture. This was part of a broader effort to support the regime appealing to the Afro-Cuban population, which had been largely neglected during the sovietizing period.

As a result, identity and culture started to be portrayed as analogous to "tradition: and to something that various others possess. Heritage started to be used to exhibit these distinct cultural and identity features as proof of open-mindedness. The notion of culture as constructed by the regime thus equated culture with alterity and specifically with the oppressed. This is revealing of how the Cuban regime does not question its own hegemonic culture, even as it projects the oppressed as having a distinct and progressive voice. It is not surprising, then, that the rhetoric of cultural localism has often manifested as the addition of new rooms devoted to local cultural figures or to ethnography. However, most new rooms devoted to cultural identity have ultimately become exhibitions of a folkloric version of Afro-Cuban culture. These rooms usually display objects from Santeria, a syncretic religious practice developed in the Caribbean among people brought to Cuba from West Africa by slave traders.

The regime also filtered international and scholarly efforts to highlight the Afro-Cuban legacy through revolutionary ideology. This involved, for instance, the celebration of the past of slave resistance and its incorporation into the romantic narrative of revolutionary struggle. Routon (2008:635) has aptly described this sea change in Cuban cultural policies after 1990 as "the socialist fetishization of Afro-Cuban 'fetishism.'" The regime's efforts to enshrine Afro-Cuban heritage became apparent in the promotion of the UNESCO project "The Slave Route: Resistance, Freedom and Patrimony" from 1994 onward. The project aimed to raise awareness of the history of slavery and involved the heritagization of various historic sites and the creation of a museum. But the project also crafted a narrative of slave resistance and connected it to revolutionary struggle, designed for both national and foreign audiences (Flikke 2008). One of the practical achievements of the project was the declaration as national heritage of *nganga*, a central feature of *palo* Afro-Cuban religion. Another important event was the inauguration of the monument Triunvirato in 1991, a further celebration of slave resistance. As previously mentioned, the monument was slated for inauguration in 1983, but it was considered a priority only after 1990. Along similar lines, in 1997, a solemn ceremony was performed in the presence of foreign dignitaries and scholars for the inauguration of the Monumento al Cimarron (Monument to the Runaway Slave) in El Cobre. In it, Alberto Lescay's sculpture depicts a runaway slave standing over an *nganga* made of an iron cauldron brought from a local sugar plantation. In his ethnographic account of the inauguration, Routon describes its ideological work as "appealing to a familiar, romantic trope of revolutionary discourse," which was, for him, "the ideological identification between forms of slave resistance like marronage and the political culture of the 1959 revolution" (Routon 2008:635).

The regime therefore enacted a sea change in its self-representation, embracing its identity as a maroon nation under siege by globalization and neoliberalism and abandoning the long-standing revolutionary neglect of Afro-Cuban religions and folklore. The heritage processes described above reveal how post-1990 Cuban multiculturalism draws on the partial acknowledgement of cultures and ethnicities to advance the state's political agenda. The new rhetorical strategy used Ortiz's idea of transculturation to create a more inclusive image of the local and the nation, but social dynamics and social change were neglected. The shift in the role accorded to indigenous peoples within the national narrative, for instance, revealed this determinism, namely, the fact that, despite transculturation talk, actual transculturation is neglected and processes of social change and social dynamics are concealed. If the class-based master-narrative had represented the indigenous as a subaltern but rebellious group exterminated by the Spanish, then, after 1990, and again without historical evidence, the new narrative represented the indigenous as a homogeneous ethnic group that blended with the Spanish colonizers in a process of transculturation. This narrative sees the Spanish conquerors as becoming Cuban creoles through their encounter with the indigenous and with the American natural environment.

These narrative shifts can be grasped in recent rearrangements in museum exhibitions, where the rooms with indigenous remains are located alongside the vernacular tools and objects representative of the supposedly authentic culture of the Cuban creole rural peasant, the reworking of Holguín's provincial museum being the most illustrative case. as a further sign of historical determinism, however, the Marxist-Leninist division of history into stages has not been altered. Museums moved from demonstrating revolutionary commitment to demonstrating local identity. In turn, these signifiers—revolutionary commitment, local identity, and cultural history—stand for the same master signifier: the hegemonic narrative developed and monitored by the state.

The reach of the transformative power of the state in terms of heritage production was, however, undermined by economic crisis. State propaganda highlighting the expansion of culture and the quantitative data on most cultural institutions—culture houses, cinemas, theaters, art galleries, museums—cannot conceal the fact that the economic crisis of the 1990s dealt culture and heritage a severe blow. There was a contradiction between the views of different interviewees in the heritage field and the official data. For instance, while a 2002 assessment by MINCULT showed no decrease in the number of museums, both high and low-ranking heritage workers reported that dozens of museums had closed down completely or partially, that their staff numbers were decimated, and that collections had been lost or damaged. The few new museums that were created were closely related to specific political campaigns such as the Batalla de Ideas and Libertad para los Cinco or to the action of the OHCH.

Occasionally, some museums continued functioning as centers for community gatherings, and the museum staff went beyond the museum walls to teach children in schools and do other museum-related work. Throughout the fieldwork it became apparent, through observation and also through the interviews conducted, that the scope and reach of museums has diminished dramatically: they have become gathering sites for those aligning with the "official view"—veterans' associations, leaders of mass organizations, local official intellectuals and artists, and so on—and are disconnected from the local community. The new directorship of the CNPC, under the aegis of the OHCH, has recently set up new provisions to close down some museums and conduct performance and sustainability tests to gage profitability and community involvement. These measures have been highly contested. They have challenged the original humanist revolutionary drive to spread a free and universal culture through the museum network and irritated those who still see museums as key propaganda instruments.

The Detachment between Nation and Marxism-Leninism

The symbolic separation of the nation from Marxism-Leninism manifested most clearly in the creation of the Memorial José Martí, conceived and designed for a national and international audience. The memorial followed the MR in abandoning Marxist-Leninist symbols and rhetoric, but it did so in a subtler way. While the MR relinquished references to Marxism-Leninism and left the rest of its exhibition mostly untouched, the memorial developed a new discourse, aesthetic, and exhibition that encapsulated the ideological transformations of the period.

The reemergence of nationalism was intrinsically connected to a renewed emphasis in the figure of Martí. The Cuban intellectual had always been a key ideological reference for the Revolution, but during the institutionalization period there was a tendency to label Martí as simply one of the several heroes of the War of Independence. This tendency was countered by the creation of a Martí Studies Center in 1977, but the relevance of Martí then pales in comparison to that of the post-1990 period, when there was a return to "monotheism" of Martí. As in the early revolutionary years, the regime used the connection between the War of Independence, Martí, and the Revolution to establish its legitimacy.

The reappraisal of Martí was another of the regime's efforts to simulate a founding substance behind the new ideology that could withstand the pressures of globalization. This showed the great flexibility of revolutionary ideology to adapt to new contexts, as well as its capacity to detach the nation from Marxist-Leninist ideology and reject its immediate past. The interviews I carried out reflect this; many interviewees who had once advocated prosoviet positions in heritage and museums now considered Marxism-Leninism to be no more than a transient and superficial ideology. The process that Navarro (2002) has called "ideological transvestism" and "recycling" was embodied by the architect and designer of the memorial to Martí, José Linares Ferrera. He studied in Socialist Czechoslovakia, designed hundreds of soviet-style museums throughout Cuba, and wrote museology papers based on soviet ideas. However, as he argued in one of our interviews, he embraced the new museology and Martí's ideals after the 1990s, designing the memorial in a minimalist fashion in contrast to soviet models (J. Linares Ferrera, interview, March 20, 2013, and April 3, 2013).

The memorial was supposed to be inaugurated in 1995 to commemorate the centenary of Martí´s death, but it was not finalized until 1996. It is situated at the base of the monument to Martí in Havana's Revolution Square, which had remained empty since the MR there was dismantled in 1967. It comprises a performance hall, a room for temporary displays, and a permanent exhibition presenting an in-depth account of Martí's life. The use of heritage serves to establish the symbolic connection between Martí and Fidel by emphasizing their shared concerns: the education of young Cubans, internationalism, and anti-imperialism. Indeed, the narrative and aesthetics of the memorial intermingles the characters and ideas of Fidel and Martí, creating ambiguity. The exhibition provides a historic account of the transformation of the old republican Plaza Cívica into Revolution Square, which symbolically sanctions the connection between Martí and Fidel. The room denounces the corruption of the Republic in belligerent language and presents Fidel as the redeemer of Cuba, highlighting the events of popular support for Fidel that had been performed in the square (Figs. 5.1 and 5.2).

The narrative of the memorial, however, differs in important ways from the narrative of the early revolutionary period, fundamentally in its emphasis on memory and heritage. In the 1960s, the images of nation and Revolution coalesced in an ongoing social process. The massive public performances and rituals in Revolution Square established the symbolic relation between Martí and Fidel. In them, the links between Martí, Fidel, and the masses were direct and unmediated. Since the 1990s, there has been a gradual decrease in the frequency, size, and intensity of public rituals and mass demonstrations in the square; since Raúl came to power in 2008, these have almost disappeared. Instead, the symbolic link between Martí and Fidel has been mediated through the manufacture of heritage via the memorial, that is, through a metacultural discourse based on heritage. The masses, no longer able to experience a direct encounter with their leaders, now have to do it indirectly through the museum exhibition. The display of the history of the monument to Martí within the narrative of the memorial itself, as well as the transformation of Fidel's rituals into museum displays, is aimed at providing legitimacy and factual historic (rather than symbolic) grounds for the Martí-Fidel connection.

The gradual abandonment of mass mobilization as a political strategy after 1990 was apparent at the inaugural ceremony of the memorial. It was no longer a public performance of the leadership in front of the masses but a restricted private event for the elite inner circle. The masses were allowed to celebrate and occupy the streets only the following day (Gonçalves 2001). The transformation of the symbolic landscape of Revolution Square, which surrounds the memorial, reinforced this sense of sacralization and reification via heritage. The monument-image of Guevara that used to change annually was made into a fixed monumental image in 1992, followed soon after by a similar monument to Cienfuegos. This carefully arranged commemorative landscape aimed to reinforce the legitimacy of the regime by conveying a sense of stability.

Figures 5.1 and 5.2. The Memorial José Martí emphasizes the symbolic links between Martí and Fidel through the revolutionary myth of "youthism," representing the care both Castro and Martí took "for the new generations" of Cubans. Source: Author.

These transformations suggest that the Revolution is no longer using the past and cultural heritage as resources to produce and project an image of the future revolutionary prospects; rather, it is using cultural heritage as a way of naturalizing its own roots and deriving a sense of legitimacy. However reified and instrumentalized, the past is engaged as meaningful in itself, instead of being seen as mere raw material for propagating new revolutionary ideas, as it was during the future-oriented institutionalizing era. In its attempt to establish a historical connection between past and present using heritage to create representations of nation and identity, the Revolution is in fact turning itself into heritage: the social dynamism and mobilizations taking place in the square during the 1960s are now represented via heritage rather than reenacted. If anthropologist Barbara Kirshenblatt-Gimblett (1998) is right and what is dead is often removed from social life and transferred to the museum as metacultural discourse, the Revolution might be sanctioning its own coming of age and farewell to the years of passion.

Monuments and the Transformation of Ideology into Heritage

Understanding the changes in monument production and their meaning is highly significant for understanding the roots of the symbolic hostility between Cuba and the United States in recent decades, and the potential impact of this hostility on the process of reconciliation between the countries. The aligning of public heritage symbols and narratives with the new ideological climate made use of belligerent language and emphasized a form of banal anti-imperialism geared toward countering the threat represented by the United States. This process involved the reworking of traditionally symbolic spaces of Havana, such as Avenida de los Presidentes and Plaza del Maine. The extent of this reworking was limited by economic shortages and by the state's lack of clarity about the content and forms of the ideology to be represented. Because of this lack, the regime resorted to a new use of heritage that expanded a process begun with the Memorial José Martí: the transformation of ideology into heritage. This does not mean that heritage and ideology become autonomous fields, because heritage is always conditioned by ideology. Rather, the notion of the transformation of ideology into heritage tries to capture a paradoxical process that reduces the number of mediations between new developments in official ideology and their transformation into tangible symbols in the form of monuments and other urban transformations.

After 1990, there was a dearth of monuments, owing to the political and economic crisis. If the crisis had opened the door for artistic experimentation and creativity, then the collapse of heritage institutions ended such debates and led to the direct control of monument production by political commissioners. According to various CODEMA interviewees, most members of CODEMA disbanded after the 1990 crisis, and the state, wanting to keep public representations of ideology under strict control, downplayed CODEMA's role. Monument building was put under direct command of the leadership, which partly explains the reduction of mediations between ideology and heritage representation that characterized the period. Indeed, the lack of mediation and control provided by institutions like CODEMA transformed monuments and some museums into straightforward representations of power.

The ideological shift entailed a change in heritage policies and the people involved in them. The large monumental programs were suspended, and commissions for the construction of new monuments were given to trusted sculptors trained in the USSR. Sculptors such as Andrés González replaced Thelvia Marín and José Delarra, at which point Delarra paradoxically shifted toward abstract art, after his bold commitment to socialist realism for decades (Menéndez-Conde 2009:222). The case of González is surprising, as he received official monument commissions only after 1990, despite finishing his art studies in the 1970s. He has designed the monuments to Sánchez in Coppelia, Bernabé Ordaz in Mazorra, and Martí in the Tribuna Antiimperialista José Martí. He also added the monuments of Eloy Alfaro and Omar Torrijos to the new statues of Simón Bolívar, Benito Juárez, and Salvador Allende in the Avenida de los Presidentes, one of the key spaces of republican symbolic display that the government coopted after 1990. These monuments reflect the new symbolic needs of the Revolution in relation to the new geopolitical context, wherein Cuba has aligned itself with Latin American leftist governments from Venezuela, Bolivia, and Ecuador.

The few monuments built between 1990 and 2014 were the result of official state requests and followed realist standards, such as the memorial to the peasant guerrilla leaders Los Malagones. At the same time, two large monumental complexes approved by CODEMA and designed by leading architects and sculptors were cancelled. These were the Conjunto Monumentario en Homenaje a los Ejércitos Libertador y Rebelde (Monumental Complex to the Liberation and Rebel Armies) in Santiago, and the Monumento a las Víctimas de la Reconcentración (Monument to the Victims of the Reconcentration), to be built in Santiago and Havana, respectively. The documents of the projects that won the competitions revealed not only their commitment to Socialist and revolutionary content but also their abstract aesthetics (CODEMA 1998, 2001). For Lara Franquis, sculptor of one of the winning teams, the reasons for discarding of monument were "not exclusively economic but also and mainly aesthetic. We thought that we had made enough concessions to the political power, because we knew that if the monument was completely abstract we could not win. But seemingly it was not realist enough [to be approved]" (interview, April 29, 2013). The cancellation of these projects was revealing in many ways. First, it signaled the end of the previous procedure for producing monuments. This usually required mediation between the demands of different actors, such as the commissioners and the actual representation, including CODEMA, artists, urban planners, and historians. After 1990, this system gave way to the unmediated relationship between ideology and heritage. Second, and contrary to the transformations in the rhetoric of museum practice, monuments remained attached to realist aesthetics. Third, the cancellation showed that the contentious relationships between the leadership and artists continued, but now under more severe economic limitations and fewer concessions to artists. When I asked sculptor José Villa Soberón, who led one of the teams, about the cancellation of the monuments, he argued that current Cuban monument construction goes against the idea of public art and replaces it with a mere multiplication of statues of leaders and heroes. For him, these monuments are meaningless because "people identify them as political and consequently they disappear from their memory immediately" (interview, May 15, 2013).

The cancellation of these projects also had to do with the fact that they were designed as complements to the revolution squares of Havana and Santiago. The monumental typology of the squares was gradually being ignored by the regime owing to the decrease in public rituals, parades, and rallies. Most provincial capital cities have remained without revolution squares, and the ones that existed lost their physical and symbolic maintenance, that is, what Nora (1996:6) describes as the "commemorative vigilance" necessary to render monuments symbolically active. The only new square built after 1990 was the Vicente García square in Las Tunas, which, according to the original program of the competition, "had been a local dream since 1982" (CODEMA 1990b). Calling it a competition was mere rhetoric, as the authorities commissioned the project directly from a group of architects and sculptors who replicated previous square models. They created a fifty-two-meter-long frieze representing a culture-history narrative of the independence and revolutionary wars in semireliefs. The monumental area of the square was dominated by a huge realist statue of the local hero of the War of Independence Vicente García, who, according to the original project, "symbolizes the rebelliousness of the people of Las Tunas" (CODEMA 1990b). In line with the new ideological context, the Marxist-Leninist master-narrative was abandoned and replaced by the nationalist-revolutionary narrative of the 100 years of struggle that had characterized the early revolutionary period. Consequently, the frieze did not include representations of the class-based struggles of the indigenous people and the slaves and instead focused on the independence and revolutionary wars.

The construction of Vicente García square could not conceal the fact that the revolution squares were being neglected as the preferred monumental typologies for the representation of power. For architect Choy López, they became symbols of decadence and testimonies of the revolutionary failure to create new city centers consistent with Socialist utopias of progress and modernization. As he argued,

> The Squares are damned [. . .] because they are dead spaces disconnected from life [. . .] Given that one day we will need to reconstruct our cities, there is no place for the Squares because of their tight links to the symbols of power [. . .] I think we will need to recycle and transform them into public spaces of cultural and social use, recovered by society. (Interview, May 17, 2013)

These transformations reflect ongoing changes in the perceptions of the Cuban nation and identity. In terms of narrative content, there has been a clear return to the plot of revolutionary nationalism based on rebelliousness. Conversely and paradoxically, the aesthetic paradigm has remained strictly socialist realist, the official representational idiom of power and the symbol of order and tradition.

The Politics of Antagonism: The Batalla de Ideas as Heritage

The Batalla de Ideas channeled the revitalization of anti-imperialism and animosity toward the United States. This was a nationwide cultural program for the ideological and moral reinvigoration of the Revolution promoted by Fidel that started after the controversy between Cuba and the United States surrounding the case of Elián González. When Elián was six, his mother took him illegally to Miami by boat, dying in the attempt. Elián survived and stayed in the United States, but his father's subsequent claim to bring back to Cuba triggered an escalation of diplomatic tensions. In the claim to repatriate Elián, the regime saw a symbol that could rally Cubans under a common cause and launched a campaign in 2000 to strengthen the ideological commitment of Cuba's youth to fight against neoliberalism and individualism. In terms of heritage, the Batalla de Ideas drew on a combination of the resignification of place and the creation of new museums and monuments based on melodrama, that is, on a narrative plot that contrasts a powerful villain with a morally pure but weak victim. Although melodrama had provided a metaphor for the core meaning of Fidel's speeches and public rituals since 1960, the Batalla de Ideas gave it new emphasis.

Elián's campaign provides a paramount case for analyzing the transformation of ideology into heritage and illustrates the underlying ethos of the Batalla de Ideas. Soon after the Elián campaign began, the government decided to build the Tribuna Anti-imperialista in front of the U.S. Interests Section and next to the monument to the victims of the *Maine* in Havana. This had historically been the central area for the symbolic negotiation of U.S.-Cuban relationships. The monument consisted of a long platform presided over by a huge realist statue of Martí designed by the aforementioned sculptor González. He represented Martí holding Elián and pointing toward the U.S. Interests Section with an accusatory finger.

The concrete pillars of the monument were covered with plaques commemorating Cubans killed by U.S. forces. In addition to this, the site was adapted to changing degrees of antagonism toward the United States. Thus, when the U.S. Interests Section started displaying political messages on its façade in 2006, the Cuban government countered with the erection of hundreds of black flags intended to symbolize the 3,400 Cuban victims of the U.S. forces since 1959 and to hide the messages from public

Figure 5.3. Statue of Martí holding Elián and pointing to the U.S. Interests Section. Source: Author.

view. The Tribuna was openly intended as a political intervention to gain international legitimacy. For the developers of the Tribuna, "the architectural design had to seize the privileged location of the U.S. Interests Section, while at the same time providing easy access to the media and good aerial shots to report everything that happened there [. . .] It should also become a cultural platform" ("Tribuna Anti-imperialista" 2000:26). The monument accomplished the twofold task of resignifying the space surrounding the U.S. Interests Section and of providing an adequate setting for media coverage of performances in the commemorative landscape created by the Tribuna. In fact, the monument and the mass demonstrations in support of Elián's repatriation received the expected international media coverage. Cubans soon popularly referred to the Tribuna as the *protestódromo* (protestdome), because it turned into the preferred setting for mass mobilizations, replacing Revolution Square, which was thereafter reserved for specific commemorations, such as May Day, 1 January, or 26 July, only.

Few know, however, that the Tribuna was a remaking of a 1991 project called the Complejo Monumentario por la Dignidad del Pueblo Cubano (Monumental Complex for the Dignity of the Cuban People), planned well before Elián was born. The original project in the archive of CODEMA set out the theoretical grounds for the project in accordance with the post-1990 situation, justifying its location in the square of the *Maine* monument:

The building of the embassy of the United States, built nearby the monument to the victims of Maine, had become the symbol of U.S. hegemony in Havana. The Cuban Revolution put an end to this situation. The people tore down the eagle from the monument [...] and the area has served on countless occasions for Cubans to manifest their opposition to the aggressive and arrogant U.S. policies. (CODEMA 1991)

The stated objectives of the 1991 project were clear: to underscore the dignity of the Cuban people, to highlight Cubanness, and to mark the presence of the Revolution on the square of the *Maine* symbolically. Furthermore, the complex was seen as a way of reinterpreting contentious past events in U.S. relations, such as the 1898 blowing up of the USS *Maine* that triggered U.S. intervention in Cuba's war with Spain. This was the intent of the original project, which stated that the monument should become a symbol "to help us explain from our perspective the blowing up of the Maine" (CODEMA 1991). The existence of the 1991 project, never publicly mentioned by the authorities, is significant, because it shows that the official ideology for years to come, and the uses of heritage associated with it, had been carefully designed since the very beginning of the Periodo Especial, in 1990. Elián's campaign simply provided the pretext for the implementation of the project. Now it would serve not only to mark space via heritage but also to trigger new sociopolitical mobilizations in an effort to reinvigorate revolutionary passion.

Overall, this process reflected the flexibility of the Revolution and its capacity to adapt the substance of history in the making to the unchanging form of the revolutionary melodrama of a blameless victim beset by a powerful evil force. Moreover, it illustrated the regime's attempt to disguise ideology in cultural idioms for the purpose of fostering a fictitious sense of political openness and participatory democracy. Accordingly, the press did not refer to the mass assemblies that Cubans were largely compelled to attend as "demonstrations" but rather as "open forums" and "political-cultural acts" (De la Hoz 2000:6). The official version provided by the media insisted that the agency of the campaign rested on civic actors: "[It was] the role of the cultural field and Cuban artists who, together with the people, created a mass movement that entailed a shift in U.S. public opinion towards Cuba" (Rivas Rodríguez 2000:9).

The official promotion of the monumental Tribuna as a cultural endeavor could not conceal the highly ideological connotations of the process. The Tribuna openly collapsed past and present to serve the ideological purposes of the regime. The project brought Martí back to life and portrayed him not as an intellectual, an apostle, or the father of the nation but as an aggressive anti-imperialist warrior protecting Elián, who symbolized the oppressed Cuban nation. The creation of the museum of the Batalla de Ideas reinforced this aggressive representation of Martí. Because of the commitment to cultural localism, the museum was established in Elián's birthplace, the city of Cárdenas. An analysis of the procedure for creating the museum revealed the functions of heritage during that time in Cuba. First, the project documents were sent for review to the CNPC, who then provided technical assessment and some advice in terms of museum display before granting its approval. Meanwhile, CNPC director Arjona Pérez sent a letter to Lara Franquis at CODEMA commissioning seven realist busts of Cuban heroes for the future museum, without opening a public competition, as had been common in the previous period. Indeed, although the legal framework had not changed, in practice CODEMA became simply a workshop for producing sculptures on demand, with no say in terms of the conception, content, or form of the monument or museum projects. This illustrates the fragility of Cuban governmentality at the time and confirms my argument that the number of mediations between power and heritage has decreased.

As with the Tribuna, the new museum resulted from the reworking of a previous project stored in the CNPC archives called the museum of the *Lucha Ideológica del Pueblo Cubano* (Ideological Struggle of the Cuban People), which was renamed the museum of the *Lucha Antiimperialista* (Anti-imperialist Struggle) (CNPC 2001). The original project, as quoted in the new museum script, conceived the museum as a "school to cultivate the love for the fatherland, the Revolution, Fidel, the party, and the ideals of Socialism in the spirit of the younger generations" (CNPC 2001). The museum was inaugurated in 2001 and comprised three exhibition areas. The first is devoted to the sculptures of seven Cuban independence and revolutionary heroes that CODEMA artists had produced, the second provides an exhaustive account of all U.S. aggressions toward Cuba, and the third presents a detailed history of the Elián campaign. In doing so, the museum transformed on-going social dynamics into heritage, a rhetorical strategy aimed at the fixation of official historical discourse.

The process of transforming ideology into heritage is apparent in the central room of the museum, devoted to the display of a replica of the statue of Martí and Elián that had been recently erected on the Tribuna in Havana. According to the museum script, the statue "shall have the maximum hierarchy, and must, consequently, become the point of greatest attraction for the museum" (CNPC 2001). However, the replica was displayed without any explicative panel or reference to its original location in the Tribuna. In addition, large banners portrayed mass mobilizations in Havana's Revolution Square, images of the monument to Martí with anti-imperialist quotations, and a scale model of the Tribuna, as in the Memorial José Martí. Thus, the museum discourse is a clear example of how the regime used heritage to appropriate the individual identity and biography of Elián and reframed them as symbols of national identity.

The transformation of ideology into heritage is a process that establishes a series of metacultural relations between heterogeneous heritage features. For Kirshenblatt-Gimblett (2004), metacultural production implies the selection and conversion of selected aspects of culture and social life into heritage. This picture was complicated in Cuba by the fact that

Figures 5.4 and 5.5. *Left*: replica of the statue of Martí holding Elián in the Tribuna Antiimperialista in the museum of the Batalla de Ideas. *Below*: model of the Tribuna Antiimperialista in the museum of the Batalla de Ideas. Source: Author.

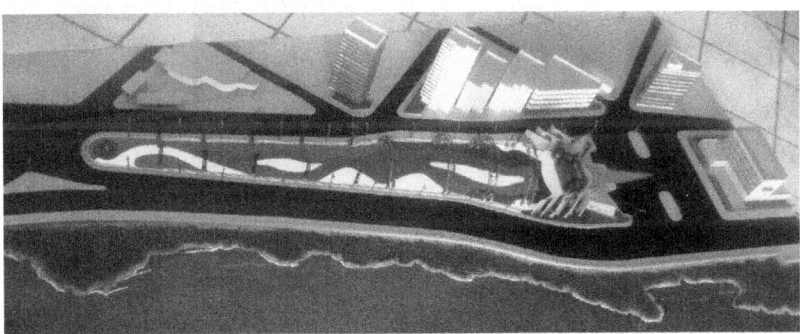

the heritagized elements were part of an on-going heritage process that was taking place outside the museum walls almost contemporaneously. Indeed, the replica of the statue of Martí and the model of the Tribuna on display at the museum of the Batalla de Ideas were neither neglected nor outdated features of contemporary cultural and social life. This had been the case, for instance, with the statues of Spanish monarchs when they were brought into museums after Cuban independence. In other words, there was overt intentionality in establishing a symbolic set of references between the heritage features on the Tribuna and the replicas in the museum of the Batalla de Ideas, probably with the aim of making this heritage process referential, spreading out and replicating its significance. However, if the symbolic power of monuments derives from their uniqueness, hosting replicas of them in museums could undermine their significance rather than increase it.

This situation can be read as a transformation of museums and their traditional role, which throughout their history in Cuba and elsewhere was to be repositories of "dead" objects, those elements that have lost their connection with life in the community (Kirshenblatt-Gimblett 1998). Contrarily, the museum of the Batalla de Ideas has served as a repository of objects that were still "alive" outside the museum walls. According to Boris Groys' (1994) deconstruction of Socialist aesthetics, the highly ideological nature of public symbolism in Socialist countries would make the idea of relocating statues of revolutionary leaders after the end of Socialism in museums similar to returning Warhol's *Campbell's Soup Cans* to the supermarket. However, this is precisely what Cuba has done—even if the regime was not officially transitioning toward capitalism and democracy.

The transformation of ideology into heritage partially resembles the recent shift in Chinese heritage policies of not acknowledging the historicity of the revolution and the party and the deliberate commoditization of the memories of the war and the revolution through the promotion of Red Tourism (Long 2012). However, this has happened in Cuba to a much lesser extent. For instance, for years, the directorship of the MR has attempted to include the museum in official tourist tours, facing the reluctance of state tourism institutions to do so (interview, J.A. Pérez Quintana, March 27 and May 2, 2013). This evinces the regime's will to maintain two different heritage images, one shaped for tourists and another for Cubans. It also points to a different relationship with the revolutionary past, one that emphasizes respect and continuity instead of a break and push toward commoditization and historic disruption.

When the thrust of the Elián campaign diminished and the case was settled, new anti-U.S. campaigns were launched. What mattered was not the content of these campaigns but maintaining a belligerent climate. The next campaign was the Libertad para los Cinco, which concerned a group of Cubans who had been accused of terrorism and imprisoned in Miami since 1998. The regime had turned these men into anti-imperialist heroes and fought for their liberation until they were freed, in December 2014. The campaign was announced everywhere in the media and public spaces and took on heritage form in the museum of the Comités de Defensa de la Revolución 28 de Septiembre (Committees for the Defense of the Revolution 28 of September). Since its inauguration in 2007, the museum has accorded a central role to "the Five" and has become a leading promoter of the campaign for their repatriation. The exhibition includes objects and pictures that underscore Cuba's international relations with other Latin American countries such as Venezuela and Bolivia. The heightened and overt ideological charge of the museum is surprising given its location in Obispo street, the heart of the OHCH heritagization project in Old Havana and the most touristic Cuban street. For foreign and local visitors to Old Havana, the museum appears to be an island of state ideology in the midst of the more welcoming and friendly aesthetics favored by the OHCH. In yet another example of the ambiguity and complexity of the regime, the OHCH director Leal Spengler fully supported the creation of the museum.

Similar symbolic actions materializing the ideology of the Batalla de Ideas were implemented throughout the country. In Santiago, various museums, including Moncada and the Granjita Siboney, were reworked to emphasize the figure of Martí. As in Havana, there was a symbolic return to the sites of dissonance with the United States during the republican period, both tangible (San Juan Hill) and intangible (the interpretation of the War of Independence). Thus, a large plaque commemorating the centenary of the battle on the contested site of San Juan Hill, installed in 1998, put an end to the lack of an official heritage narrative at the site. The plaque provided the official historical interpretation, affirming that the war was a Spanish-Cuban-American War—rather than solely Spanish-American—that resulted in the United States' neocolonial domination over Cuba until 1959:

One century ago, on this hill, we fought to put an end to Spanish colonialism in the island of Cuba and America. The young

North-American Empire subjected Cuba to its neo-colonial domin-
ion, and thus was born the subordinated Republic [*República depen-
diente*]. In 1998, the Cuban nation is proud of its history, freed from
domination [. . .] since the revolutionary dawn of 1959.

The plaque had been one of the projects aimed at reinterpreting key sites
of memory that the PCC included in its monumental program during the
institutionalization period. This is significant because its implementation
was considered relevant only when the Revolution abandoned its future-
oriented projection toward Socialism and began to revisit its own past in
a search for identity, after 1990.

Meanwhile, in an affirmation of the new logic of transforming ideology
into heritage, the museum of the Spanish-Cuban-American War was inaugurated in 1998 (CNPC 2003). It resembles the museum of the Batalla de
Ideas in Cárdenas and the new museum of the Marcha del Pueblo Combat-
iente (Rally of the Combatant People), inaugurated in 2002 in Havana. The
exhibition presents a history of U.S. aggressions toward Cuba and ends
with praise for Fidel and the Revolution for freeing Cuba from imperialism. A large placard displays pictures of the different Cuban monuments
commemorating the war in the oriental provinces: again, "real" heritage
is included in museum display as metacultural discourse. The museum
employs a symbolic strategy aimed at transforming the Spanish-Cuban-
American War, which had become a repository of negative heritage, into a
positive Cuban event. Now, Cubans are commemorating the war in Cuban
territory. In line with the politics of antagonism, the museum provides
an interpretation of the war as an extended and unresolved conflict with
the United States that did not conclude with the revolutionary triumph
over imperialism but rather is ongoing. This suggests that the process of
transforming ideology into heritage was not a transient event but a form
of relating to the past and generating representations of identity and nation that were characteristic of the ambivalent period between 1990 and
2014.

Conclusion

Do we not encounter in Cuba [. . .] a kind of negative Messianic time: the social standstill in which "the end of time is near" and everybody is waiting for the Miracle of what will happen when Castro dies, and socialism collapses?

(Žižek 2001:7)

The philosopher Slavoj Žižek has further argued that, in Cuba, "revolutionary mobilization conceals social stasis" (Žižek 2001:7). Indeed, the transformation of ideology into heritage and the politics of antagonism as reflected in the Batalla de Ideas and other campaigns reflect the standstill of the Revolution despite the renewed attempt to mobilize the masses. In parallel with attempts at mobilization, there has been a paradoxical requirement that heritage be put at the service of the ideology of cultural localism. This shift reveals an effort to abandon the abstract and universal sense of self of the previous period and to root identity in the particularity of place; it is this sense of place that heritage is expected to both produce and represent.

The post-1990 period signals the separation of Marxism-Leninism from the nation as well as the revival of the figure of Martí, now portrayed as a revolutionary anti-imperialist warrior who is symbolically analogous to Fidel. For nearly three decades, the ideas of nation and Socialism blended until they became inseparable: both were essential to being Cuban (Martínez Heredia 2005:100). The shift toward local—not necessarily Socialist—identity since 1991 and the acknowledgement of the need to engage with history in other terms have opened space for a more inclusive national narrative. As the various campaigns of political mobilization show, however, different narratives about the past and the historic legitimacy they provide are still contested in the memory-war between the Cuban regime and the United States, and, specifically, the Cuban-American exile community (Rojas 2007:237). This leads to abuses of memory on both sides and results in a context of permanent conflict monopolized by discourses of resentment, victimization, and blame.

Cuba has mobilized the potential of heritage to generate dissonance, with the aim of reviving past conflicts and producing a state of uninterrupted symbolic war against a timeless and transhistoric enemy. My analysis of heritage policies, representations, and practices suggests that Cuba has not come to terms with its history and is still trapped in a messianic interpretation derived from the former master-narrative, which was influenced by Marxism-Leninism. According to the philosopher Giorgio Agamben (1999), messianic temporality is distinctive of sovereign powers that place themselves outside the law and historic time to establish that there is nothing outside the rule of power. This state of affairs is paralleled by the political exploitation of a Manichean and oversimplified narrative that presents Cuba as the isolated David fighting Goliath, who is sometimes represented by the United States, sometimes by the more abstract threat of "neoliberal globalization." Indeed, as the anthropologist Arjun Appadurai has shown, the postcolonial state usually posits "global commoditization (or capitalism, or some other such external enemy) as more real than the threat of its own hegemonic strategies" (Appadurai 1996:32).

Heritage has both reflected and served to articulate the simplification of political meanings and the messianic conception of time that still prevails in Cuba. Heritage is central to this purpose, because it can transform materiality into a symbol of ahistorical inalterability. As the archaeologist Reinhard Bernbeck (2013:535) has shown, the reheritagization of heritage in contentious political contexts is often associated with the emergence of a distinct aesthetic configuration. The process of transforming ideology into heritage attempts to capture this shift in the dominant aesthetic canon of post-1990 Cuba. This new configuration of heritage endows materiality with meaning by evicting historical context. The paramount example is the monument representing nineteenth-century-intellectual Martí holding a late-twentieth-century Elián—a conflation of spatiotemporal coordinates exacerbated by the exhibition of a replica of this monument in a museum almost immediately after the monument's inauguration.

The complexity of the meanings elicited by heritage becomes clear with the oxymoronic move of musealizing a new monument. This situation produces a tension between the different temporalities of heritage: the contemporary desire for evermore usable pasts and the actual production of pasts through social dynamics and history in the making (Trouillot 2012). Indeed, the distance between ongoing social dynamics and their representation via heritage has diminished exponentially in Cuba: the Batalla de Ideas officially started on December 5, 1999, the Tribuna Antiimperialista was inaugurated five months later, and the museum of the Batalla de Ideas opened a year and a half later. Interpreting the process through the lens of Kirshenblatt-Gimblett (2004:59), Cuba might be running out of pasts to consume, as the need for legitimacy in increasingly changing conditions gains pace. In these situations, ideology can become heritage even before it has had a chance to have a social life.

The transformation of ideology into heritage reflects the difficulty of addressing the challenge of reuniting the messianic time of ideology and the historic time of social dynamics. The regime's intention was to gain legitimacy with Elián's campaign and to materialize it via heritage to provide a sense of historic depth. However, the whole process conveys the sense of decadence in which the regime has reached its "end of history," bringing its latest propaganda campaign into the museum for contemplation. Certainly, the perception of time created by monuments can suggest permanence, eternity, and the end of temporality. However, grounding ideology in monumental time might not have the desired effect if the time span between the processes of monumentalization and the musealization is too short and as a result conveys the sense that heritage and the ideas it represents are vulnerable, changing, and transient. Assessing whether these processes of heritagization have an effective and enduring impact will require some time, especially given the rapid sociopolitical transformations currently taking place in Cuba.

What this analysis suggests is that Cuba is running out of not only pasts but also prospective futures to reclaim from the ever-changing symbolic and ideological repository of the Revolution. Despite the new discourse of transculturation and ethnicity, the nation is still conceived as an unchanging essence. Tribuna Antiimperialista's representation of a timeless Cuban spirit of rebelliousness symbolically fighting the United States ultimately raises the question of why it was deemed necessary to place a replica of the new monument in a museum. This might be an effect of the loss of a sense of historic time and the concomitant demise of Socialist utopia. Alternatively, it might be nostalgia for the lost sense of timelessness provided by the Marxist-Leninist philosophy of history. Understanding these dynamics of heritage politics and policies is fundamental to making sense of current developments and of the regime's future prospects at a time of overriding change. We have yet to see how the context of post-2014 Cuban-U.S. rapprochement will affect the politics of antagonism, and its associated forms of heritage production, so eagerly promoted during this period, as one of the Cuban government's persistent fears has been excessive U.S. cultural influence over Cuba.

The Office of the City Historian of Havana and the Nation as Heritage after 1990

A Path toward Reconciliation or toward Touristification?

Our project was to create a new social and communal utopia based on cultural heritage. And I say this because when a project is not rooted in culture it can be under risk. A time ago, for example, we knew that Cuba would bet on tourism as the underpinning of our economy, but we do not work for tourism

(Leal Spengler 2006:19)

The previous chapter described the effects of cultural localism and the transformation of ideology into heritage. This chapter addresses another tendency of heritage production after 1990, namely, the transformation of the traditionally neglected colonial area of Old Havana into a heritage site under the aegis of the OHCH. The OHCH follows international and local preservation agendas, combining market reforms, entrepreneurialism, privatization, and the intermixing of global capital with Socialist institutions and the state's ideological agenda. The OHCH seeks to meet two crucial objectives: first, to create a tourist destination through the heritagization of Old Havana and to become an instrument for the capture of hard currency after the opening of Cuba to tourism in 1990; and second, to use heritage to construct a new representation of national identity. For the OHCH, the abstract essence of the nation was not just any rebellious spirit, as the state official narrative had it, but Cuban culture and heritage. According to OHCH chief Eusebio Leal Spengler, the colonial heritage of

Old Havana "reveals the invisible soul of the country," which is embodied in the Cuban transculturation that is "imprinted on the character of the people who inhabit it" (quoted in Guerra 1999:5). It is therefore important to shed light on the reasons for this apparent about-face in revolutionary urban and heritage policies and their meaning in the broader Cuban context.

After the Revolution, in 1959, the regime adopted antiurban policies and neglected the colonial and republican periods, which it considered symbols of an exploitative past. This dynamic entailed an almost complete commitment to the future-oriented myth of the new in all aspects of social life—the new man, new city centers, and new heritage. The tension that existed between humanistic calls for heritage preservation and the Socialist call for the creation of new public spaces and heritage was usually resolved in favor of the latter. Contrarily, the post-1990 period has almost exclusively become identified with the various projects of city-center restoration. Similar to what happened during the republican period, the preservationist wave has gone beyond Havana to include Camagüey, Santiago de Cuba, Trinidad, Cienfuegos, Sancti Spíritus, Bayamo, Remedios, and Baracoa. Seven of these cities have been nominated for the UNESCO World Heritage list, and two have achieved this status after the 2000s.

The cities of Camagüey, Trinidad, Cienfuegos, Sancti Spíritus, Remedios, Bayamo and Matanzas are now part of the Red de Oficinas del Historiador y el Conservador de las Ciudades Patrimoniales de Cuba (Network of Offices of the Historian and the Curator of Cuban Heritage Cities). These institutions, however, do not enjoy the autonomy of Havana's OHCH. This notwithstanding, the overall good performance of all Cuban historian and preservationist offices signals the definitive return of investment and interest in the historic centers and the almost complete abandonment of the new Socialist city centers created around the revolution squares. Unlike in the Marxist-Leninist argument, progress has started to be equated with the incorporation of old heritage into new social life. In other words, heritage has become meaningful for its sociocultural historic significance, rather than for its potential use as "raw material" in the creation and propagation of a master-narrative.

This chapter analyses the role of the OHCH in the heritagization of Old Havana, a UNESCO World Heritage Site and one of the largest and best preserved Spanish colonial cities in Latin America. Heritagization is a process that involves the establishment of a regime of representation that results from the deliberate selection, omission, or suppression of certain material features and symbols. The aesthetics and narratives defining notions of Cuban identity are intrinsically connected with this process. This is interesting in terms of the potential divergences between OHCH and state heritage policies, that is, whether the OHCH heritage work might challenge, undermine, or complement that of the state. The chapter ends with a case study of the musealization of the Palace of the Segundo Cabo (PSC) in Old Havana. The restoration and musealization of the PSC encapsulates many of the conflicting discourses and practices of the OHCH, their relation with state policies, and the OHCH's ways of representing national identity. The symbolic and political relevance of the project is enormous, especially because it is intended to become the central site for the normalization of relations with the European Union (EU). It was not by chance that the first visit of a top EU diplomat to Cuba, in March 2015, lasting one day, included a visit to the PSC.

Because the OHCH raises partisan views, both inside and outside Cuba, the views presented here draw on my own ethnography in dialogue with both critics and supporters of the OHCH. The use of heritage as a hallmark of national identity for global tourism within an isolated Socialist island cannot but become a highly controversial and ambiguous process. The heritagization of Old Havana does not fit any standard model of capitalist gentrification, as some authors have attempted to argue (Scarpaci 2000). Not only is there not a significant social group of "gentrifiers" in Cuba, but the well explored relationship between conservation and landed property in liberal capitalist contexts is also completely distorted by the logic of state capitalism's central allocation of resources, by the difficulties in buying and selling properties, and by the residential program established by the OHCH in Old Havana. Likewise, according to the director of the Master Plan of Old Havana, it cannot be exclusively framed within the field of Latin American historic centers management, where the OHCH is considered "a *rara avis* [. . .] that cannot be taken as a reference because it operates within a different socio-political system" (Rodriguez Alomá 2009:iii).

The conjuncture of global heritage discourses, international capital, tourism, and urban conservation in Old Havana reflects how the cultural logic of globalization leads to very different outcomes in different places.

The OHCH has become the focus of international and national interest because it has transformed Old Havana into Cuba's privileged gateway for international tourism and because of its frantic construction activity, which contrasts with the complete paralysis of the building industry throughout the rest of the island.

The OHCH operates in the limited space of Old Havana, where only eighty thousand of Havana's population of more than two million live. However, it has a significant national impact in terms of economic performance and the definition of national identity. This is partly because its theoretical and institutional framework differs from that of state heritage institutions and partly because the OHCH has gone beyond the boundaries of Old Havana to carry out, on demand, different heritage works, including restorations and museums, in other Cuban regions. It functions as a highly autonomous parastatal institution, bypassing state legislation and, when working on demand, operating in a sort of legal vacuum within the legal framework of the state. However, the state has curtailed the autonomy of the OHCH after financial scandals affected the institution in 2014, when Leal Spengler's right-hand woman Raida Mara had to resign after three decades of leading the OHCH's Department of Cultural Heritage.

The crux of the matter in terms of the political interpretation of the OHCH is how its autonomy relates to state power. Most foreign scholars and some relevant local figures, such as Linares Ferrera, see the hand of the state behind the OHCH and criticize the conversion of Old Havana into a touristic theme park (Linares Ferrera 2002; Ponte 2011). However, most of the Cuban professionals and academics I interviewed during fieldwork were supportive of the OHCH overall. They considered it more politically open, dynamic, and efficient than the state. Most young professionals and academics decidedly preferred working for the OHCH than for the state for many reasons, including the potential for self-realization, internet access, better salaries, sociocultural benefits, more freedom, less racial, gender, and sexual discrimination, and fewer ideological commitments.

The OHCH differs from other Cuban institutions in that its revenues do not come from the allocative power of the state but from commercial activities, which include heritage works, hotels, restaurants, and land estate management and require appealing to a public. Drawing on research in Romania, Katherine Verdery (1995:95–96) has made the case that this shift can challenge the hierarchies of Socialist states, not because of the creation of a public demand but because new sites for the production of meanings and ideas emerge outside the control of the apparatus. The introduction of market logic threatens the bureaucratic establishment, because it challenges the customary distribution of resources and centralized power.

Open political opposition could not exist in Cuba until recently without facing state repression. However, institutions such as the OHCH, which were irrelevant before 1993, have been able to become powerful and challenge those who sit higher up in the bureaucratic ladder but who lack resources. The work of the OHCH can be indirectly challenging, because, as Václav Havel points out, under Socialism "every piece of good work is an indirect criticism of bad politics" (Havel 1985:36). More importantly, the OHCH produces history outside of state control and has social aims and programs within Old Havana, including a university. This provides a certain space of freedom for improving the people's quality of life, making apparent the shortcomings of the state system of social provision. Moreover, the OHCH clings to universal heritage charters and conventions beyond the boundaries of the national legislation. It works based on the principle of legality, insisting that respect for culture and the law is one of its key objectives.

Therefore, although the OHCH is far removed from the resistance movements that emerged in Socialist Eastern Europe, it sets the stage for a subtle conflict of subjectivities that is eminently political. Indeed, those working in the state heritage apparatus often engage in bitter polemics with OHCH workers. For instance, in 2011, the OHCH was attempting to take over CENCREM, a state heritage institution and UNESCO chair in Cuba. A heated polemic emerged after an anonymous author published a harsh critique of the OHCH, describing it as a "technocratic autocracy" that was implementing neoliberal reforms in Cuba (Sabio 2011). Despite its anonymity, it was widely known throughout Havana that a member of the state heritage ranks, probably from CENCREM, had written it.

Despite these tensions, most interviewees and most Cubans I informally engaged with agree that the efficient OHCH semimarket model should be replicated throughout the country, as it works better than the inefficient state apparatus. According to architect Felicia Chateloin Santiesteban, however, the state "refrains from expanding this model, because they [the leadership] fear losing control over history, power and finance" (interview, May 8, 2013). In fact, the OHCH can afford a media apparatus—radio and television programs, book and journal publishing—and thus is able to produce its own history to ground its legitimacy as an autonomous social actor. Accordingly, it has been able to create a historic lineage assumed by many Cuban and international scholars and professionals to affirm a line of continuity with the OHCH during the Republic and with the works of former city historian Emilio Roig de Leuchsenring. The aim of this narrative is to situate the OHCH as the only legitimate institution in charge of the recovery of Old Havana, a narrative that requires deconstruction.

A Brief History of the OHCH and Old Havana

The colonial Spanish Laws of the Indies created the figure of the city historian to record the main events of the Spanish conquest. After independence, however, the Cuban Republic recovered the position of city historian, in which capacity de Leuchsenring implemented numerous heritage projects during the first phase of the OHCH's existence. Although the official revolutionary narrative sustains the widespread idea that Old Havana was in a state of decay and degradation at the time, it was actually the financial and business center of republican Havana (interview, D. Taboada Espiniella, May 9, 2013).

When the Revolution triumphed, financial buildings and offices slowly disappeared, and the area gradually fell into decay (see Cabrera Infante 2013:94–95). Most buildings became *cuarterías* (poor overcrowded communal buildings) mostly occupied by nonwhite newcomers to Havana, who still inhabit them. At the time, under increasing pressure from the state to centralize power, the OHCH disappeared with the death of de Leuchsenring in 1964. Nonetheless, the contemporary OHCH uses its machinery of history production to promote the false idea of continuity in its function. It was during the 1970s that Leal Spengler first started to function in practice as city historian and the OHCH retook control over the Capitanes Generales. The palace was reopened as a city museum, and the OHCH gradually began to participate in some preservation works under the mandate of the local People's Power.

At the time, Old Havana was not seen as a heritage site or treated as a monument (Coyula Cowley 1984). Rather, revolutionary political discourse condemned it as a space that symbolized colonial and neocolonial exploitation. Some interviewees recall that certain politicians and professionals advocated its demolition for the sake of modernization. A group of architects working for the CNC, however, started isolated restorations focusing on key sites such as the Cathedral, the Plaza de Armas, and Plaza de San Francisco. They made inventories, catalogues, and architectural studies and prevented buildings from total collapse with little budget and recognition, which reflected the government's disinterest in the colonial past. However, this did not prevent the looting and decay of Old Havana. For instance, in a his autobiography, writer Reynaldo Arenas (1992:273) describes his participation in the looting of the convent of Santa Clara, which would later become the headquarters of CENCREM's UNESCO-Cuba Chair. Similar descriptions of Old Havana's decadence can be found in Cabrera Infante's *Mapa de un espía* (2013).

The studies and restorations of this group of architects laid the foundation for the first Master Plan of Old Havana, in 1976. This allowed Arjona Pérez to launch a large international campaign that resulted in the declaration of Old Havana as a World Heritage Site in 1982. Even then, culture workers envisioned the restoration process as a modernizing endeavor, considering that "Old Havana will be in 2000 as it was in 1900, but articulated within a modern and dynamically growing city" (UNESCO Cuba 1983:31).

Despite Cuba's mistrust of UNESCO at the time, the state supported the project to create the CENCREM. CENCREM was a state institution connected to UNESCO and was in charge of implementing the five-year restoration plans for Old Havana and developing a network of heritage subinstitutions, including the Escuela de Museología, and restoration workshops on metal, pottery, paper, canvas, stone, furniture, and mural painting. Thus, although the OHCH claims to have always been the leading institution in the heritagization of Old Havana, it actually played a secondary role. Back then, the biggest political tension was between the more preservationist attitude of CENCREM and the Dirección General de Planificación Física, which advocated the modernization of Old Havana inspired by Marxist-Leninist ideas of progress. Another important but more subtle conflict was between Arjona Pérez, chief of the Department of Cultural Heritage and indirectly of CENCREM, and Leal Spengler, director of the OHCH. Their tensions were not publicly relevant until the 1990s, when the OHCH gained power and autonomy, although they were palpable in the 1980s (UNESCO Cuba 1983:31).

The declaration of Old Havana as a World Heritage Site in 1982 implied the selection of an aestheticized image of the Spanish colonial city and its fortifications that privileged monumental aspects. In 1983, in the midst of a crumbling Havana, UNESCO's director general Amadou-Mahtar M'Bow argued that it was one of the most representative architectural works to emerge in the Caribbean as a result of the "cultural encounter between indigenous, African, and Spanish cultures" (quoted in Rigol and González 1983:7). Overall, the five-year campaign implemented by the state to safeguard Old Havana was a failure and did not achieve the expected results (Novel 1984; Rigol 1986). Not only was the state making more resources available to CODEMA for the implementation of its large monumental program and of the revolution squares than to city-center preservation, but also the philosophy of the project and the institutional overlapping resulted in only a few, and low-quality, architectural works (Moreno García 1988).

By the end of the 1980s, the start of the Proceso de Rectificación and the Cuban opening to international tourism raised awareness that Old Havana was both an embarrassing self-portrait and a potential source of hard currency. The state abandoned policies of urban neglect, and the authority and centrality of Havana was restored (Fornet 1998; Marín 1990). Nonetheless, many professionals considered the development of tourism to be a negative and were concerned with issues of authenticity. The minister of culture mediated the polemic, arguing that tourism "can create a distorted image of our cultural identity, if the image offered to the tourist is not authentic" (Hart Dávalos 1989:n.p.).

The turning point came when an outstanding colonial building at Plaza Vieja collapsed in front of a British reporter in 1993. The state then decided to grant full autonomy to the OHCH and put it under the direct oversight of the Council of State. The state commissioned the OHCH with the marketing and packaging of Cuban heritage for tourism. The OHCH had to capture hard currency while being committed to heritage preservation and social aid. Soon, the OHCH created a series of companies to operate real estate investments, hotels, restaurants, and tourist travel. The state allowed the OHCH to operate with dollars at a time when these were banned in the mainstream economy, to grant visas, and to negotiate exports and imports without state mediation. It adopted a plan of human sustainable development, created an office of international cooperation, and drafted a master plan in 1994.

With these extraordinary powers—unique in Socialist Cuba—the OHCH became the main investor, planning, housing, and zoning authority, parks commissioner, and tax collector in Old Havana. The OHCH leadership, led by Master Plan director Patricia Rodríguez Alomá, developed their entrepreneurial model from the Latin American tradition of city center management. Their aim was to foster a "managerial rather than bureaucratic approach [. . .] to ensure self-financing" (Rodriguez Alomá 2009:36). The OHCH replaced five-year plans with market and entrepreneurial strategies developed in partnership with foreign capital and in tune with heritage charters of universal character, adapted to the national context.

The OHCH philosophy became manifest in the resolution of a long-standing debate about the future of the modern republican garage in the Plaza Vieja. CENCREM adopted a social approach, advocating the rehabilitation of residential facilities before any heritage intervention, and the municipal government wanted to preserve the garage as a bomb shelter in case of U.S. invasion. Contrarily, the OHCH focused on the recovery of the square as a public heritage and touristic space. Accordingly, and to nationwide concern, the garage was demolished and the square immediately heritagized to adopt a colonial air manufactured for tourism. The recovery of the central square became the symbolic milestone of Old Havana as a tourist destination. Old Havana also became a symbol of local pride and national identity amid a traumatic economic crisis, promoting the recovery of local memories and history, cultural identity and diversity.

Clearly deviating from the Marxist-Leninist credo sustained by state politicians, Leal Spengler declared that "cultural heritage is a timeless [. . .] face of patriotic identity, with its physical expressions, but also [. . .] made up of traditions, customs, ways of doing, behaving and thinking, and different cultural practices" (quoted in Plan Maestro 2012:115). Despite the heated polemics, most academics and professionals in the heritage field supported the heritagization process. As Ángela Rojas, ex-president of ICOMOS Cuba, summarized, "The only way to preserve heritage is with economic resources and not only with good will. Therefore, the problem is not the contradiction between culture and economy, but the management model and its ethical position" (Rojas 2000:22). She was clearly shifting focus from the prevailing ideological criticism of touristification and loss of authenticity to the need to adopt pragmatic criteria of performance and reflect on the ethics involved in the restoration process. In a way, this change encapsulates the main transformation of the period in terms of heritage values and ethics.

Drawing on financial power and entrepreneurial strategies, the OHCH gradually took over the contested space of Old Havana. Since 1993, the OHCH has subdued or expelled other institutions, including the municipal government, Physical Planning, ICOM, ICOMOS, the Comisión Nacional de Monumentos, the various workshops of CENCREM, and lastly CENCREM itself in 2012. The OHCH also started to manage, directly or indirectly, many libraries and state museums, such as the Natural History and Colonial Art museums, and beyond the boundaries of Old Havana, the Museo Napoleónico, Vedado House, and the Capitolio. After 2010, it has started to control appointments in high-rank state positions in the fields of heritage and culture, such as the director of the CNPC, gradually imposing its philosophy upon the heritage sector at a national level. Many people wonder about the limits of the OHCH's expansion, some with trepidation, others with hope for a better future.

OHCH Heritage Production: Creating Public Space

And don't tell me that is heritage
That it cannot be knocked down because it is of Eusebio [Leal Spengler]
This request is not a sham
It is a demand of the people!
KNOCK IT DOWN!

(Lyrics of "Obsesión" by Calle G, 2011, referring to the statue
of José Miguel Gómez in the Avenida de los Presidentes)

José Miguel Gómez was a Cuban president known for having ordered the massacre of thousands of black protesters during the Republic. When the Revolution triumphed, his statue was removed from the huge monument presiding over the Avenida de los Presidentes. During the 2000s, the

OHCH restored the statue to its place in the name of heritage preservation and historic authenticity, causing a wave of discontent and contestation among the Afro-Cuban community. Meanwhile, as shown in the previous chapter, the state built a series of monuments to Latin American revolutionary leaders down the avenue under a completely different logic. Nearby, and again outside the boundaries of Old Havana, the OHCH inaugurated Vedado House in 2007. Vedado House is a museum displaying an ideal republican bourgeois house full of luxuries. The OHCH was rehabilitating not only the colonial past but also the neocolonial past and its symbols. For the first time in revolutionary Cuba, these pasts are being exhibited without any belligerent, didactic, or critical intent, a move that was unimaginable before 1990. I analyze the meanings elicited by the OHCH's new attitudes to heritage production and their place within state heritage policies by drawing on interviews with various OHCH workers at different departments and on the documentation found in different OHCH archives.

The OHCH is enmeshed in complex power struggles within the state apparatus, but it also has a polarizing effect on the public. The OHCH is affecting the construction of meanings by deciding what places and heritage sites are preserved, restored, and heritagized. It creates the main symbols of collective memories and local identities that are then consumed as tourism by foreigners. Thus, although the focus of the OHCH is the restoration of Old Havana, it also promotes certain views of the past related to specific identities and memories. The identity created by the OHCH, however, is elusive and contradictory and requires the articulation of local identities to suit tourists' demands for a homogenized traditional past.

Ángel Rama (1996) describes Spanish colonial cities and their postcolonial rearticulations as the results of a complex interaction between political, technical, and literary discourses generated by a class of intellectuals, bureaucrats, and politicians: the *letrados* (lettered people). A group of urban conservationists reminiscent of Rama's *letrados* are in charge of the heritagization of Old Havana. Urban conservationists are elite academics and professionals who share preservationist interests and a similar aesthetic paradigm. As the *letrados*, they shape the city symbolically and materially in the image of their historic interpretations, which define "colonial authenticity." But they also shape Old Havana through their figurative imagining of the city in poetry, essays, and novels, an attitude clearly reflected in Leal Spengler's works, values, and personality. They work in the key heritage-producing departments of the OHCH: the Master Plan, Architecture, Cultural Heritage, and Museums. Normally, the state or the OHCH fund these *letrados'* postgraduate degrees in foreign universities (mostly in Spain), they travel and have internet access, and therefore they possess high levels of cultural capital. Their role is fundamental in the design, monitoring, and implementation of the dozens of restoration and musealization projects that the OHCH manages contemporaneously. They shape specific aesthetic regimes and urban designs, which are associated with specific memories and intended to project an authentic heritage object.

Although some authors highlight the central role of UNESCO in the heritagization of Old Havana (e.g., Hill 2007, 2012; Pichler 2012), its agency has been actually tangential, especially when compared with for-profit joint ventures and nonprofit institutional and NGO cooperation funding managed by the OHCH. These funds are invested in the creation of a heritage landscape through various strategies that differentiate the historic center from the rest of Havana. These strategies include, first, the creation of a different atmosphere and heritage space for tourists in Old Havana and, second, the selection and highlighting of certain architectural and aesthetic styles and the exclusion of others that fail to fit the aesthetic colonial canon, along with the memories and social elements attached to them.

The first strategy, which aims to create a differential heritage atmosphere in Old Havana, produces a simplified image of space to help tourists navigate the site. This reinforces the idea and feeling of Old Havana as a living museum or artwork. The broad lines of the heritagization plan are provided by the Master Plan, which is in charge of studying and managing the 242 blocks and 4,000 buildings of the site, 900 of which are considered of heritage value (Rodríguez Alomá and Ochoa Alomá 2002). The purpose of the Master Plan is to rehabilitate the three main colonial squares—Plaza de Armas, San Francisco and Plaza Vieja—and the streets connecting them to create tourist-friendly promenades. The Master Plan is a representation of space, which is understood as the conceptualized field of academics and urban planners that generates a system of signs

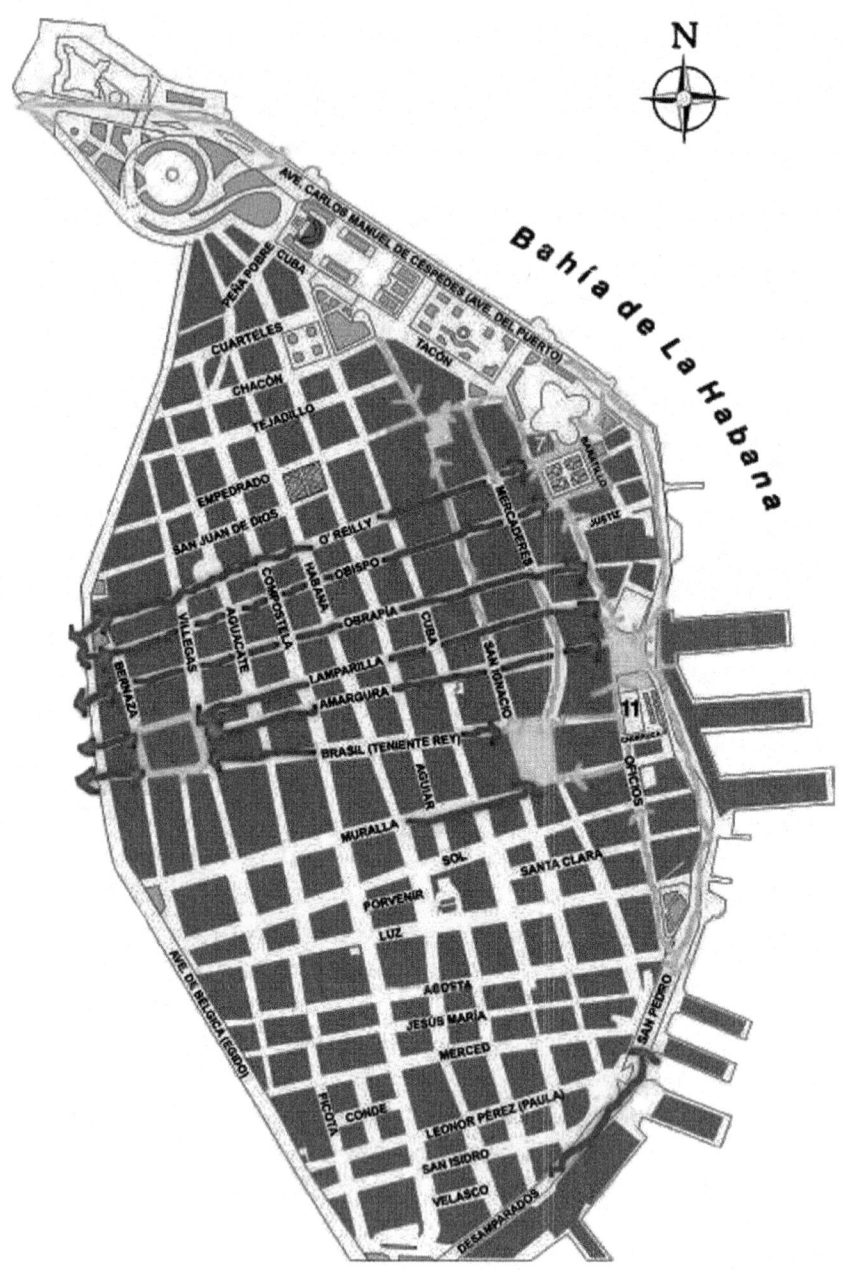

Figure 6.1. Picture highlighting the main corridors and squares that are being restored in Old Havana. Source: Portieles Fleites (2005).

(Lefebvre 1991:39). It envisions the separation of residential and touristic areas, the reduction of the area population of eighty thousand by nearly half, and the attempt to avert the collapse of buildings of heritage value.

The creation of a heritage atmosphere also involves the design of a coherent colonial heritage canon in Havana's diverse assemblage of styles (eclectic, baroque, neoclassical) and periods (colonial, republican, revolutionary). This assemblage requires a strict imposition of spatial order. The Master Plan assigns specific functions to certain spaces in order to generate a new aesthetic paradigm through the selection, hierarchization, and segmentation of the existing symbols and material culture of the area. Sites possessing most of the monumental colonial architecture are highlighted for tourist consumption, highlighting convents, cathedrals, fortresses, and government buildings. Museums, old-looking and expensive shops, and buildings with restored façades, suggestive of a coherent heritage landscape, surround interconnecting corridors. In turn, the urban regulations ensure a restricted set of allowed uses of public and private space, establishing the kind of activities that can be performed in each space of Old Havana, including hotels, guesthouses, businesses, and recreational areas (Suárez García 2006). The colonial and tropical atmosphere is emphasized by folkloristic performances by groups of dancers, musicians, and street artists employed by the OHCH. These groups create images and symbolic meanings that aim to satisfy tourist expectations of a musical and colorful Caribbean culture, which contrasts with the grey aesthetics and physical decay of other Cuban urban areas.

Similarly, the few public sculptures created by the OHCH reinforce the deterritorialized and symbolically neutral atmosphere of Old Havana. These include the sculpture of the Spanish dancer Antonio Gades, the religious figures of Saint Francis of Assisi and Teresa of Calcutta, and the Knight of Paris, which commemorates a famous street man who lived in Old Havana during the 1950s. The interpretation of these sculptures is ambiguous. On the one hand, they reflect the difficulty of carrying out meaningful and authoritative representations in the public sphere. This is so because these sculptures constitute unique examples of figurative monuments placed at street level, without pedestals, whose symbolism deviates from the official ideology. Therefore, these sculptures can be interpreted as symbols of deideologization and of the opening of the public symbolic space in Old Havana. On the other hand, their connection with Cuban and local themes and identities is virtually nonexistent.

The various sculptors I interviewed during my fieldwork noted that Leal Spengler would allow artists to make only these kinds of neutral projects, rejecting any form of abstract or contemporary art in Old Havana. Because introducing nonrevolutionary meanings in the public space can be politically contentious, the OHCH tolerates only aesthetic projects of neutral, universal, or humanistic meanings. This attitude is criticized by Antonio Ponte as "exhibitionist extravagance" (Ponte 2011:253) and is interpreted by Rojas as a reflection of "a sort of carnivalesque simultaneity that makes it difficult to establish the new sovereignty" (Rojas 2011:129). Although these critiques are partially correct, they miss the crucial point, revealed by my analysis of the long-term trajectory of Cuban heritage production, that they are radical precisely because their meanings are ambiguous and elusive, unlike the straightforward meanings conveyed by state monuments.

Another contested form of heritagizing Old Havana is the exclusion of many quarters from the UNESCO designation, which splits colonial Havana in half. Many interviewees question the definition of the city center boundaries, arguing that the Colón, Jesús María, Guadalupe, and Cerro quarters have been integral parts of the city since the late eighteenth century (Chateloin 2008). With the exception of Cerro, these residential areas presented a vernacular and scarcely monumental built environment, which rendered them uninteresting for UNESCO and unsuitable for the heritagization process.

This issue has political connotations within Havana, for many would like to see the OHCH model of rehabilitation and self-management extended to other quarters of the crumbling city, which have been facing the upsurge of inequalities after 1990 (M. Coyula Cowley, interview, May 15, 2013). This poses the question of whether the half-capitalist model of self-financing other quarters would be sustainable; indeed, various OHCH workers I interviewed consider this endeavor unfeasible. Indeed, the OHCH prefers to carry out only isolated actions outside Old Havana, arguing that the preservation of the center is its primary focus and the job the state has commissioned it to do.

The second main heritagization strategy has to do with the selective highlighting, creation, or destruction of specific architectures and

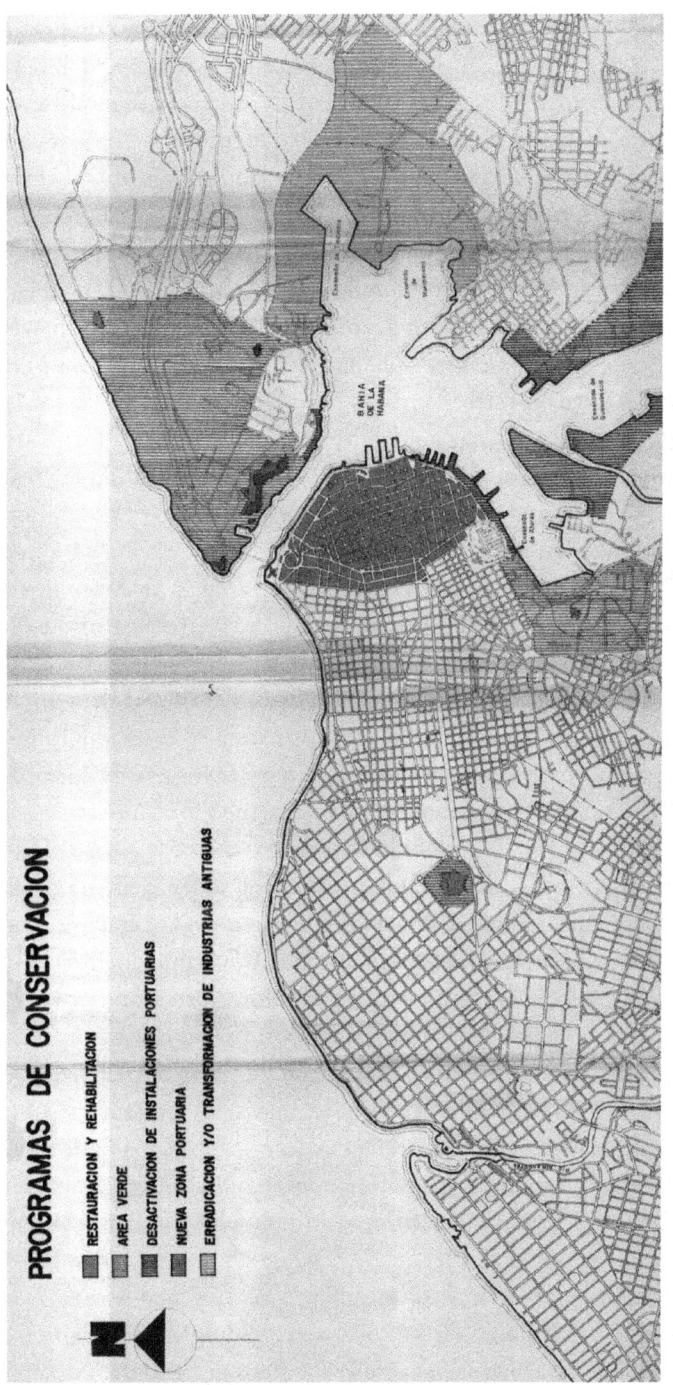

Figure 6.2. UNESCO's map highlighting in red the World Heritage Areas of Old Havana and its Fortification System in 1982. *Source:* UNESCO: http://whc.unesco.org/en/list/2o4/documents/.

aesthetic styles. Critics of the OHCH question the ethical implications of constructing a private cemetery, gardens to Lady Diana and Teresa of Calcutta, or two costly Greek and Russian Orthodox cathedrals amid a daunting nationwide residential crisis, not to mention the lack of coherence that these actions have with the overall colonial air of Old Havana (Ponte 2011). This incoherence is even more striking given there are few Orthodox Christians on the island, while the OHCH does not provide any place of worship for the millions of followers of Afro-Cuban religions. Although their social presence has been historically more relevant than that of the Orthodox believers, Afro-Cubans are deemed unsuitable as part of the OHCH heritage narrative.

In a further example of the ambiguity of the OHCH, new bizarre architectural elements that coexist with the colonial aesthetic canon re-created throughout Old Havana are freely added. The imposition of the canon involves removing republican elements that fall outside it, which indirectly helps to create an atmosphere of atemporality that in turn reinforces a sense of continuity with Old Havana's colonial past. The case of the Plaza Vieja provides an example of the underlying philosophy of the OHCH regarding urban space and heritage. The aforementioned collapse of a building on the square and the subsequent razing of the republican-era modern garage were followed by a reconstruction of the collapsed building from scratch and the creation of a square designed for tourists to enjoy, respectively.

The reconstructed building established the standards of the colonial aesthetic canon, including fan-shaped windows, carpentry and iron works, Persian blinds, tile roofs, and walls painted with bright tonalities of yellow, blue, and green. This manufacturing of colors, forms, and ornaments to create a monumental atmosphere is known in Old Havana as *fachadismo* (façadism), the aesthetic transformation of the external envelope of the building into heritage. This aesthetic regime is not random: urban conservationists, drawing on the works of architect José Capablanca, select specific features as representative of colonial architecture (see Capablanca and Daubar 1983). In my experience, most non-OHCH Cuban academics and professionals prefer OHCH's *buen gusto* (good taste) to what they interpret as the state's lack of architectural aesthetics.

After the reconstruction of the collapsed building and the demolition of the republican garage, the Plaza Vieja was flattened and then decorated with a fountain made of Italian marble, as was customary during the republican period. However, the antiquarian approach and the meanings created by the OHCH were at odds with people's own strategies for producing locality. Indeed, the fountain had to be fenced off because the impoverished population in the surrounding areas used it to do laundry, bathe, or play. Clearly, the OHCH did not want locals to use the fountain. It was to be purely decorative and was designed to become part of various elements in the square that shared similar symbolic and aesthetic features, that is, those that generated the colonial aesthetic canon.

The antiquarian mentality is also evident in the accumulation in the center of the square of sculptures that sculptor Rivero Mas considers "mere copies of European styles" that are far from "reflecting our Cuban identity" (interview, May 21, 2013). He asserts, "The colonial city never had those sculptures; they are created for the contemplation of the tourist" (interview, May 21, 2013). This raises the question of whose histories and collective memories the OHCH is forging. Critics of the OHCH consider that Old Havana and Plaza Vieja are becoming living museums or thematic parks where OHCH urban conservationists commit to meeting tourists' expectations of an authentic nineteenth-century colonial city, or at least what they imagine it to be.

However, authenticity is always elusive in historic-center heritagization projects, as different social classes have dissimilar symbolic allegiances to the built environment, which consequently leads them to have differing ideas about the places they want to create. The exclusion of contemporary architecture from the city center is another matter of dissonance and an example of the antiquarian mentality of the OHCH. For architect Choy López, OHCH restoration philosophy is "clearly conservative":

It is surprising that contemporary architecture has no room in the historic centre [. . .] There is no intellectual and theoretical background to let contemporary architecture into the historic centre. It is good to restore, but where buildings collapse, it is also legitimate to construct new buildings. (Interview, May 17, 2013)

The first attempt to introduce contemporary architecture in Old Havana actually reinforced and reflected the underlying antiquarian ethos of the OHCH. In a key passageway for tourists, the OHCH decided to rebuild the first Cuban university, which had been demolished in 1956, as a modern structure. The costly and contemporary design projected by architect Linares Ferrera for the University College of San Gerónimo, managed by the OHCH, is based on the original convent, employing contemporary materials and designs. Its defining trait is its large windows arranged to reflect the immediate built environment. The building is not only an architectural failure that is currently at risk of collapse but also a symbolic self-denial of the contemporary architectural intervention: its assigned role is to "reflect" the surrounding buildings of heritage value rather than possess any inherent meaning.

Although the OHCH develops many social initiatives for children, the elderly, and the poor, if we look beyond the façades and areas presented to tourists, there are signs of heritage apartheid in Old Havana. Forms of exclusion include police control in the main streets such as Obispo and O'Reilly, where poor, and usually black, Cubans are stopped and checked regularly. But more structural forms of exclusion also apply, such as the gradual closure of businesses operating in local Cuban pesos and the prevalence of CUC businesses whose prices are unaffordable for average Cubans. CUC stands for Cuban Convertible Peso; it is equivalent to the U.S. dollar and is not normally paid to workers, who receive their pay in *monedanacional*, or Cuban pesos. The OHCH pays part of its salary with CUCs to ease the lives of workers in Old Havana. Since 2014, only one business (a cafeteria) has operated with Cuban pesos in the OHCH area.

The OHCH also rehabilitates deteriorated but densely inhabited residential buildings of heritage value and turns them into offices, museums, or elite residential areas rented to tourists or foreign companies or given to OHCH workers, although the latter is officially denied. This process usually involves signifying the local inhabitant as a threat to heritage, which legitimizes the heritagization process and the expulsion of people from Old Havana. Indeed, the people are constantly called on to respect and educate themselves about heritage properties. However, it would be misleading to portray the OHCH as the only actor responsible for the heritagization of Old Havana. Often, local residents demand the heritagization of their areas in the hope of attracting tourists. For instance, Adrian Hearn (2004:78) discusses the case of a health education project involving the performance of Afro-Cuban music implemented by the OHCH in the San Isidro quarter. Part of the local population attempted to turn it into a

tourist attraction to earn money in hard currency, until the OHCH inter-
vened to restore the project's original focus, that is, health education.

Because the OHCH privileges the monumental and symbolic over the
residential, many residential areas away from the main tourist corridors
deteriorate rapidly. In addition, the OHCH relocates residents dislodged
from rehabilitated buildings in the distant quarters of Alamar and Habana del Este, which most Cubans dislike. The ultimate aim is to gradually empty out Old Havana, thus easing the heritagization process and
the creation of a coherent touristic space. This includes removing Old
Havana from most customary revolutionary events, such as political parades and rallies organized by mass organizations. This does not mean
that Old Havana is completely devoid of the revolutionary, ideological visual landscape. As seen in the previous chapter, a museum of the CDR and
billboard men who announce the latest political campaign are situated
in the strategic Obispo Street, along with other state actors, such as the
municipality, who express ideological messages. Nonetheless, the visual
landscape of Old Havana is largely devoid of ideological content compared
to other areas of the city. This reveals that the regime promotes two faces
and symbolic orders, one for internal consumption and another for external consumption.

The OHCH Museum Network: From Ideology to Aesthetics

Concerning questions of Culture and heritage preservation, but only in this area,
the more conservative we are, the more revolutionary.

(Leal Spengler 1986:104)

Leal Spengler's play on words summarizes OHCH museum work, which
equates the commitment to promoting national identity and the Revolution with a highly conservative and static view of culture and heritage.
By 2013, the OHCH was managing a network of twenty-nine museums,
most of them located in Old Havana. To address how these museums differ from those of the state network, I focus my analysis on their process
of creation, the cultural representations and narrations they portray, and
their social life within the community. In general, OHCH museums are
versatile devices functioning as "contact zones" that become part of the

aesthetic colonial canon of Old Havana. They also fulfill other functions in terms of community, social work, and international relations. Because OHCH museums avoid creating historical narratives, they usually feature uncontroversial displays that highlight the aesthetics of objects, making museology and museography equivalent to interior design. My analysis of the OHCH museum network and comparison of it with state museums reveals the ambiguous and contradictory articulation of heritage production and representations of national identity in Cuba.

The Department of Cultural Heritage is responsible for the creation of museums in the OHCH. Museum designers and curators, however, recognize that museum work has always been conditional on the process of restoration and architectural preservation. The usual procedure involves the selection of a building for rehabilitation, according to the ranking of buildings with heritage values provided by the Master Plan. When a building is designated for musealization, the higher-ranking personnel in the Department of Cultural Heritage sets the theme and entrusts the task to a group of experts. The Office of International Relations then seeks foreign financial support to fund the work, which is usually carried out by Puerto Carena, the OHCH construction company. Decisions about the future uses of the building are made after the rehabilitation has been completed.

The post-1990 museum projects stored in the OHCH Archive of Architecture reveal the lack of standard procedures in museum creation and the prevalence of aesthetic concerns over thematic ones. The projects provide detailed accounts of how to use materials, colors, styles, and showcases, how to create the overall atmosphere, and how to integrate the museum display with the built environment. The language and style used in the projects is that of interior design rather than museology. This partly explains the prevalence of form and aesthetics over content. There are no museum scripts, and narratives are almost nonexistent, as museums are intended to create an affective environment in line with the general colonial aesthetic canon, rather than to convey a meaningful narrative.

Therefore, OHCH museums clearly deviate from the logics of state museums, which still largely emphasize the museum script over aesthetics. The aesthetization of museums tends to blur the distinction between them and other OHCH institutions, such as *casas de la cultura*, schools, cafes, and hotels, which have similar aesthetics, collections, and exhibitions. Although overall urban preservationists are happy with this blurring of

Figure 6.3: Examples of restorations of deteriorated buildings in Old Havana according to the colonial aesthetic canon. *From left to right*, the house of the Arabs, Casa Villalonga, Café la Marina, and Santo Ángel building. The collapse of the Santo Ángel building triggered the start of the heritagization process of Old Havana. Source: Compiled by the author at the Archive and Library of Architecture of the OHCH.

differences between institutions, it enhances the perception of Old Havana as a living museum where heritage permeates social life.

My analysis of the cultural biographies of museum objects revealed that most OHCH collections consist of diplomatic presents received by Fidel and then donated to the OHCH. This is especially so in the case of the houses oriented toward diplomatic relations, such as the museum-houses of Africa, Asia, and the Arabs. The exhibitions of diplomatic museum-houses are straightforward accumulations of objects displayed in showcases, selected according to commonsense criteria of perceived beauty.

This procedure contrasts with the management standards of state museums set out by the CNPC. Those have a nationwide validity that, in theory, should apply to the OHCH museum network. As we have seen, CNPC museums require their staff to follow strict procedures and provide detailed accounts of the research behind the museum script and inventories, thereby justifying the objects and forms of representation chosen. Contrarily, OHCH museums do not have scripts, detailed inventories of collections and museological objects, or any concern for museological aspects, and thus disregard the guidelines established decades ago by the Escuela de Museología. This difference reflects an underlying conflict between OHCH and CNPC professionals. The former argue that state professionals lack "good taste" and are inefficient and slow, and they openly criticize bureaucratism and the endurance of soviet-style museology. In turn, state professionals criticize the lack of rigor and disregard for historic narratives in OHCH museology. Mercedes García Santana, ex-director of CENCREM, considers that OHCH museums "lack a thesis to demonstrate, something to work on. All their museums are collections of objects and arts and crafts, or just for tourists or for academic disciplines" (interview, March 13, 2013). Similarly, for the vice-president of CNPC,

the OHCH is either unaware or disregards ministerial heritage laws. They do this because they can buy and sell freely, thus working quicker than our bureaucratic framework. They do not send us their scripts, they worry more about aesthetics than scripts and museology, about which they know little [. . .] Their concept of museum reflects scarce theoretical reflection and, in fact, they undermine the museum idea as such [. . .] They only use the concept of "new museology" to argue that museums of other kinds, those with a historic narrative, are outdated. (A.C. Pereira Escalona, interview, February 15, 2012)

In fact, the OHCH takes care to dissociate itself and its museums from the revolutionary narrative and aesthetics. Only one of the twenty-nine museums, the Armería 9 de Abril (9 April Armory), commemorates a revolutionary event. Urban preservationists also selectively erase some traces of the OHCH's past to convey an image of an institution that has always been present in Old Havana and maintained a similar aesthetic and preservation ethos. The aim is to emphasize that the OHCH is the legitimate heir and curator of the colonial legacy. We have already seen how the OHCH City Museum adopted soviet museography and museology during the 1970s and 1980s. After 1990, the OHCH rapidly abandoned this style and adopted the colonial aesthetic canon that prevails today. Similarly, the OHCH has erased from memory the traces of the museum dedicated to Lenin in the Plaza de Armas. Few current OHCH professionals know about this museum. I could find only one picture (see figure 6.4), and only the former director and two custodians recalled the museum's existence.

Figure 6.4. Sala y Biblioteca Lenin, subsequently renamed Sala de las Revoluciones. Source: Archive and Library of Architecture, Photography Section, OHCH.

The Sala y Biblioteca Lenin (Lenin Room and Library) functioned from 1989 until it was renamed the Sala de las Revoluciones (Room of the Revolutions) in 1994. The room included a reproduction of Lenin's studio and a script consistent with the Marxist-Leninist master-narrative, exhibiting the main revolutions in history using imported soviet holograms. Soon, however, the OHCH dismantled the museum and established the first administrative office of its Department of Cultural Heritage on the site, erasing every trace of the museum. This comes as no surprise, as the Plaza de Armas was meant to be the hub of the colonial aesthetic canon, and the heritagization of Old Havana required burying every vestige of Marxist-Leninist narratives.

Yet it would be misleading to put all OHCH museums in the same boat and judge them against the same standards. Like the Cuban state, the OHCH is a Janus-faced institution that sets out many different and sometimes contradictory projects, symbols, and functions. Accordingly, different groups of museums fulfill different roles. A series of state museums recently taken over by the OHCH—such as the Numismático, the Cartas (Cards), the Napoleónico, the Automóviles (Cars), the Bomberos (Firemen), the Cerámica (Pottery), the Armería 9 de Abril, and the museum-house of José Martí—exhibit classic museum displays. Addressing why each of these museums has fallen under OHCH control is beyond the scope of this study, but each case reveals that the process is often troublesome and contentious. Some museums, such as the Numismático and the Napoleónico, were simply so deteriorated that the state could not afford to pay for rehabilitation; in other cases, such as the Museum-house of José Martí, the OHCH specifically targeted the museum for acquisition.

All museums undergo a process of aestheticization to bring them in line with OHCH standards after their incorporation into the institution. Although directors and staff of state museums usually reject this process, the will of the OHCH has ultimately prevailed in all cases. For instance, the national museum of Cerámica crossed paths with OHCH plans to musealize the colonial castle, the Castillo de la Fuerza, where it was located. The OHCH offered the museum a new location in Mercaderes street and promised to respect the museum profile, which focused on contemporary art and pottery. As the museum director Alejandro Alonso notes, however, "after the museum fell into OHCH hands it turned from being artistic to become like other museums of the OHCH [. . .] We were forced to adopt an aestheticizing appearance and to abandon contemporary art and experimentation" (interview, April 4, 2013). Other groups of museums, such as the museums of Tobacco, Chocolate, and Rum, are exclusively aesthetic devices, with shops intended for tourist consumption.

While the former museums function as performative devices for aesthetic display, another group of museums has a pedagogical aim. Those include the museums of Simón Bolívar, Guayas Amín, Juan Gualberto Gómez, and Benito Juárez. These are hardly different from other institutions that the OHCH does not consider to be museums, such as Factoría Habana and the houses of Victor Hugo and Alejo Carpentier. They fulfill didactic and cultural roles and carry out most of the OHCH's social works, including programs for the elderly, such as free museum breakfasts, a maternity hospital for women, and learning courses for children. Tourists can visit the exhibitions during academic lectures, while children are in class, or while diplomatic events are taking place.

This combination of functions integrates heritage and social life in Old Havana, providing one of the few contact zones between the popular and the elite, the local and the foreign. Among these institutions, the museum-houses present more symbolic content because their exhibitions work to highlight specific aspects of Cuban identity. They exhibit the cultures of those who have been represented as subaltern in Cuba and whose identities had been previously disregarded in the national narrative, including the Arabs, Asians, and Africans. According to Alberto Granado Duque, director of the house of Africa, the institution is committed to "divulging African culture and art, using the presents made to Fidel to put them at the service of the Cuban people. Contrary to foreign museums, there is nothing colonial here" (interview, March 2, 2013). He emphasizes the decolonizing character of the museum by referencing the fact that not a single object was bought or looted in Africa. He recognizes that the museum plays a role in diplomatic relations with Africa but argues that the main reason for its creation in 1986 was the emphasis placed on cultural identity in Cuba, especially Afro-Cuban identity, in line with the Proceso de Rectificación and desovietization.

The diplomatic and cultural functions of the museum-houses serve to articulate the national image in an apparently neutral and aesthetic form. Homi Bhabha's concept of "non-pluralistic politics of difference" (Bhabha 2004:222) aptly describes the underlying politics they stand for. This is so because museum-houses do not engage with the history or current realities of the communities that they intend to represent but rather exhibit abstracted and monolithic representations of them through the aseptic display of isolated objects. For Granado Duque, museum-houses aim to represent the ideal of the Cuban nation resulting from the transculturation of Spanish and other cultures. Ortiz' idea of transculturation, now celebrated in official discourse, is manifested more clearly in the house of Africa than anywhere else. The households Ortiz' collections of African musical instruments and follows his ethnographic research agenda.

The unavoidable question for an institution working to restore a Spanish colonial city and assuming a narrative of transculturation is the place of Spanish influence, culture, and tradition in the postcolonial national narrative. When asked about the absence of an OHCH museum, state museum, or cultural center dedicated to the Spanish legacy—aside from the regional houses of Spanish migrants—most OHCH museum curators and directors either replied that it is unnecessary or avoided the question altogether. However, Granado Duque openly considered that "there is no exhibition of Spanish values because they do not fit in the national narrative and are not considered fundamental" (interview, March 2, 2013).

I interpret the lack of representation and engagement with the Spanish past and symbols as evidence of the OHCH's assumption as official discourse of nonpluralistic politics of difference. As in other postcolonial articulations of identity, the narrative of transculturation draws on the metaphor, so aptly articulated by Bhabha, of the national community as a representation of the "many as one," which totalizes "the social in a homogenous empty time, and the repetition of that minus in the origin, the less-than-one that intervenes with a metonymic, iterative temporality" (Bhabha 2004:222). The "less-than-one" is represented in Cuba by the indigenous and Afro-Cuban subaltern cultural identities, in a sort of postcolonial reframing of the revolutionary narrative of rebelliousness in terms of ethnicity rather than class, culture rather than ideology. In this regard, the OHCH follows the overall tendency of the state heritage apparatus to focus on local and minority identities, but it does so by articulating a different aesthetics rather than a different narrative, as state museums do. The downplaying of Spanish culture can function as a way of constructing a specifically Cuban heritage, paradoxically evicting the symbols of colonial influence while restoring it materially.

There is, however, an enduring contradiction between cultural identity and the state's national narrative that affects the OHCH and reflects all the underlying tensions of Cuba in terms of identity and cultural memory—what Julia Kristeva calls the "loss of identity" and Frantz Fanon describes as a profound cultural "undecidability" (see Bhabha 2004:222). First, there is an attempt to come to terms with the cultural identity of postcolonial Cuba as both different from and heir to the Spanish cultural legacy, with which, by the way, the predominantly white, national cultural elite identifies, as opposed to the "subaltern" identities with which the new dominant discourse requires them to identify. The resolution of this problem is complicated, however, by the second challenge, which involves doing without the atemporal master-narrative of political struggle and rebelliousness, which still permeates education and most history handbooks. Moreover, as we know, this master-narrative condemns all things associated with Spain and Europe as colonial and as a threat to the timeless spirit of the Cuban nation.

In this sense, the OHCH is attempting to replace the sense of timelessness of the previous Marxist-Leninist narrative with a similarly atemporal focus on aesthetics. The aesthetic mode of representation is supposedly neutral in relation to different academic, historical, or artistic registers and serves to replace meaning and content with a purely aesthetic form. Deborah Root (1996) has argued that whenever objects are displayed aesthetically, they are symbolically placed beyond culture and context. The OHCH museology uses material culture as an aesthetic device. Objects stand for and represent the nation as an absolute and ahistorical entity. This representation is in contrast to Socialist museology's emphasis on the contextual meaning of objects as representatives of broader socioeconomic, cultural, and political processes.

At the same time, the OHCH resituates aesthetized objects *within culture*, rather than make them function simply as representatives of historic periods or social classes. However, the cultural framework of reference wherein the OHCH locates objects represents the nation as an ahistorical, aseptic, and unproblematic reality. This form of aesthetization reflects the OHCH's evasive and uncritical stance. It avoids addressing the contentious history of Cuba, its discontinuities and racial, cultural, and economic conflicts, which could undermine the authoritative national narrative. Against this background, the project for the musealization of the Palace of the Segundo Cabo (PSC) will require coming to terms with the double temporality generated by, on the one hand, the master-narrative inherited from previous periods and, on the other, the "real" historic time of Cuban cultural identity and its relations with Europe.

The Palace of the Segundo Cabo: Narrating a (Different) Nation?

Beginning in 2008, the PSC demanded that a multicultural historic narrative of the relations between Europe and Cuba be developed for display in the future museum. For the first time, OHCH urban conservationists and museum experts had to generate a heritage narrative based on a historically grounded account of identity and cultural change. The PSC started immediately after the reestablishment of diplomatic relations between the EU and Cuba, as part of an agreement between the OHCH, UNESCO, and EU representatives. The project is in line with EU global cultural diplomacy, which invests in symbolic sites of national significance to influence politics and policies in developing countries. The PSC was originally slated for completion by 2012, but when funding run out its opening was delayed until 2014. The deadline was pushed back further, to July 2015, and had additional economic support from the EU. The stated objective is to restore the highly deteriorated building and to create in it a "space of encounter between Cuba and Europe in the fields of culture and heritage [. . .] to promote intercultural dialogue and foster cultural diversity and cultural expression, gender equality [. . .] and [to] preserve cultural heritage under risk" (OHCH 2012:n.p.).

Leal Spengler laid down the guidelines of the ambitious project in a 2010 workshop. He emphasized the need to get rid of bureaucratism and to do "something completely different," which would entail creating "neither a museum nor a cultural centre [but] a place for the interpretation of the cultural relationships between Cuba and Europe" (Leal Spengler, April 29, 2010). Because the OHCH is highly dependent on the figure of its leader, OHCH professionals have been trying to interpret and implement Leal Spengler's hour-long poetic speech. For Yainet Rodríguez Rodríguez, a museologist at Factoría Habana and a member of the management team for the project, this is problematic, because "Leal speaks metaphorically and elliptically, thus leaving open the interpretation of his words. But people here strive to understand him and follow his criteria" (interview, March 16, 2013).

The development of the PSC involved a process of mediation and learning among a large group of OHCH professionals in various departments. They tried to come to terms with Leal Spengler's words and the discourses of the EU, UNESCO, and the foreign museology companies hired by the OHCH. The PSC posed a challenge for the group in charge of imagining and designing it, because there are no museology books, new technologies, or similar projects in Cuba that might aid in its construction and because most Cubans are limited in terms of travel. Moreover, this group was fragmented, changing, and heterogeneous: at different times, it numbered between twenty and sixty people and included investors, designers, architects, historians, museologists, and archaeologists. Because the group is not highly paid by the PSC, putting it together and gathering its members for meetings proved to be a challenge for the organizing team. Consequently, the process of developing the project's content and ideas has been discontinuous and slow, which explains its delayed inauguration, in May 2017.

In our interviews, the actors involved tended to present their stories about the PSC according to one of two patterns. Some interviews were highly incisive and critical, while others presented an *oficialista* (official) version that mimicked institutional reports and provided uncritical versions of the process. Consequently, knowledge about the PSC remains always partial and incomplete, especially given the continuous delays in the project's completion. The aim of this section, therefore, is not to reveal the representations that will appear in the final museum display but rather to explore the meaning of the discussions that have taken place between the various actors and what they tell us about the relation between heritage and notions of nation and identity.

It is useful to interpret the PSC as the creation of a postcolonial autoethnographic text. Mary Louise Pratt (1991:35) describes autoethnographies as discourses and images through which people describe themselves in ways that mimic the representations others have made of them. For Pratt, autoethnographies are not autochthonous strategies of self-representation but instead involve "a selective collaboration with and appropriation of idioms of the metropolis or the conqueror" (Pratt 1991:35).

The reception of autoethnographic texts is highly indeterminate, because they have to address metropolitan audiences and the local community producing them. This is the case with the PSC, which was commissioned by international actors such as UNESCO and the EU and implemented by the OHCH, who has to take into account the views of both Cubans and foreign tourists. To advance the interpretive hypothesis presented here, I understand the PSC as an autoethnographic representation that perpetuates the undecidability of Cuban national identity after 1990. In turn, this undecidability reflects the endurance of the coloniality of power and a new form of adaptation to Western hierarchies of heritage value. For in the challenging process of negotiating heritage and identity, Cubans see and represent themselves through the eyes of an other, against which they reaffirm their identity.

According to Marie Agou, a leading EU representative, when the project started in the EU headquarters in Brussels in 2008, no one could have predicted the "symbolic world and expectations created around the Palace, with the most prominent figures in the heritage field in the Caribbean area interested in it and coming to check its evolution" (interview, April 23, 2013). She affirms that although the OHCH was always the main actor in the process, the EU and UNESCO had some requirements that forced the OHCH to deviate from its customary working patterns. First, they wanted the palace to become the gateway to world tourism. It should function, they believed, as the central visitor center for the millions of tourists visiting Old Havana. Second, as UNESCO Regional Director Herman Van Hoof argued in the inaugural ceremony of the project, the palace should serve as an engine of "human development, social improvement, communication and dialogue" (Van-Hoof 2009:1). Third, the palace's museology had to be contemporary and employ new technologies to convey ideas and meanings. This explicitly forced the OHCH to abandon its museology based on design, aesthetics, and isolated objects.

In theory, these ideas seemed clear for OHCH workers. For instance, Margarita Suárez García, director of Museums of the Department of Cultural Heritage of the OHCH, considered that "the *Segundo Cabo* project has to be completely original, moving beyond the New Museology. It has to be the door to the visitors to Old Havana, facilitating their arrival and the interpretation of the site to tourists [. . .] explaining to them the emergence of Cuban culture and nationality" (interview, March 26, 2013). However, UNESCO rejected the OHCH's first proposal. UNESCO Cuba Director Víctor Marín Crespo saw the first draft as

> an attempt to put some spare objects from the *Capitanes Generales* [OHCH City Museum] in there and to tell the same story as always, about the caravels and the indigenous, with a linear history based on politics and antagonism with Europe [. . .] The relations between Cuba and Europe cannot be reduced to a Manichaean narrative; they comprise many different registers. (Interview, March 19, 2013)

After that, UNESCO and the EU demanded an explicit focus on gender, ecology, and human rights and a participatory and democratic methodology in the development of the main guidelines. This forced different and usually quite isolated OHCH departments to start a dialogue and to deal with issues for which they are scarcely theoretically equipped.

The first years of the project focused on architectural restoration. This involved making the palace fit the aesthetic colonial canon promoted by the OHCH elsewhere in Old Havana. The OHCH removed interior walls and ceilings, plasters, and a modern construction that had been added to the roof. Discussions about the "cultural uses" of the building began in September 2011, with a workshop on museology and new technologies offered by European museology companies. Some members of the working group traveled to Europe in January 2012. The trip resulted, in March 2012, in the first general outline of the future museum, whose main features were discussed throughout 2012 and 2013 and have remained mostly unchanged.

The working group presented a draft of the Guiding Document in January 2013, in which they establish the general guidelines of the project. The document affirms that the PSC must become a "national referent of museums with contents [. . .] using new museology and new technologies," with the objective of "enhancing the multicultural dialogue between Cuba and Europe" (Equipo Coordinador 2013:5). The museology of the exhibition should represent "relevant events in Cuban-European relations [. . .] reflecting our cultural exchanges" (Equipo Coordinador 2013:6). In turn, museography should be "in line with the heritage values of Old Havana and assume a preservationist perspective [. . .] fostering the interaction of all kinds of publics with the contents" while avoiding the inclusion of "physical objects of heritage value," thus creating a "museum where heritage is immaterial" (Equipo Coordinador 2013:5).

Nonetheless, these advanced theoretical notions became mere intellectual posturing within the Document, which equated new museology with new technology and "immaterial heritage" with digital representations of objects. Moreover, the script proposal presented a positivist and political history of Cuba and Europe, starting in 1492 and finishing with the Revolution in 1959. The document situates the discovery of America as the milestone that "dialectically linked" European and American cultures and made it impossible "to tell the story of each of them without referring to the other. The European influence was key in the formation of Cuban culture and, at the same time, was transformed by this relation" (Equipo Coordinador 2013:14). Contrary to the project's stated intentions to avoid heroic historic characters, disciplinary divisions, and static views of the past, the museum was divided into rooms according to academic fields of knowledge, and each room was assigned to a different working group.

The first room of the museum was called The Arrival. It initially re-created Columbus' farewell to the Catholic Monarchs in Spain, his crossing of the Atlantic and arrival in Cuba, and his encounter with the indigenous. The room aimed to reflect "nature and men, and the beings inhabiting unknown seas and lands" (Equipo Coordinador 2013:19). The "Dramaturgy" of the room, as the Document puts it, positions the visitor as the European landing in Cuba and encountering the indigenous, thereby emphasizing the strangeness of the environment to the newcomer through the use of lights, sounds, and smells.

Another series of rooms would exhibit traditional contents divided into fields of knowledge and represented with new technologies: music and dance, cartography, urbanism, and books. These rooms highlighted famous characters—prominently European—along with dates of particular inventions or discoveries. Cuban contributions to Europe and a dynamic approach to cultural and social exchange and transformation were largely absent. As a UNESCO representative rightly argued, the rooms "are traditional museography converted into digital form: it is just a warehouse designed with Photoshop" (B. Guzmán, interview, March 19, 2013).

More interesting than the content of the document, which is charged with positivist, historicist, and colonial epistemology, were the discussions about its contents and aesthetic representations. While aesthetics were seen as the task of designers and technicians, contents were debated in different meetings among a wide array of professionals. According to Onedys Calvo Noya, director of the working team, one of the main contentious issues among the professionals involved in the design was the emphasis on making the museum aesthetically appealing and "making technology an end in itself" (interview, March 21, 2013). This contentiousness reflected a conflict between both the competing narratives to be represented by the museum and the generations, namely, between Soviet Union–trained museologists and younger museologists enchanted by design and technology. Younger designers, museologists, and the investors wanted, in the words of Chief Investor Norma Pérez Trujillo, "the museum to become more similar to a show than to a traditional museum" (interview, April 1, 2013). In turn, older OHCH museologists complained that they were not ready to conceptualize a museum without objects and that designers should not take over museum planning. As one of them argued, in reference to the designers,

they have not made a museum in their lives and now they come with big designs and machines without underlying ideas [. . .] We are used to letting objects tell the story without interpretation, letting collections dominate the exhibition in traditional museums. The challenge here is that we must narrate an abstract history, a history of ideas, and to deal with our heritage and its problems and narratives [. . .] without talking about imperialism and our story of struggles. (A. Quevedo Herrero, interview, March 20, 2013)

The more traditional museologists strongly advocated as the museum's guiding principle a political and historicist narrative of Cuban-European relations. Moreover, they wanted to end the historic narrative of the museum in 1959. As such, they sustained the official attitude of avoiding historicizing the Revolution and of overlooking past Cuban relations with Socialist countries. The problem with this stance is that many formerly Socialist countries are now part of the EU. The higher OHCH ranks originally supported these museologists' conservative standpoint. A document produced by the OHCH leadership for internal circulation among members of the working team clearly stated that the PSC had to exalt the values of the nation, implying that the narrative should have a conservative and nationalist bent. Thereafter, as Calvo Noya argued, it became fundamental to highlight "the evolution of the Cuban nation in time" (interview, March 21, 2013) and, regarding cultural identity, "to show foreign tourists who we are" (N. Pérez Trujillo, interview, April 1, 2013).

Another question was how to position Hispanic culture, whose definition goes hand in hand with a certain understanding of Cuban culture and identity. Anthropologist Christine Ayorinde (2004:198) has argued that there has always existed in Cuba an underlying dissonance between Afro-Cubans and the mostly white and Hispanic leadership. She probably overstates the racial content of the conflict but is clear, if we follow Carlos Franqui, that the Cuban cultural elite assumes a European worldview that sees Caribbean culture and way of life in a negative light (quoted in Moore 1988:103). In the case of the PSC, all members of the working team are white. However, only the group of older and more conservative museologists openly advocates a Hispanicist reading of Cuban history and culture, as is apparent in many discourses and practices and in their Hispanicist allegiance, which periodically surfaced during interviews. Some argued that Cuban culture was a variation of Hispanic culture and legacy. Others, such as Suárez García, stated that "the formation of Cuban culture happens before all that [Cuban independence]; it was not the Americans, the Polish or the Hungarians that had influence, but the Spanish" (interview, March 26, 2013).

Thus, discourses about the Cuban nation are ambivalent and stand halfway between overt Hispanicism and what Mignolo defines as a "saying out of place" (Mignolo 2000). This "saying out of place" is an abstract and ahistorical site of enunciation seeking identity in the difference from the indigenous, Afro-Cuban and Spanish realities. As Rodríguez Rodríguez aptly puts it, "Among us there is a prevailing idea that these cultures [Spanish, indigenous and African] are somewhat 'loaned' to Cuba: we see the spirit of the nation as preceding both the Spanish and black cultures" (interview, March 16, 2013).

Thus, while the narrative of the state positions Spain as a representation of atrocity and colonialism, the white cultural elites and their unofficial understandings of history, which serve to reproduce their internal cultural hegemony, see Spain as the cultural *madre patria* (motherland) from which Cuban identity and ways of life derive. This group behavior is captured through Herzfeld's (2005) concept of "cultural intimacy," through which a group of insiders who share a similar understanding of their history of identity are also aware that this commonality could be source of external embarrassment and political problems.

Most young and critical members of the working team reject both the official and the pro-Hispanic narrative templates. Young museologists and designers are closer to the concerns of UNESCO and EU representatives, who seek a more dynamic account of cultural interaction. It is clear why in our interviews the project leaders always characterized the PSC as a process of coordination and translation of discourses representing different understandings of history and identity. As a member of the Department of International Relations argues,

> we are learning the languages of the institutions: the EU focuses on gender, multiculturalism, and ecological sustainability. UNESCO wants us to mention all the conventions and put their logos all over, while state bureaucrats do not want texts stating that this or that program is aimed at eradicating poverty or fostering people's democratic participation, because officially there is no poverty and people already participate democratically. (M. Rojas Vidaurreta, interview, March 5, 2013)

Similarly, the coordination process has to consider diplomatic relations. For instance, the room devoted to Columbus and the Spanish Monarchs was suppressed to avoid any reference to problems with Spain. In this context, UNESCO does not play the role for which it is so often criticized—of supporting the agendas of nation-states. Rather, UNESCO representatives have emphasized the need to open up the museum narrative to new themes and histories other than the official national discourse of antagonism with Europe. According to Marín Crespo, Cuban authorities were suspicious of EU intentions with the project. For this reason, UNESCO has

> helped in showing that there is no will to create conflict or an aggressive discourse [. . .] There was concern that the project could escape from state control [but now] Leal has started to talk about alternative possibilities, about representing a different past, a past of science and exchange rather than antagonism. (Interview, March 19, 2013)

Indeed, after February 2012 the museum narrative expanded gradually to highlight the concept of transculturation and cultural exchange and, according to Calvo Noya, to include how "the nation was forged in contact and relation with Europe" (interview, March 21, 2013). This was particularly challenging for the organizing team, because decades of soviet historiography had denied historical links with Europe beyond oppression and imperialism. A deeply rooted epistemological legacy from the sovietizing period is the Hegelian notion that identity has to be constructed dialectically with reference to an enemy, first represented by colonial Europe and then by the United States.

My interpretation is that the difficulty of developing a narrative that moves away from colonial and modern tropes is a reflection not so much of political will but of underlying epistemological colonialism. The agendas of EU and UNESCO that request the OHCH to highlight gender and multicultural issues, sociocultural relations, and different historic narratives cannot be handled by the PSC working team, owing to the overriding empiricism and positivism pervading Cuban epistemology in most fields, a legacy of decades of antitheoretical thought and reified Marxism-Leninism, and disconnection from critical scholarship.

Along these lines, Agou considers that "the OHCH does many things and very efficiently, but this is not reflected in official reports and meetings, which are just empirical and factual descriptions of what is being made [. . .] This lack of analytical depth is a deeply rooted cultural feature" (interview, April 23, 2013). Even Calvo Noya acknowledges that "the project is not theoretically grounded; everything is pragmatic and empirical" (interview, March 21, 2013). For Laura García Méndez, the librarian in charge of the room of the Book, the theoretical shortcomings "have created many problems, because we did not define terms and concepts beforehand [. . .] We started from the relations between two regions, but the terms of these relations were not clear, and different people understand them in different ways" (interview, March 11, 2013).

The result of this atheoretical stance is a constant interplay between positivist history and the official narrative of anticolonialism and antagonism that leads to overt contradictions in terms of content. For instance, the guidelines of the room of the Book argue, on the one hand, that European books were "utmost representatives of transculturation" and, on the other, that they were produced "to legitimize the hegemony of the Old

Continent" (Terrón and García 2012:3). In theory, the museology of the room aims to present cultural processes "as symbolic representations of a cultural group, rather than of the erudition of a few characters" (Terrón and García 2012:8). Surprisingly, then, the room's design presents a positivist and linear historic evolution of the main European figures and editorials in the manufacturing of books in Cuba. This standpoint is the result of overriding historicism, which creates an empty and homogeneous time that favors hegemonic identification with the perspective of the victor. It discards other views and possibilities of history and conveys the underlying idea of the impossibility of changing reality.

Early in 2013, the investors forced the working team to incorporate a historian from the Instituto de Historia to impose order on the timeline and to fulfill the objective of "reflecting the cultural links between Europe and Cuba" (Equipo Coordinador 2013:2). Although this has changed lately, the institute traditionally advocated orthodox positions and sanctioned the "right" understandings of Cuban history. In a meeting in February 2013, the historian presented a one-hundred-page-long historicist report focused on political and military history with an overtly Hispanicist bent. He was followed by a traditional museologist who presented a vast list of objects that supposedly represented the history of Cuba classified according to academic disciplines. He then supported the historian, arguing that "chronology must be the common narrative thread of the museum" and that "the Spanish came and did everything here" (General Meeting, February 9, 2012).

Their presentations prompted a heated debate and strong reactions from those advocating a more dynamic perspective and the abandonment of positivist history as the guiding principle of the museum. Conservative museologists and historians were criticized for their impoverished definition of Europe, which was sometimes equated with Spain only. The scholar and museologist Rosa María González López harshly criticized the historian and museologist for excluding the ex-COMECON countries, with which "Cuba established all kinds of cultural, human, scientific and educative relations" (interview, March 21, 2013). Critics also emphasized that both presentations had avoided addressing Cuban-European relations during the Republic and the Revolution.

However, the emphasis on Hispanicism should not be understood as an affirmation of Cuban similarity to or derivation from Spanish identity or culture. The historian's narrative was in line with the "saying out of place" that portrays the Spanish as "the others." He constantly referred to the Spanish as "they," the ones who "came" and against which Cubans fought for independence, thereby implying a preexistent "Cuba" forged through struggle. In other words, the official narrative had to conceal Hispanicism and leave it in the realm of cultural intimacy. This narrative accorded a prominent role to Spanish identity only negatively, as the mirror against which Cuban identity emerged dialectically.

The incorporation of the historian complicated the creation of the museum narrative even further for different reasons. Both the heritage narratives of the state and those of the OHCH tended to highlight the subaltern memories and identities of Afro-Cubans, rather than of the Spanish. For Rodríguez Rodríguez, this complex Cuban conundrum derives from "the political fear to deal with real history, when in reality, if the narrative is based in scientific facts, there should be no problems [in terms of political censorship]" (interview, March 16, 2013). For her, while the state tries to

> enhance Afro-Cuban culture [. . .] we are terrified to acknowledge the influence of Europe in Cuban culture and identity, because we are taught to think that everything coming from Europe is negative, but the European influence is obvious if we look at our skin color, physical constitution and demography. We fear to consider ourselves as Europeans in public, but have no problems to identify with the blacks, with the subaltern, in theory [. . .] Examining and exhibiting what real cultural relations are there between Cuba and Europe would be fundamental to decoloniz[ing] our thought. (Interview, March 16, 2013)

The team struggled to reconcile different views of identity, nation, and memory in the creation of a meaningful narrative that could satisfy the different actors involved in the project. The room of The Arrival reflected this challenge. The narrative of transculturation required the inclusion of the indigenous people, that "minus in the origin" with which the white workers in charge of the PSC struggle to identify. As with every other traditional Cuban museum, the developers' initial idea was to create a room for the indigenous people. However, according to Calvo Noya, "we faced the problem of representing them; we lacked an accurate form of expressing their reality" (interview, March 21, 2013).

The solution devised, in January 2014, was to display a replica of an abandoned indigenous village that showed their material culture from the standpoint of the European conqueror. Rodríguez Rodríguez criticized this decision, arguing that "in trying to tell our story, we are representing ourselves as the one who arrives to Cuba [. . .] We have this stigma of inferiority, of feeling like second-level Europeans" (interview, March 16, 2013). She rightly pointed to one of the key markers of the authoethnographic colonial text: shaping self-representations of identity based on images created by others. Although the Guiding Document developed a narrative based on transculturation that included the indigenous, various interviewees despised indigenous history and culture. In a sentiment I heard expressed more than once, members of the group said that the indigenous people were there making pictures in the sand with sticks when the Europeans came, implying their inferiority.

The museum's provisional narrative highlighted the significance of the "discovery" of Cuba and disregarded alternative views. This narrative has been criticized in working meetings and has been repeatedly equated with the pan-Hispanic celebration, which Cuba also observes, of Columbus Day on October 12 to commemorate the "discovery" of America and its "new peoples" by the Spanish. Critical professionals who disagreed with this narrative saw it as a continuation of the previous Marxist-Leninist master-narrative, because transculturation is similarly understood as a series of reified features and characteristics possessed by certain social groups.

For Rodríguez Rodríguez, transculturation from this perspective ultimately becomes an "essentialized 'Cuban product' [. . .] that defines the specific Cuban features according to some fixed patterns, seeking the creation of a stable identity" (interview, March 16, 2013). Indeed, "within the colonial narrative," she further argues, "we assign ourselves the role of rebelliousness and struggle, but there is not real anti-colonial discourse. This would imply accounting for dynamic cultural fluctuations, differences, hybridizations and for the Cuban contribution to world culture" (interview, March 16, 2013). She aptly illustrates that beneath the revolutionary, anti-imperialist rhetoric lies a highly positivist historicism that reflects colonial epistemology. This is the same epistemology criticized in the 1960s by Carbonell, who considered it "regrettable that the colonialist conception of culture keeps force among us" (Carbonell 2005 [1961]:40).

In reality, the PSC team was largely unaware that the historicist narrative reproduced colonial themes and understandings of identity and left little room for the role of Cuban culture and identity in the outside world. Ultimately, the narrative proposed for the future museum focused on how "the others" should see "us," without accounting for the other side of the relation: how we see and have influenced them. This reflects a sense of inferiority that facilitates the assumption of colonial epistemologies.

Cuba shares this adhesion to Eurocentric narratives with other Latin American countries. In these countries, the different liberation ideologies contested only the political and economic exclusion from the West but largely accepted a Eurocentric epistemology. The mainstream postcolonial theories (e.g., Chakrabarty 2009) have a difficult fit in the Latin American context, and even more so in Cuba and other Socialist countries, owing to their separation of the cultural and institutional orders and their disregard for how the postcolonial discourse can turn into an instrument of power. Indeed, the rhetoric of multiculturalism or transculturation, which in Cuba is disengaged from its political and institutional context, can conceal the underlying colonial meanings implicit in the dominant discourses. The Latin American theorization of the coloniality of power proves useful in highlighting how early modern colonialism—the variety practiced by Spain and Portugal as opposed to by later British and French colonialism—continues to pervade the ways that labor, race, humanity, and nature are perceived in the region (Quijano 2000).

Today, the universalism implied in heritage values and channeled through global actors such as UNESCO and the EU serves to reproduce the peripheral status of the global South and to assimilate it to the modus operandi of the Euro-American North. For the PSC, the underlying problem of creating a narrative lies in the paradoxes of this troubled postcolonial situation. The uncritical assumption of foreign values, together with the request by foreign institutions to represent local cultural dynamics on their own terms, generates a tension with the dominant national narrative. Because this narrative posits the nation as an abstract entity that is outside history, relations are seen as occurring between isolated cultural and ethnic wholes: Cuba and Europe, or the Spanish, the Indigenous, and the Afro-Cubans. However, every attempt to elucidate the European and

American cultural contributions in isolation hinders the understanding of cultural processes.

Epistemic coloniality has practical consequences in the field of heritage. For instance, the emphasis on colonial monumental architecture to the exclusion of intangible elements or other architectonic features reflects the imposition of colonial values. Because Cuban vernacular architecture does not fit Western criteria of value, the UNESCO World Heritage designation comprised only the area with buildings of imported colonial styles and left aside the vernacular. Epistemic coloniality should not be interpreted as another "external" imposition of Western values by UNESCO but rather as an internal reproduction of epistemic colonialism: the World Heritage proposal was designed in Cuba by Cubans, with committed Marxist Arjona Pérez leading the initiative. Because Western notions of culture were exported through conquest in ways that re-created Europe and its colonial values, those were reproduced in local contexts, including those, as in Cuba, where Western dominance was rhetorically contested (Dirks 1992:3).

Thus, unlike the crypto-colonial relationship with the USSR, the Cuban subjection to the global hierarchy of value and epistemic coloniality can be interpreted as a more abstract form of domination, one that imposes Western values and criteria without necessarily creating a relationship between nation-states. The abstract quality of this form of domination is captured in the Cuban government's fears of "neoliberal globalization" rather than of the United States or "the West" exclusively. This is also a more insidious and profound form of hegemony, for it cannot be located in a particular nation, system, or ideology and therefore cannot be simply rejected by political orientations, as was the case with soviet influence after the Rectificación de Errores in 1986.

Even through the PSC has not been completed, the discussions about its creation reveal the adoption of a colonial narrative and set of values whereby Cubans see and represent themselves through the eyes of the other. The World Heritage declaration focused on enhancing colonial monumentality that is representative of Western material culture and values. The OHCH has furthered this task by manufacturing a colonial aesthetic canon and reproducing an epistemologically colonial national narrative, concealed by the discourse of transculturation and its underlying nonpluralistic politics of difference.

Conclusion

I have shown that the OHCH's approach to history deviates from the official narrative of antagonism and is less openly ideological. However, its historicist approach is geared toward tourist consumption rather than toward reconciliation or political opening. This is apparent in the PSC project, which does not even mention that the problem of Cuban identity has little to do with immigration (as it does in Europe) and more to do with emigration and the exiled community. In other words, issues of Cuban identity have more to do with multinationalism than with multiculturalism. Even if Leal Spengler openly talks about emigration and "the others" outside Cuba—a highly controversial and unspoken theme—it is another thing altogether to acknowledge their existence and political voice in a museum display. In a PSC meeting, a technician proposed the creation of a room with voice recorders whereby people could leave their messages, thereby making cultural exchange between Cuba and the world ongoing and dynamic. Rapidly, however, a historian from the Instituto de Historia argued that such a room could cause political trouble because *los de allá* (those on the other side, in Miami) would use the room to criticize the regime, and thus a system of censorship would need to be established. When I asked about this issue, Pablo Riaño Fanjul, director of the OHCH Architecture Department, provided a description of his institution that concurs with my interpretation. He argued that the OHCH

> shows a clear tendency to mimic what the leader says, with the paradox that Leal is more open and courageous than those working for him, who fear political problems [. . .] Anyway, the OHCH is a replica of the state in a small scale. Its companies and departments are just efficient copies of the ones of the state and, as the state, it resists change and democratization, enforcing a pyramidal internal power structure. (Interview, March 8, 2013)

He continued, affirming that

> the OHCH is multifaceted and polyfunctional, as well as ambivalent [. . .] Bureaucrats see it as a threat because it goes against their anti-utilitarian ideas, which go against making money with cultural heritage. The OHCH, however, has privileged the capture of hard

currency over the integration of the population. This involves a shift in the dominant discourse: there were state heritage policies in the 1980s, but heritage was seen as something from the past, related to the nation and its values exclusively [. . .] The OHCH is the mirror of the country, and the national narrative it sustains is similar to the one of the state because they have shared aims: to enhance and magnify national identity. What varies is the form of telling the story, the openness to other cultures and the promotion of collaboration rather than antagonism. (Interview, March 8, 2013)

In line with Riaño Fanjul, the OHCH could be best understood as one of the many faces of Cuba, a complex heritage-based experiment that redefines Cuban identity and the national narrative. It interacts in different ways with other state dynamics, in its attempt to leave behind the soviet legacy and to dissociate culture from power. For the average Cuban, the OHCH raised the hope that things could be different, that aesthetics, cultural heritage, and efficiency mattered, and that these could be achieved in Cuba even during a devastating economic crisis. The OHCH is undoubtedly more efficient and provides a freer work atmosphere for its members. Ultimately, however, it is only slightly more concerned with historic truth than the state is and for the most part simply provides a more aesthetically pleasant and friendly self-image of Cuba for tourists. Contrary to the state use of heritage at the service of a fixed and ideological historic narrative, the OHCH gives heritage different social and economic uses and integrates it with social life. It also helps by dealing with certain troublesome issues of the undesired colonial and republican pasts, by recovering and generating sites for memory and history.

However, in symbolically and materially recovering and restoring the heritage of these pasts, the OHCH may be indirectly reproducing some of the negative forces the Revolution so stubbornly fought against: socioeconomic inequality, relentless commoditization, and the imposition of foreign aesthetic and social values. The heritagization of Old Havana creates a disjunction that both includes some people, through social care and educational programs, and excludes others, through the suppression of affordable businesses for locals. The OHCH does combine the popular and the elite and allow them to coexist, but this transpires under a top-down approach whose ultimate aim is the simplification of Old Havana's complexity with the goal of facilitating and capitalizing on tourism. Rather than a process of gentrification, the OHCH is creating a tourist space through the heritagization of Old Havana. This approach shows the impracticality of implementing the OHCH self-management and semi-capitalist model in the whole of Havana, or, for that matter, in entire provincial cities, where the model is applied to city centers only.

In summary, the state heritage apparatus is Janus-faced: it simultaneously promotes the transformation of ideology into heritage and the restoration of the colonial heritage of Old Havana, two apparently contradictory processes. Revolutionary Cuba is, then, a living paradox. Its policies should not be understood as intentional designs for social control but instead as pragmatic efforts to rearticulate the distribution of populations, investments, functions, and meanings that effectuate the practical continuation of the regime in times of change: a task in which heritage has a central role to play in the coming years.

7

The Coloniality of Heritage in Postcolonial Cuba

This book started with an event that will be remembered as a turning point in Cuban history, namely, the reopening of the U.S. embassy in Havana. It concludes with two vignettes that reflect both change and continuity in Cuba after 2014. The first was the tearing down of an imposing neoclassic building in September 2015. The building had been neglected for years, despite its privileged position in front of the Capitolio. Now, the government and the OHCH have poured millions into making this area a symbol of the new Cuba, more open to the outside world—and especially to the United States. This marks the continuation of Havana's infrastructural problems but also points to the end of official policies of urban neglect and disregard for historic preservation.

The second event took place the same year in Camagüey, where a new Wi-Fi system had been installed in the central Plaza Agramonte after decades of severe internet restrictions. Looking for better Wi-Fi coverage, a man climbed the monument to the *patria* that dominates the square and tore it down. In less than twenty-four hours, the local authorities performed a solemn ceremony of reparation emphasizing nationalist values and restored the statue with a floral offering. Although the authorities were using heritage to reassert the continuity of traditional values, what lurked behind the event was the growing disconnection between official heritage discourse and the needs and interests of Cubans.

Figure 7.1. Neoclassic building facing the Capitolio being torn down in September 2015. Source: Author.

Both vignettes illustrate one of the arguments of this book, namely, that heritage is a present-centered process that is always in the making. Not only do the meanings of heritage shift, but they can promote mutual understanding to the same degree that they can perpetuate social divisions. For decades, the Revolution used heritage to remind others of the revolutionary triumph and to structure public meanings and symbols in terms of "winners" and "losers." Without overemphasizing its political relevance and reach, the post-2014 turn of events offers an opportunity to revisit this symbolic landscape based on the rhetoric of "us" and "them," and this requires understanding the long-term uses of heritage to prolong violence and opposition. This also begs the troublesome question of the status of Cuba as a postcolonial nation in constant search of its own identity, an issue that has haunted Cuban politics and culture since the country's independence from Spain, in 1898. In this conclusion, I address these questions by examining the changing forms that the coloniality of power has adopted in Cuba, tracing the links between different nationalist

Figures 7.2 and 7.3. *Top*: a man tears down a statue looking for coverage in the newly established Wi-Fi hot spot in Camagüey in 2015. *Bottom*: ceremony reinstating the value and significance of the fallen statue. Source: Author.

ideologies, types of colonialism, and logics of heritage production. Finally, I characterize the main tenets of heritage under Socialism, highlighting the similarities and differences between Cuba and other Socialist countries.

This enlarged trajectory confirms my theoretical insight that heritage is relevant to postcolonial nation-building because it can project the narratives and symbols that suit nationalism and make them pass as authentic and natural. As I pointed out at the beginning of this book, making things pass as natural—in other words, reifying them—and linking them with an ideal of authenticity in the past is central to nationalism and the legitimization of political regimes. Heritage's potential for nationalism derives from its capacity to assemble history and materiality. History can create narratives of political identity that emphasize how individuals and groups have maintained their particular sets of "essential" characteristics through time, while materiality can structure symbols in public space to facilitate the inculcation of history and ideology.

From this perspective, heritage is a process whereby social actors produce certain pasts and signify material culture according to shifting values, knowledges, ideologies, and power relations. This goes beyond a simple conception of heritage as the uses of the past in the present, for to use the past in the present, an image of the past must be constructed. In other words, heritage is not renewable. What is renewable is the social capacity to attach meaning to past or newly produced places, performances, or material culture and the uses made of these meanings in the present. This capacity to signify is intrinsically linked to the fascination with authenticity and the past, and this fascination is a specific trait of Western modernity. Rather than a close-cut definition of heritage, then, we need a complex understanding of the dynamic interactions between the social construction of heritage, history, and materiality, and the different actors involved in the definition of heritage ontology, that is, that which exists both physically and symbolically.

In the postcolony, the definition of heritage ontology was central to the state's efforts to subsume the diverse cultural, ethnic, and political identities inherited from colonial times into a unified national community. But the cultural and heritage policies behind this process were in most periods unclear, uncertain, and even fragmented. Achille Mbembe has argued that postcolonies are "characterized by a distinctive style of political improvisation" (Mbembe 2001:102), and Cuba is no exception to this. Indeed, Kapcia (2014) has recently advocated analyzing Cuba as another postcolonial state, rather than comparing it to Socialist or Latin American countries. The argument here builds upon this assertion and complicates it, showing how problematic it is to compare Cuba with other postcolonial nations from a heritage perspective. The concept of the coloniality of power proves useful in this context for its emphasis on process and its contention that both capitalist and Communist regimes remain colonial whenever they impose the values of Western modernity on others. This concept is useful for examining the future paths of the Revolution and its heritage policies, because, as this book has attempted to demonstrate, throughout its postcolonial trajectory, Cuba has reproduced and institutionalized, but also rejected and challenged, Western epistemic categories and the hierarchies of knowledge, value, and culture that they imply.

At the outset, this book challenged the view that Cubans did not look inward and to the past in their nation-building process. It revealed the close relationship between the emergence of Cuban national identity and the creation of modern museums and monuments that portrayed the past in different ways. Certainly, Cubans reproduced the colonial episteme when they sought to imitate the heritage values and criteria of Europe and the United States, which they saw as successful civilizational models. At the same time, however, they revisited their own heritage, looking for the right historical periods, material culture, ideas, and values to shape the newly created national community. Similarly, heritage was used for the negotiation of Cuban identity against both the colonial Spanish past and the growing influence of U.S. neoimperialism.

Intellectuals developed various heritage institutions—inconsistently supported by the state—that selected elements from popular culture, constructed them as folklore, and presented them as distinctively Cuban. The characterization of popular culture as folklore is a common, albeit paradoxical, postcolonial attitude that can be interpreted as cultural colonialism. Intellectuals resignified popular culture as high culture according to the terms of the ex-colonial or neocolonial powers. That is, they produced nationalist categories in ways that naturalized the structures and values of Western modernity. Indeed, they sought recognition among an international cultural community—first in Spain, later in the United

States—that regarded folklore and heritage preservation as signs of modernity and scientific achievement. The constant calls among intellectuals to build modern museums, monuments, and heritage legislation imitating Western models were often justified by affirming "this is what developed countries do."

Heritage logics reproduced the European cultural modernism that had characterized late colonial periods. For museum curators, building a modern nation implied not only collecting the relics of Cuban heroes but also acquiring European artworks of "universal value." Cuban nationalist monuments were built by Italian artists employing a neoclassical style. This also revealed the close relationship between materiality and nationalism. In their publications, projects, and speeches, social actors always linked the discussions about the materials to build monuments, the preservation of past material culture, and the styles employed with the ethics and values that were necessary to cement national identity.

It was considered, for instance, that Italian marble, neoclassic aesthetics, and the heritage of King Carlos III encouraged the Cuban national spirit, whereas wood, baroque aesthetics, bullfighting, the remembrance of King Felipe II or the practice of Afro-Cuban religions damaged it. In other words, the definition of official heritage and the constitution of national identity were consubstantial processes. In turn, citizens were implicitly conceived as passive actors to be incorporated into the nationalist agenda through the definition of official heritage. This could be perceived in the absence of heritage performances and the separation between subjects and objects promoted by most heritage processes and explicitly theorized by heritage professionals such as Labatut.

The Revolution emphasized a rupture with the past and the reinterpretation of republican symbols and heritage. The early revolutionary heritage practices and ideas broke with certain republican heritage processes, such as the separation between subjects and objects and the idea that monuments and museums were static elements to be passively viewed. The republican conception of the citizen as a passive receptor of meaning gave way to the revolutionary requirement for the masses to participate in heritage production and to perform political parades at heritage sites, linking revolutionary symbols to individual and group experiences.

Heritage reflected the endurance of the coloniality of power on various levels. Heritage professionals predicated the expansion of heritage upon

Western humanist and so-called universal values embodied by UNESCO. The example of the French Revolution inspired the conversion of barracks and bourgeois mansions into museums. In addition, the regime sought to reconcile revolutionary identity and popular culture—especially Afro-Cuban "superstition"—with Western schemes of progress. The rearrangement of museums downplayed Cuban archaeological and ethnographic collections while highlighting European paintings along with Egyptian, Greek, and Roman archaeological objects, and galleries with reproductions of "universal art" were created. To be modern and educated, Cuba had to use heritage to play catch-up, proactively inscribing itself within Western modernity. The creation of the MR encapsulated the complexity and ambiguity of Cuban heritage policies. While creating a museum of the revolution meant the explicit adoption of soviet heritage categories, the contents of the museum avoided references to Marxism-Leninism and were consistent with the leadership's nationalist narrative.

As the regime wavered between different values, political projects, and ideologies, a contradiction emerged regarding the materiality of heritage. Republican intellectuals had constantly emphasized the need to employ the appropriate materials and styles for shaping national identity. However, in the early Revolution, the intrinsic connection between materiality and identity was questioned. Fidel maintained that what mattered for national-revolutionary identity was content rather than form and aesthetics. Architects and artists critically targeted monuments and museums and the bourgeois values of beauty and contemplativeness they implied. These professionals were operating in a manner consistent with the Socialist ideals of egalitarianism and therefore criticized the potential of heritage to generate hierarchies and impose hegemony.

But this rhetoric was contradicted by practice. It became apparent that the state's need to forge a new national-revolutionary identity could not be fulfilled without the power of heritage to gather together materiality and history. Therefore, heritage continued to function as an assemblage of history and materiality, which also implied continuity with republican heritage logics. The competitions to build new monuments required the bidding teams to carry out historical research, to interpret the past, and to give it tangible form in public space. Certainly, the contents and themes represented changed, but the lack of an alternative aesthetic canon implied the continuation of neoclassical monuments and museums.

The institutionalizing period accentuated the future-oriented tendencies of the Revolution, which prioritized the production of new heritage to convey Socialist ideology and abandoned the former emphasis on the reinterpretation of previous heritage. In contrast to early revolutionary times, the connection between the materiality of heritage and national-revolutionary identity was not contested. Gradually, the dominant monumental canon became socialist realism, which, as the orthodox intellectual José Antonio Portuondo had put it, expressed the true identity of "the nation for itself" (Portuondo 1963a:57). Museum objects had to 'demonstrate' the meaning prescribed by ideology, and monuments had to be built with Cuban materials and be realist. Artists' resistance to socialist realism shows that they did not see it as a mere style but as a means of representing political power and national identity.

The close connection between heritage and history continued through the institutionalizing period but became more complex and bidirectional. At times, the production of heritage and that of history were dissociated. For instance, monument competitions started to impose the official historical content that bidding teams had to represent, rather than requiring them to carry out historical research. On other occasions, however, heritage and history went together, as when museums were required to produce local histories and represent them in exhibitions.

The debate about the postcolonial status of Cuba during this period unavoidably leads to the question about the relationship with the USSR. Written documentation between 1975 and 1990 reflects an almost complete official acceptance of soviet heritage categories, aesthetics, and narratives. However, in practice the Cuban case was more ambiguous. Unlike North Korea and other Socialist countries, Cuba did not officially embrace Stalinist ideas, did not promote the demolishing of traditional city centers, and forbade the monumentalization of living leaders. Indirectly, the constant efforts of high-ranking heritage workers to correct "ideological deviations" in heritage projects reveals a superficial assent to Marxism-Leninism among heritage professionals. This assent concurs with the explicit rejection of socialist realism by artists and with the present-day interpretation that most interviewees in the Cuban heritage field tend to provide about the institutionalizing period. The latter argue that only a small group of Cuban politicians promoted soviet ideas about heritage and that Marxism-Leninism and socialist realism were seen as the official canon rather than as the epistemological base of heritage work.

The above interpretation has three drawbacks. First, it denies the active role of Cuban heritage actors in the adoption and promotion of soviet heritage ideas, which most had, in fact, done for decades, and disregards the marginalization of dissenters such as Montenegro. Second, it provides a pretext for many to argue that Cuba assimilated soviet ideas on a superficial level only, thus aligning with the official rejection of alleged soviet excesses after the start of the Proceso de Rectificación. Third, it overlooks the complex interactions between the leadership and soviet ideology. Not only MINFAR but also the PCC and the Council of State promoted Marxist-Leninist narratives and socialist realist forms. Monuments of ex-guerrillas were socialist realist—even those of Guevara, who openly despised socialist realism. However, the adoption of socialist realism can also be interpreted as a pragmatic decision by Cuba's leaders rather than a straightforward imitation of soviet ideas. Socialist realism provided a language of power that the regime lacked and was used in such a way as to appear as if it were in continuity with tradition and a manifestation of the regime's ideology rather than an external imposition to it. The fact that even three decades after the soviet collapse socialist realism remains the official heritage canon supports this assertion.

Thus, rather than a traditional form of neoimperialism or cultural colonialism, Cuban-USSR relations constitute a pragmatic hybrid, incorporating the objectives, ideas, and symbols of the leadership of Cuba and the USSR and those of Cuban radical nationalism and Marxism-Leninism. Because Cuba was dependent on the USSR, however, this relationship can be understood as a crypto-colonial process (Herzfeld 2002:901). Crypto-colonialism is a variant of cultural imperialism whereby aggressive nationalist rhetoric is expressed through heritage and culture, using the principles and categories of an external power while concealing effective dependence on that external power—in this case, the USSR.

The collapse of the Soviet Union disrupted the clear relationship that existed between heritage, nation, and Marxism-Leninism. The logics of heritage changed as the emphasis on the revolutionary disjuncture from the past and impulse toward the future shifted to a search for identity in the past. This was a painful shift for the regime, given that care for tradition, the past, and its remains had for decades been considered bourgeois obsessions. This contradiction was partially resolved by the division of labor between the OHCH and the state to produce different expressions of national identity.

As in the early Revolution, the state heritage apparatus emphasized the reinterpretation of heritage sites rather than the construction of new heritage due to the lack of a given ideology. This contrasted with the OHCH, which bound together the production of history and heritage, the restoration of colonial remains, and the representation of national identity. The work of the OHCH altered the relation between history and heritage, as both became mutually supportive processes informing one another. This marked an important shift from the previous period, when a predetermined master-narrative conditioned heritage production. Of course, ideology also informed OHCH heritage production, pervaded by capitalist and antiquarian tendencies, but the engagement with past material culture and history was not a given.

In contrast with the previous period, the materiality of heritage was no longer considered to be intrinsically connected with national identity. For instance, socialist realism endured as the official heritage canon despite the official rejection of soviet ideology and legacy. This was because socialist realism had become detached from the ideology that had made it the dominant canon of internationalist Socialist identity and now remained simply the authoritative language of power. This development illustrates a consistent feature of heritage that is related to its material aspect: its capacity to naturalize ideas and values and make them appear authentic and familiar.

The collapse of the Soviet Union entailed the end of the crypto-colonial relationship between Cuba and the USSR. Then, after 1990, the coloniality of power in Cuba adopted two new and more abstract forms. The first was a dependency on the global hierarchy of heritage value, whereby Cuba celebrated its national identity but did so by enforcing the categories, principles, and values established by those dominating the global gradient of economic and cultural significance. Not only has Cuba started to restore its European colonial heritage to create an image of authenticity that would satisfy the demands of tourists, mostly European until 2015, but heritage processes also have been increasingly conditioned by the requirements of global actors such as the EU or UNESCO.

The second was the epistemic coloniality of power that endured among most heritage professionals, who still find it difficult to engage critically with history and materiality and to abandon culture-history, Marxism-Leninism, and socialist realism. Although epistemic coloniality can be related to the amnesiac quality that is characteristic of most future-oriented regimes, this is not a unique tenet of revolutionary Cuba or Socialist countries and can be broadly associated with the postcolonial condition. Republican intellectuals were already complaining about the forgetfulness of Cubans, as epitomized by Aldo Baroni's (1944) *Cuba, Country of Poor Memory*. What is specific about the Cuban Revolution is its capacity to generate a selective production of amnesia about the republican and colonial pasts and even between the different periods of the Revolution, such as the denial after 1990 of previous soviet influence. This has hindered the possibility of a critical engagement with previous historical periods. Drawing on Connerton's (2009) apt concepts, the prescriptive erasure of certain pasts has turned into structural amnesia.

This long-term trajectory allows me to supersede Harrison and Hughes' (2010) question about whether postcolonial heritage is defined by the end of foreign influences or by their profusion. Having illustrated the complexity of Cuba's postcolonial condition, I hope the difficulty of providing dichotomous answers, as well as the need to address heritage as a process in order to avoid binary logics, is apparent. Thus, from this perspective, Cuban postcolonial nation-building can be defined as a multilayered process whereby foreign influences were adopted and recombined in various forms according to present needs, in a trajectory of nested degrees of coloniality—political, economic, cultural, and epistemic.

Certainly, as Kapcia (2000:135) argues, there is a constant tension between two conceptions of Cuban national identity throughout the period: one externally oriented, searching for inspiration and legitimacy outside the island, and another internally oriented, seeking the constitutive elements of Cubanness inside the country. However, at a deeper level, even when Cubans tried to search for their identity on the inside, they did so inspired by, and sometimes imitating and imposing, Western categories and criteria.

Understanding heritage as a dynamic process is fundamental to avoiding the reification of heritage categories and any easy yes-no simplification of an otherwise complex and ongoing process of national construction.

This is not to deny the relevance of broader processes and categories in the definition of heritage, such as the gradual adoption of Marxist-Leninist ideology and the centralization of the means of production. Indeed, the question of postcolonialism cannot be disconnected from a subject that has troubled scholars and political commentators for decades, namely, the definition of the differences and similarities between Cuba and other So-cialist countries. Two caveats are in order. First, twentieth-century Social-ist countries were not monolithic and differed among themselves cultur-ally and historically, but all saw the USSR as the revolutionary heartland and imitated it to different extents. Second, the Socialist uses of heri-tage differed only in degree from other political regimes, either liberal or totalitarian, because Socialist regimes not only assumed and imposed Western values of rationality, progress, and science but also developed an alternative process of capital accumulation. Therefore, we need to exam-ine the distinctive features of Socialist countries while respecting their heterogeneity.

The features Cuba shared with other Socialist countries were central Party rule, total control over heritage institutions, a hyperbolic ideolo-gization of society, a rational plan for transforming human subjectivity, and a historical master-narrative. While other regimes could draw upon preestablished religious and cultural traditions, aesthetics and ideologies, the challenge faced by Socialist countries was developing heritage from scratch, given their insistence on breaking with the past and suppressing religion. Henceforth, I present the main tendencies of Socialist heritage production, to demonstrate the distinctiveness of the Cuban case by com-paring it with those of other countries.

First, it is vital to determine the *relevance of heritage* for Socialist coun-tries. In Cuba, almost every political institution—from the PCC and MINFAR to factories, hospitals, and schools—accorded heritage a central role, one that heritage seldom plays in capitalist societies. The importance of heritage in Socialist contexts is confirmed by soviet heritage scholar Baller, who affirms that the "assimilation of the cultural heritage is a nec-essary condition for creating communist culture and a most important constituent of the cultural revolution" (Baller 1984:165). The reason for this significance is the close connection between heritage and history. Be-cause Socialist states and their ruling parties presented themselves as a scientific outcome of inevitable historical processes, the control of history and its materialization via heritage was fundamental to their claims to legitimacy.

Second, the question of *change and continuity* has more heritage implications than in pluralist societies. The Socialist claim to break with the past often resulted in the destruction of sites of memory, city centers, and monuments after the outbreak of revolution. In Cuba, although there were proposals to demolish Old Havana, the destructive urge appears restrained compared to that of countries like Vietnam, Russia, East Germany, and Romania (Giebel 2004; Răuță 2009). In practice, however, Socialist states always struggled to break with the past. In Cuba, a contradiction emerged between the revolutionary commitment to build a new nation and man, on the one hand, and the claim to be recovering authentic national traditions, on the other. Because Socialism judged progress in terms of modern scientific rationality, it struggled to engage with popular heritages, especially with those considered "unscientific" and backward. For instance, Afro-Cuban Santeria could only be incorporated into the national imaginary as folklore.

A more problematic contradiction was that the revolutionary call to abandon tradition was antithetical to the ideological and popular sources of revolutionary impetus: an independent Cuban nation grounded in a tradition of rebellion. This explains the early revolutionary concern for generating a sense of continuity and collective belonging and the endurance of previous heritage ideas. The first consequence stemming from this contradiction was that the initial avant-garde calls to do away with museums, monuments, and bourgeois cultural legacies were restrained by the regime, in a similar fashion to events in the aftermath of the Russian and Chinese Revolutions (Groys 1992).

The second consequence was related to Lenin's theory of the "two national traditions," which affirmed that heritage had to be preserved, reinterpreted, or produced according to whether it was "progressive" or "regressive." As Baller explained, progress meant "the incorporation of the lower (old) into the higher (new)" and "the subordination of the former to the latter" (Baller 1984:15). In Cuba, this conceptualization of heritage entailed a massive process of resignification of previous heritage and an enduring ideological reluctance to restore colonial city centers. The uses of heritage were subordinated to the imperative of progress toward a future Socialist state. This explains the relation between future-oriented ideologies and the establishment of priorities in terms of heritage production: because past heritage was denigrated, the production of new heritage was emphasized.

The third consequence is the *use of heritage to inculcate ideology*. In theory, Socialist countries divided this process into two phases: (1) the redistribution of cultural heritage, and (2) its assimilation and internalization (Baller 1984:177). The redistributive phase focused on spreading heritage to the masses. In this phase, heritage was conceptualized as an external feature to be appropriated by subjects. In the assimilation phase, the new man had to internalize ideology to make him the producer of the new Socialist heritage. The Cuban case can be interpreted in this light, as the early revolution emphasized the redistribution of heritage through the expansion of schools and museums, while the institutionalizing period focused instead on its internalization.

Socialist states subordinated heritage to the inculcation of ideology and explicitly considered it a propaganda tool. Because content (Marxism-Leninism) and form (socialist realism) could not be discussed, heritage became a science concerned with technical procedures. Handbooks of heritage originating in the Eastern Bloc and widely utilized by the Cuban state rationalized heritage as a process of mass production, talking of divisions of labor, methodological recollection, operative chains, or scales of value assessment. The aim was to establish a nationwide heritage network to express ideology using similar aesthetics and sets of objects and subsuming ethnic and cultural differences under a common master-narrative. The most prominent example of this approach was Poland, which created a national museum in each provincial capital (Kaluza 2014). The institutes of history of the various Communist parties provided the narrative content, and institutions like the Soviet Department for Agitation and Propaganda or the Cuban Department of Cultural Heritage monitored the ideological purity of heritage throughout the country (Khazanov 2000:38).

Fourth, the uses of *material culture* changed. Heritage legislation established that any private object could become part of public heritage collections. As shown in Cuban museology handbooks, the collection of objects and their categorization as heritage depended on their capacity to demonstrate or evoke events and theories, rather than on their artistic or scientific value. Objects had to create a sense of authenticity, to "teach lessons" and be "witnesses of history." For that purpose, objects were never left uninterpreted. This explains the proliferation of panels and texts surrounding objects that characterized Socialist museology.

The fifth issue concerned *aesthetics and socialist realism*. Aesthetics was considered a branch of science linked to social engineering. The concept of beauty was rejected and forms were standardized under socialist realist criteria, which posited that ideology had to be equal to its material representation. Socialist realism had to incorporate the progressive contents of the past to represent the objective conditions of historical development and provide a revolutionary vision of the future (Baller 1984:149). Socialist realism was seen as a way of forging Socialist identity and inculcating ideology. In a way, socialist realism is the extreme manifestation of the impossibility of disconnecting history and materiality in official heritage discourse. The Cuban case was distinct from other Socialist countries in the prohibition on representing living leaders and the way that artists openly contested socialist realism. Artistic resistance targeted the heart of the heritage process, as it questioned the relation between history and materiality, content and form, and posited abstract aesthetics as a sign of autonomy and freedom against power.

The sixth distinctive feature is *spatial politics*. Most regimes use space to represent power and ideology, but the distinctiveness of Socialism lies in its belief that old and new infrastructure (e.g., urbanism and buildings) would directly determine the superstructure (e.g., the psychological behavior and identity of the masses). This explains the downplaying of traditional city centers and the creation of new Socialist ones, in which ideology and the institutions of power could be structured in space and proletarian rallies held. Revolutionary Cuba adopted such practices but oriented public space to emphasize the connection between future-oriented urbanism and past nationalistic heroes and themes via heritage, as illustrated by the revolution squares.

In examining the distinctive features of Socialist heritage in comparative perspective, we may also shed light on what makes Cuba exceptional. First, Cuba was part of a group of countries in which strong national traditions and popular support grounded Socialist revolutions and where nationalist and internationalist identities merged strongly. The legitimacy of revolutionary Cuba, China, Vietnam, and Laos rested on the recovery of national sovereignty after colonial occupation, with many nationalists becoming Marxists (Long 2014:204). This differentiates Cuba from Eastern

European countries, which—with the exceptions of Albania and Yugoslavia—became Socialist by external imposition and therefore framed their opposition to Communism as a nationalist project (Schöpflin 1996:153). Consequently, Eastern European countries clearly differentiate Socialist and nationalist heritages and deploy belligerent attitudes toward any remnants of Socialism.

Second, but related to this, is a problem Cuba shares with most Asian and European post-Socialist states: the difficulty of extricating Socialist heritage ideas and symbols from the nation-state at various levels (Light 2000b; Myhrberg 2012). Drawing on the case of Slovakia, Shari Cohen (1999) argues that these problems have resulted from the historical amnesia produced by Socialist ideology. However, Cuba differs slightly from this pattern because of the relative autonomy and deep-seated nationalist outlook of its leadership. Similarly, Cuba did not follow the pattern of post-USSR states where the Communist Party fell, precipitating the frantic destruction of Socialist monuments, the construction of nationalist ones, the musealization of the Socialist past, and the increasing popular nostalgia for Socialist material culture. These tendencies have clearly emerged in countries that have developed critical discourses about Socialism, such as Germany, Hungary, Poland, and the Czech Republic (Light 2000a). However, countries like Russia and Romania have a more ambivalent relationship with Socialism, and elements of Socialist heritage management endure (Bădică 2014; Khazanov 2000).

Third, Cuba also differs from countries in which the Communist Party still holds power. While the North Korean case prevents any easy comparison (Kwon and Chung 2012), China, Laos, and Vietnam are characterized by the difficulty of harmonizing official heritage discourse with the expansion of capitalist values and the commoditization of the Socialist past (Denton 2005). Although the tendency to transform ideology into heritage after 1990 points in that direction, this process has unfolded in Cuba to a much lesser extent, in part because Cuba until recently has maintained a planned economy. Similarly, despite post-1990 Cuba sharing with China the shift toward cultural identity, tradition, and heritage, it has not actively promoted Red Tourism or the commoditization of the Socialist past as China has (Long 2012).

Finally, regarding the kind of heritage celebrated by each country, Cuba differs from most post-Socialist Asian and African countries that actively engage with the Socialist past and emphasize the precolonial past. The priority accorded to precolonial pasts tends to be greater in countries that can establish connections with great ancient civilizations, such as China, Cambodia, and Ethiopia (Donham 1999; Varutti 2014). Cambodia presents some similarities with Cuba in that it has commoditized its classic heritage in Angkor—as Cuba has done with its colonial heritage. Like Cuba, Cambodia has not heritagized or critically engaged with its Socialist past, partly because the shadows of the Khmer Rouges still linger long in the country (Winter 2008). This may be a sign either that the Socialist past is not really over or that it is at least still too close to be recognized as something that requires ideological management from a new perspective.

Cuba also contrasts sharply with post-Socialist Ethiopia, where national identity is based on a narrative denying that colonization ever took place in the country (Donham 1999). Other African postcolonies, such as Namibia, Tanzania, Zimbabwe, Mali, and South Africa, use ethnic heritages to cement national identity but also commoditize them and encourage ethnic groups to do so (Arnoldi 2006; Fairweather 2006; Meskell 2012). Cuba differs from this pattern, because Cuban national identity is not based on the celebration of ethnic difference and heritage. Rather, the incorporation of difference into official heritage representations in Cuba is a state-led process that promotes commoditization but discourages participation, the supposed emphasis on difference being in the end self-referential.

These unique characteristics evince the complexity of Cuba, which can be interpreted as a postcolonial nation-building Socialist process that is difficult to locate within any broader paradigm, either Latin American, post-Socialist, or postcolonial. The uniqueness of Cuba also makes it difficult to predict its future avenues, as the country enters yet another period in its complex postcolonial trajectory. The future political challenge for the regime is to move toward an open and democratic society with a free market while preserving a single party structure. From a heritage perspective, the central terrains of dispute will be Old Havana and the fate of the OHCH, which will have important consequences for national cultural politics and for other Cuban heritage cities.

Nearly 55 percent of tourists arriving to Cuba visit Havana, and 90 percent of them go through Old Havana, which makes the OHCH a highly lucrative institution. After August 2016, however, corruption scandals affecting the institution led to the dismantling of OHCH for-profit enter-prises. The Grupo de Administración Empresarial (Business Management Group), a consortium under control of the army and trusted by Raúl, took over OHCH building and real estate companies, hotels, and restaurants. The powers of the OHCH have been restricted to the management of mu-seums, restorations, and cultural promotion. The official rhetoric behind these changes is the need of a more pragmatic management of businesses in Old Havana by specialized companies. The fate of Old Havana can give us clues about the future avenues of the revolution and its heritage pro-duction structure. Many in Old Havana wonder whether the military will be capable of continuing the mission accomplished by the OHCH, and whether they will consider the well-being of locals or focus instead on profit-making via tourism. Will the army centralize heritage production and suppress the multivocality involved in the narrative of cultural na-tionalism deployed by the OHCH? Does the takeover by the army imply the return of a national-revolutionary narrative of hostility and antago-nism in Old Havana, or is it a pragmatic adaptation to globalization and to the demands and expectations of Western tourists about an exotic Carib-bean island?

Be that as it may, Cuba hereafter will be beset by the following complex conundrum: if the country denies the revolutionary past to move on and to forget the causes and the society that provoked the Revolution, then it might reproduce the revolutionary conflict. However, if Cubans deal with the heritage of the Revolution, they will most likely cling to partisan views and be conditioned by their past involvement with the system. Without doubt, heritage will be a terrain of dissonance for Cubans, both on the island and abroad, in the years to come.

APPENDIX

Primary Sources

Owing to the restricted access and heterogeneous nature of many Cuban archives, I have included this appendix to clarify the written sources of my research. This list includes the main archives I consulted and from which I retrieved most of my documentation. Archival research is fundamental in many ways, because it provides new documentation produced by the state apparatus and thereby offers insight into the state's internal functioning and power relations. The degree of indexation in Cuban archives varies, and part of an archive's documentation is usually not indexed or (intentionally or unintentionally) concealed. Thus, access depends on the degree of trust built with the archivist and the level of local institutional support. This state of affairs does not apply to the National Archive or most OHCH archives, but it does apply to most of the others. When archives lacked any indexation, my strategy was to go through all the documentation and to decide on the spot whether the data were relevant for the understanding of heritage processes. In addition, different archives cover different temporal eras, and therefore I had to adapt my research to the nature of each. Another characteristic of Cuban official documentation is its lack of standardization, which makes comparative quantitative approaches futile. Despite state attempts at institutional homogenization, most documents, such as inventories, catalogues, or museum collections, vary in form from province to province. Unfortunately, after the 1990s, the huge economic crisis put an end to most archival, publishing, and indexing activities in Cuba. The main archives I consulted are:

National Museum Archive
Museum of the Revolution Archive
City Archive of Havana, managed by the OHCH

Photography, Architecture and Library and Master Plan archives of the OHCH

Manuscripts and Archives, Yale University Library

National Archive

National Institute of History (IH)

Villena Municipal Library of Havana

Faculty of Linguistics

National Union of Architects and Engineers (UNAICC)

Library of the University of Havana

Félix Varela Pedagogic Library

José Martí National Library

National Center of Restoration and Museology (CENCREM)

Superior Institute of the Arts (ISA)

UNESCO information center

Office of Historic Affairs of the Council of State Archive (Consejo de Estado)

Advisory Council for the Development of Monuments Archive (CODEMA)

Central Archive of the Ministry of Culture (MINCULT)

Ministry of Construction Archive (MICONS) managed by the OHCH

National Center of Cultural Heritage Archive (CNPC)

National Commission of Monuments

Archives of various provincial and municipal museums throughout the country

Personal archives:

José Linares (ICOM)

María Mercedes García Santana (CENCREM, UNESCO chair)

Nérido Pérez Terry (ISA)

Héctor Montenegro (ISA-National School of Museology)

Lelis Marrero (Museo de la Música).

List of Interviewees

Name	Position	Date and Place
Ayleen Robaina Barcia	Department of Architecture, OHCH	February 5, 2012
HRCDH Working Group Meeting		February 9, 2012
HRCDH Working Group Meeting		February 15, 2012
Horacio Díaz Pendás	National advisor in history of the Ministry of Education	February 15, 2012
Yainet Rodríguez Rodríguez	Cultural promotion adviser, Factoría Habana; adviser of the HRCDH	February 16, 2012 and March 16, 2013
Meeting with school-children in Fontanar	Organized by the Provincial Directorship of Cultural Heritage of Havana	February 17, 2012
Meeting with local associations at the municipal museum, Santiago de las Vegas	Organized by the Provincial Directorship of Cultural Heritage of Havana	February 17, 2012
Ana Cristina Pereira Escalona	Vice-president and director of the Museums Section, CNPC	February 19, 2012, and March 20, 2013
Ivalú Rodríguez Gil	OHCH museologist, Archaeology Office	February 24, 2012
Meeting with three members of the HRCDH		February 25, 2012
Pablo Riaño San Marful	Director of the Architecture Archive and Library; historian	March 8, 2013
Hilda María Alonso González	Institute of History, Provincial Directorship of Cultural Heritage of Havana	March 8, 2013
Jorge Moscoso Chirino	Ex-director of the Provincial Directorship of Cultural Heritage of Havana; Fondo Cubano de Bienes Culturales	March 9, 2013
María Elena Roche López	Director, Museum-House of Vedado, OHCH	March 10, 2013
Laura García Méndez	Museologist and librarian, OHCH, in charge of the Room of the Book in the HRCDH	March 11, 2013

Name	Position	Date and Place
Jorge Luis Batista Echeverría	Computing, OHCH; director of the PANGEA project	March 11, 2013
Rosalía Oliva Suárez	Historian, OHCH	March 12, 2013
Alberto Granado Duque	Director of the House of Africa, OHCH	March 12, 2013
Lourdes Millet Ramos	Director of the Museum of Guanabacoa	March 12, 2013
Mercedes García Santana	UNESCO Chair in Havana, ex-director of CENCREM	March 13, 2013
Osmany Ibarra Ortiz	Museologist, National Museum of Music	March 14, 2013
Pablo Fornet Gil	Master Plan, OHCH	March 14, 2013
Antonio Quevedo Herrero	Museologist, OHCH; in charge of the Warehouse Room in the HRCDH	March 14, 2013 and March 20, 2013
Grisel Terrón Quintero	Director of libraries and archives, OHCH; in charge of the room of the Book in the HRCDH	March 18, 2013
HRCDH Working Group Meeting		March 18, 2013
Begoña Guzmán	Adviser, UNESCO Cuba	March 19, 2013
Víctor Marín Crespo	Director, UNESCO Cuba	
José R. Linares Ferrera	President of ICOM Cuba; architect and museum designer	March 20, 2013 and April 30, 2013
Onedys Calvo Noya	Director of Factoria Havana; general coordinator of the HRCDH	March 21, 2013
Rosa María González López	Museologist and historian, OHCH, scientific adviser in the HRCDH	March 21, 2013
Amaury Mejías Torres	Director of the Complex of Historic Military Museums	March 24, 2013
Sergio González García	Director of the Numismatic Museum, OHCH	March 26, 2013
Rigoberto Menéndez Paredes	Director of the House of the Arabs, OHCH	March 26, 2013
Margarita Suárez García	Director of Cultural Heritage, OHCH	March 26, 2013

Name	Position	Date and Place
José Andrés Pérez Quintana	Director, Museum of the Revolution	March 27, 2013 and May 2, 2013
Zoraida González Albelo	Political adviser, Museum of the Revolution	March 27, 2013
Teresa Crego Fuentes	Professor of museology and art, University of Havana	March 27, 2013
Mónica Rojas Vidaurreta	International Relations, OHCH	March 28, 2013
Raquel Carreras Rivery	Cultural Heritage Preservationist	March 29, 2013
Norma Pérez Trujillo	Main investor of the HRCDH, OHCH.	April 1, 2013
Sadys Sánchez Aguilar	Director of the Napoleonic Museum	April 1, 2013
Severino Armando Rodríguez Valdés	Director of museums, OHCH	April 1, 2013
Ana Celia Pérez	Director of the Firemen Museum; ex-director of the Square of the Revolution of Guantánamo	April 2, 2013
Lelis Marrero Oliva	Museologist, National Museum of Music, in charge of the creation of the municipal museums of Havana Province	April 2, 2013
Celia Oliva Martínez	Museologist, CNPC	April 2, 2013
Nérido Pérez Terry	Professor of museology, ISA, ex-CENCREM	April 3, 2013
Liset Falero Luna	Museologist, Poey Museum	April 3, 2013
Luis Álvarez-Lajouchere	Collection curator, Poey Museum	April 3, 2013
Alejandro G. Alonso	Director of the Pottery Museum	April 4, 2013
Patricia Rodríguez Aloma	Director, Master Plan, OHCH	April 4, 2013
Juan Páez Costa	Museologist, Provincial Directorship of Cultural Heritage of Havana	April 5, 2013
Marcos Tamames Henderson	Director of the Provincial Museum of Camagüey	April 10, 2013

Name	Position	Date and Place
Fernando Crespo Baró	Historian, Historian Office of Camagüey; ex-director of the Square of the Revolution of Camagüey	April 10, 2013
Edelsi Muñagorri Salabarría	Museologist, Provincial Museum of Las Tunas	April 11, 2013
Hiran Pérez Concepción	Director of the Provincial Commission of Monuments, Holguín	April 11, 2013
David Gómez Iglesias	Museologist, Provincial Museum of Holguín	April 11, 2013
Olga Portuondo Zúñiga	Museologist, Provincial Museum of Holguín	April 11, 2013
Roberto Valcarce Rojas	Archaeologist, Holguín Province	April 12, 2013
María De Jesus Lojo Mancebo	Museologist, birthplace of Calixto García, Holguín	April 12, 2013
María Marta Rojas Álvarez and Nancy Tauler	Museologist and director of the Municipal Museum of Gibara	April 12, 2013
Laura Lina Andrés Castellanos	Museum of Natural Sciences of Gibara	April 13, 2013
Maibis Riquenes Guerra	Museologist, House-Museum Frank País, Santiago	April 15, 2013
Meiser Martín Martínez	Director, House-Museum Frank País, Santiago	April 15, 2013
Diana María Cruz Hernández	Professor of art history, University of Oriente, Santiago	April 16, 2013
Lidia Sánchez Fujishiro	Historian, Oficina del Conservador, Santiago	April 17, 2013
Yadira Parra Donet	Historian, Santiago	April 17, 2013
Isabel Rigol Savio	Professor of architecture at various universities; ex-director of CENCREM,	April 20, 2013
Margarita Ruiz Brandi	Ex-president of CNPC; ex–executive secretary of CODEMA	April 23, 2013
Marie Agou	European Union representative in Cuba	April 23, 2013

Name	Position	Date and Place
Lisette Roura Álvarez	Archaeologist, OHCH	April 25, 2013
Yessi Montes De Oca	Museologist, House of Asia, OHCH	April 25, 2013
Rubier Bernabéu García	Ph.D. candidate, Urbanism and Architecture, CUJAE	April 26, 2013
Tomas Vicente Lara Franquis	Sculptor; president of CODEMA	April 29, 2013
Israel Díaz Mantilla	Director of the House-Museum Lezama Lima	April 30, 2013
Enrique Hernández Castillo	Museologist and architect	May 5, 2013
Clara Fernández Rodríguez	Master Plan, OHCH	May 5, 2013
Rene Gutiérrez Maidata	Architecture Department, OHCH, Ex-technical chief of cultural heritage of Havana Province	May 6, 2013
Jorge Garcell Domínguez	Archaeologist and researcher, CNPC	May 6, 2013
María de los Ángeles Pereira	Professor of art history, University of Havana	May 7, 2013
Felicia Chateloin Santiesteban	Professor Architecture and Urbanism, CUJAE	May 8, 2013
Daniel Taboada Espiniella	Architect, director of the Vernacular Architecture section at the OHCH. Ex-CENCREM, Council of Culture and MICONS	May 9, 2013
Rebeca López Rodríguez	Ex-director of the Armoury Museum; Lenin Room and Firemen Museums	May 9, 2013
Zoe Nocedo Primo	OHCH, director of the Museum of Tobacco	May 9, 2013
Luz Merino Acosta	Vice-president of the National Museum	May 10, 2013
Concepción Otero	Professor of urbanism, University of Havana	May 13, 2013

Name	Position	Date and Place
Mario Coyula Cowley	Architect; director of Urban Planning of Havana; specialist in monumental design	May 15, 2013
Gladys Collazo Usallán	President of the CNPC	May 16, 2013
Moraima Clavijo Colom	President of the National Museum	May 16, 2013
José Antonio Choy López	Architect; designer of the Square of the Revolution in Santiago	May 17, 2013
Augusto Rivero Mas	CODEMA founder; professor of architecture and urbanism at various universities; specialist in monumental design	May 21, 2013
HRCDH Working Group Meeting		May 21, 2013
Yoel Cordoví Núñez	Historian and researcher at the National Institute of History	May 23, 2013
Otto Randín González	Executive secretary of the National Commission of Monuments	May 23, 2013
Sonia Menéndez Castro	OHCH archaeologist	May 23, 2013
Rafael Fernández Moya	Habaguanex historian	May 24, 2013
Velino Couceiro Rodríguez	Cultural specialist and museologist of the municipality of Plaza de la Revolución, Havana	May 28, 2013
Roberto Gottardi	Architect	May 28, 2013
Magda Resik Aguirre	OHCH radio, historian	May 31, 2013
Sergio González Cías	OHCH directorship	May 31, 2013
Héctor Montenegro Martínez, online interview	Ex-director of the School of Museology, now in Miami	June 18, 2013

REFERENCES

"Agresión"
1960   Agresión de los comunistas a estudiantes católicos cuando se disponían
            a honrar a Martí. *Diario de la Marina*:6.
"Alejandro Rodríguez"
1917   Presentación del monumento a Alejandro Rodríguez y Velasco en
            Roma. *Bohemia*.
"Bienvenida"
1960   Cordial bienvenida a Anastas Mikoyan. *Revolución*:1, 15.
"Editorial Archivos"
1924   Esta revista Cubana. *Archivos del Folklore Cubano* 1(1):4–8.
"Editorial Arquitectura"
1958   El coloso de Cuba. La nueva estatua del apóstol de nuestra independen-
            cia José Martí. *Arquitectura* 26(303):445–449.
"Exposición"
1960   Nace una exposición. *Lunes de Revolución*:4–9.
"Habana Vieja"
1955   Los propietarios y la rehabilitación de la Habana Vieja. *Revista de la
            propiedad urbana* 252:7.
"Mártires"
1960   Monumento a los mártires de la Revolución. *Carteles* 41(12).
"Monument in Cuba"
1926   Monument in Cuba to 71st Regiment Dead Is Unveiled on San Juan Hill
            by Mrs. O'Brien. *New York Times*.
"Monumento a Cristobal Colón"
1916   Cárdenas: Monumento a Cristobal Colón, patriota Tomás Estrada Pal-
            ma y museo de Cárdenas Oscar María de Rojas. *Bohemia*:3.
"Monumento a Máximo Gómez"
1919   El monumento a Máximo Gómez. *ABC*:12.
"Monuments in Cuba"
1906   Dedicating Monuments in Cuba to Our Heroes. *New York Tribune*.
"Plaza Cívica"
1951   Remodelación de la Plaza Cívica José Martí. *Revista de la propiedad ur-
            bana* 206:14.
"Pregunta"
1899   ¿Qué estatua debe ser colocada en nuestro Parque Central? *El Figaro*.

"Rodríguez Morey"

1920   El ilustre pintor D. Antonio Rodríguez Morey, director del Museo de la
            Habana, que ha regresado a su país, habiendo estrechado las relaciones
            de orden artístico entre Cuba y España. *Nuevo Mundo*:26.

"Tribuna Anti-imperialista"

2000   Tribuna Anti-imperialista José Martí. *Obras. La revista cubana de la con-
            strucción* 4(1):25–28.

Abreu Arcia, Alberto

2007   *Los juegos de la escritura, o, La (re)escritura de la historia.* Casa de las
            Américas, La Habana.

Agamben, Giorgio

1999   *Potentialities: Collected Essays in Philosophy.* Stanford University Press,
            Stanford.

Aguirre, Mirta

1963   Apuntes sobre la literatura y el arte. *Cuba socialista* 3(26):62–82.

Agulhon, Maurice

1978   La "statuomanie" et l'histoire. *Ethnologie française* 3–4:145–172.

Almeida Bosque, Juan

1983   *Letter from Juan Almeida Bosque to Rita Longa.* CODEMA Archive, La
            Habana.

Alonso, Ana María

1988   The Effects of Truth: Re-presentations of the Past and the Imagining of
            Community. *Journal of Historical Sociology* 1(1):33–57.

1994   The Politics of Space, Time and Substance: State Formation, National-
            ism and Ethnicity. *Annual Review of Anthropology* 23(3):379–405.

Alonso González, Hilda María

2012   El museo nacional en la política cultural del estado cubano, 1940–1961.
            Maestría, Historia, Universidad de La Habana.

Anderson, Benedict

2006   *Imagined Communities: Reflections on the Origin and Spread of National-
            ism.* Verso, New York.

Anoschenko, Irina. A.

1977   Soviet Museums: Results and Prospects. In *Museums in the USSR*, ed-
            ited by F. G. e. Krotov, pp. 48–63. Central Museum of the Revolution,
            Moscow.

Antuña, Vicentina

2013 [1959] Letter from Vicentina Antuña to E.R. de Leuchsenring. In *Epistolario
            III*, edited by E. R. de Leuchsenring, pp. 515. Boloña, La Habana.

Appadurai, Arjun

1996   *Modernity at Large: Cultural Dimensions of Globalization.* University of
            Minnesota Press, Minneapolis.

Appadurai, Arjun, and Carol Breckenridge

1992   Museums Are Good to Think: Heritage on View in India. In *Museums
            and Communities: The Politics of Public Culture*, edited by I. Karp, C. Mul-

len Kreamer, and S. Lavine, pp. 34–55. Smithsonian Institution, Washington.

Arenas, Reinaldo
1992   *Antes que anochezca: Autobiografía*. Tusquets, Barcelona.

Arjona Pérez, Marta
1984   *Los Museos en Cuba*. Ministero de Cultura, La Habana.
February 2, 1990   Del patrimonio: Proteger la belleza; Como se preservan los testimonies pasados y recientes de nuestra historia y cultura. *Bohemia*:86–87.
1981   Museos ¿Solo para matar el aburrimiento? In *Material de Estudio No. 1 Animación Cultural*. Instituto Politécnico de Museología, La Habana.
2003   *Recuento*. Consejo Nacional de Patrimonio Cultural, La Habana.
2004 [1986] *Patrimonio cultural e identidad*. Letras Cubanas, La Habana.

Arnoldi, Mary Jo
2006   Youth Festivals and Museums: The Cultural Politics of Public Memory in Postcolonial Mali. *Africa Today* 52(4):55–76.

Arroyo de Hernández, Anita
1947   Museo, museo, museo. *Carteles* 28(21).

Avila Mariño, Elio, and Mirta Rodriguez Peña
Ca. 1985   *La vinculación del programa de historia de cuarto grado con las visitas al Museo de la Comunidad. Museo Municipal 'Jesús Suárez Gayol,' Manatí.* CNPC Archive, La Habana.

Ayorinde, Christine
2004   *Afro-Cuban Religiosity, Revolution, and National Identity*. University Press of Florida, Gainesville.

Bădică, Simina
2014   Same Exhibitions, Different Labels? Romanian National Museums and the Fall of Communism. In *National Museums: New Studies from Around the World*, edited by S. J. Knell, pp. 272–289. Routledge, London.

Baker, Janice
2010   Affect and Desire: Museums and the Cinematic. Ph.D., Curtin University of Technology.

Baller, Êleazar Aleksandrovich
1966   *Socialism and the Cultural Heritage*. Novosti Press, Moscow.
1984   *Communism and Cultural Heritage*. Progress, Moscow.

Baroni, Aldo
1944   *Cuba, país de poca memoria*. Botas, México.

Baudrillard, Jean
1981   *For a Critique of the Political Economy of the Sign*. Telos Press, St. Louis.

Bay Sevilla, Luis
1937   Como se maltrata la plaza de la Catedral. *Arquitectura* 5(50):34.
1940   La Segunda etapa del concurso para el monumento a Martí. *Arquitectura* 8(78):21–34.
1941   Las necesidades del museo nacional. *Arquitectura* 9(90):19–22.

Bazán de Huerta, Moisés

1994   *La escultura monumental en la Habana*. Universidad de Extremadura, Cáceres.

Benet León, María Dolores, María Josefa Boan Rubiera, Floirán De Dios Lorente and David Soler Marchán

1989   *La Museoterapia. Museo Provincial, Cienfuegos*. CNPC Archive, La Habana.

Bennett, Tony

1995   *The Birth of the Museum: History, Theory, Politics*. Routledge, London.

Bens Arrarte, José María

1935   Arq. Colonial: La necesidad de la ley que salvaguarde los monumentos históricos. *Arquitectura* 3(29):7–19.

Bernbeck, Reinhard

2013   Heritage Void and the Void as Heritage. *Archaeologies* 9(3):526–545.

Bhabha, Homi K.

2004   *The Location of Culture*. Routledge, London.

Bobadilla, Emilio

1910   Sobre el museo histórico de La Habana. *La Discusión*:2.

Bofill, José

1900   *Memorias del Museo-Biblioteca de Santiago de Cuba*. Museo Emilio Bacardí Archive, Santiago de Cuba.

Bogart, Michele Helene

1989   *Public Sculpture and the Civic Ideal in New York City, 1890–1930*. University of Chicago Press, Chicago.

Bowlt, John E.

1978   Russian Sculpture and Lenin's Plan of Monumental Propaganda. In *Art and Architecture in the Service of Politics*, edited by H. A. Miller and L. Nochlin, pp. 182–193. MIT Press, Cambridge.

Boytel, Fernando

Ca. 1945   *Informe de Fernando Boytel sobre el Museo Bacardí*. Museo Emilio Bacardí Archive, Santiago de Cuba.

Bronfman, Alejandra

2005   *Measures of Equality: Social Science, Citizenship, and Race in Cuba, 1902–1940*. University of North Carolina Press, Chapel Hill.

Byrne, Denis, and Michael Herzfeld

2011   Archaeological Heritage and Cultural Intimacy: An Interview with Michael Herzfeld. *Journal of Social Archaeology* 11(2):144–157.

Cabrera Infante, Guillermo

2013   *Mapa dibujado por un espía*. Galaxia Gutenberg, Círculo de Lectores, Barcelona.

Camnitzer, Luis

1994   *New Art of Cuba*. University of Texas Press, Austin.

Cano, Miguel Ángel

1918   *La enseñanza de la historia en la escuela primaria.* Escuelas Profesionales Don Bosco, Santiago de Cuba.

Capablanca, José Raúl, and Jorge Daubar

1983   *Ultimas lecciones de Capablanca.* Oriente, Santiago.

Caravia, Enrique

1951   El Museo Nacional. *Arquitectura* 19(214):230–233.

Carbonell, Walterio

2005 [1961]   *Cómo surgió la cultura nacional.* Ediciones Bachiller, Biblioteca Nacional José Martí, La Habana.

Carpentier, Alejo

1993 [1957]   Un nuevo museo americano. In *Letra y solfa; Artes Visuales*, edited by A. Carpentier and A. Cánovas Pérez, pp. 213–214. Letras Cubanas, La Habana.

Castro, Fidel

1961a   *Comisión Nacional del Monumento a los caídos en Playa Girón,* La Habana.

1961b   *Discurso pronunciado por el comandante Fidel Castro Ruz, Primer Ministro del Gobierno Revolucionario de Cuba, resumiendo los actos del Día Internacional del Trabajo el 1 de Mayo.* Gobierno de Cuba, Plaza Cívica, La Habana.

1961c   *Palabras a los intelectuales.* Consejo Nacional de Cultura, La Habana.

1968   *Discurso conmemorativo de los Cien Años de Lucha, 10 de octubre de1968.* Departamento de Orientación Revolucionaria del CCPCC, La Habana.

1987   *Fidel Castro: Ideología, conciencia y trabajo político, 1959–1986.* Editora Política, La Habana.

Castro, Raúl

1966   *Directiva 035. Crear la sección de historia en la Dirección Política de las FAR.* Fuerzas Armadas Revolucionarias, Cuba.

Causse, Cos

1991   *Plaza de la Revolución Mayor General Antonio Maceo: La ciudad, el héroe, la plaza.* Oriente, Santiago de Cuba.

Cayuela Fernández, José Gregorio

2011   Cuba y la "república de elites": Las nuevas capas altas isleñas y el poder (1913–1921). *Historia Contemporánea* 40:187–216.

Century, Paul Reed

1991   Principles of Pitch Organization in Leo Brouwer's Atonal Music for Guitar. Ph.D., University of California.

CNPC

2001   *Museum Script "Museo de la lucha antiimperialista."* CNPC Archive, La Habana.

2003   *Museum Script "Museo Guerra Hispano-Cubano-Americana."* CNPC Archive, La Habana.

2008   *Recategorization Record "Museo 29 de Abril" in San Luis.* CNPC Archive, La Habana.

2009a   *Recategorization Record "Museo de la Clandestinidad Hermanas Giral" in Cienfuegos*. CNPC Archive, La Habana.

2009b   *Recategorization Record "Museo Histórico 26 de Julio."* CNPC Archive, La Habana.

2012a   *Museum Script "Museo Municipal de Banes."* CNPC Archive, La Habana.

2012b   *Recategorization Record "Museo Histórico de Manzanillo."* CNPC Archive, La Habana.

2012c   *Recategorization Record "Museo Municipal de Pilón."* CNPC Archive, La Habana.

Ca. 1980   *Preliminary Draft of the Museum Script "Museo del Hombre."* Academia de Ciencias; Dirección Nacional de Museos y Monumentos, CNPC Archive, La Habana.

Ca. 1985   *Museum Script "Museo Municipal de Caimito."* CNPC Archive, La Habana.

Ca. 2010   *Recategorization Record "Museo de la Primera Comandancia del Segundo Frente Frank País" in Aguacate*. CNPC Archive, La Habana.

Ca. 2012   *Recategorization Record "Museo Abel Santamaría Cuadrado."* CNPC Archive, La Habana.

CODEMA

1975   *Competition for the Construction of a Series of Memorials in the Sierra Maestra*. CODEMA Archive, La Habana.

1981   *General Guidelines*. CODEMA Archive, La Habana.

1984a   *Competition Monument "Celia Sánchez Manduley" in Manzanillo*. CODEMA Archive, La Habana.

1984b   *Competition Plaza de la Revolución "Mariana Grajales" in Guantánamo*. CODEMA Archive, La Habana.

1984c   *Report #13 Concerning the Monument to Che: Conclusions*. CODEMA Archive, La Habana.

1985   *CODEMA Regulation*. CODEMA, La Habana.

1986   *Report #10 Concerning the Monument to the Granma Landing*. CODEMA Archive, La Habana.

1988   *Competition Plaza de la Revolución "Ignacio Agramonte" in Camagüey*. CODEMA Archive, La Habana.

1990a   *Competition Plaza de la Revolución "Juan Gualberto Gómez" in Matanzas*. CODEMA Archive, La Habana.

1990b   *Competition Plaza de la Revolución "Vicente García" in Las Tunas*. CODEMA Archive, La Habana.

1991   *Project "Complejo monumentario por la dignidad del pueblo cubano."* CODEMA Archive, La Habana.

1998   *Competition "Memorial a las víctimas de la reconcentración."* CODEMA Archive, La Habana.

2001   *Competition "Conjunto monumentario en homenaje a los ejércitos libertador y rebelde."* CODEMA Archive, La Habana.

Cohen, Shari J.
1999   Politics Without a Past: The Absence of History in Postcommunist National-
           ism. Duke University Press, Durham, N.C.

Connerton, Paul
1989   How Societies Remember. Cambridge University Press, Cambridge, UK.
2009   How Modernity Forgets. Cambridge University Press, Cambridge, UK.

Consejo de Estado
1979   Preliminary Script "Museo Histórico de Manzanillo." Oficina de Asuntos
           Históricos del Consejo de Estado, La Habana.

Cordoví Núñez, Yoel
2012   Magisterio y nacionalismo en las escuelas públicas de Cuba (1899–1920).
           Ciencias Sociales, La Habana.

Cortina, José
1953   Plaza de la república: Misión espiritual del monumento a Martí. Arqui-
           tectura 21(241):331–333.

Coyula Cowley, Mario
1963   Un monumento para los contemporáneos. Arquitectura Cuba 30(335):
           13–15.
1983   Letter from Mario Coyula Cowley to Rita Longa. CODEMA Archive, La
           Habana.
1984   Por una noción más amplia del monumento. Arquitectura y Urbanismo
           2(84):8–14.
2007   ¿Para qué sirve un monumento? Artecubano 1(1):24–28.

Crego Fuentes, Teresa
1973   Panorama histórico y organización de los museos. Instituto Cubano del
           Libro, Pueblo y Educación, La Habana.

Chakrabarty, Dipesh
2009   Provincializing Europe: Postcolonial Thought and Historical Difference.
           Princeton University Press, Princeton.

Chateloin, Felicia
2008   El patrimonio cultural urbano y el criterio de centro histórico: El caso
           de estudio: Ciudad de La Habana. Ph.D., Politécnico José Echeverría.

Chávez, Lydia Chakarova Mimi
2005   Capitalism, God, and a Good Cigar: Cuba Enters the Twenty-First Century.
           Duke University Press, Durham, N.C.

Chroniqueur
1913   Inauguración del Museo Nacional. El Fígaro:210.

De la Hoz, Pedro
2000   Para que el hombre y la mujer crezcan por dentro: Actualidad y perspec-
           tiva del trabajo sociocultural comunitario. Granma:6.

de la Osa, Enrique
1949   En Cuba. Bohemia:Sección "En Cuba."

de Leuchenring, Emilio Roig

1925   ¿Se está Cuba africanizando? *Carteles* 10(48):18, 27.

1939a   En 1899 sólo 16 cubanos representativos comprendían y admiraban a Martí. *Carteles* 33(5):38.

1939b   ¿Qué estatua pensaron los cubanos de 1899 que debía ser colocada en el Parque Central? *Carteles* 33(4):38–39.

1941   Necesidad de una ley de protección de monumentos y lugares históricos. *Carteles* 22(4):46.

1942a   Aventuras y peripecias de las estatuas de Isabel II que existieron en el Parque Central. *Arquitectura* 10(108):256–258, 273.

1942b   Función social de archivos, bibliotecas y museos. *Carteles* 23(48):50–51.

1943a   Remedios: La ciudad acogedora. *Carteles* 23(23):38.

1943b   Remedios: La ciudad bien amada por sus hijos. *Carteles* 23(22):38.

1945   La ciudad de Bayamo: Monumento nacional. *Carteles* 26(15):38–39.

1955a   La más justa concepción artística de Martí. In *Veinte años de actividades del Historiador de la Ciudad de La Habana: Emilio Roig de Leuchsenring, 1935–1955*, Vol. IV, pp. 34–38. OHCH, La Habana.

1955b   Por la supresión de las cenas martianas. In *Veinte años de actividades del Historiador de la Ciudad de La Habana: Emilio Roig de Leuchsenring, 1935–1955*, Vol. IV, pp. 220–227. OHCH, La Habana.

1955c   *Veinte años de actividades del Historiador de la Ciudad de La Habana: Emilio Roig de Leuchsenring, 1935–1955. Vol. III*. OHCH, La Habana.

2013 [1942]   Letter from E. R. de Leuchsenring to E. Varela, subsecretary of Public Construction. In *Epistolario III*, edited by Emilio Roig de Leuchsenring, pp. 332. Boloña, La Habana.

2013 [1961]   Letter from E. R. de Leuchsenring to Armando Hart Dávalos. In *Epistolario III*, edited by Emilio Roig de Leuchsenring. Boloña, La Habana.

2013 [1941]   Letter from E. R. de Leuchsenring to President Batista y Zaldívar. In *Epistolario III*, edited by E. R. de Leuchsenring, pp. 308. Boloña, La Habana.

2013 [1944]   Letter from E. R. de Leuchsenring to Luis Pérez Espinós, Minister of Education. In *Epistolario III*, edited by E. R. de Leuchsenring, pp. 397. Boloña, La Habana.

2013 [1945]   Letter from E. R. de Leuchsenring to Luis Rodríguez Rivero. In *Epistolario III*, edited by E. R. de Leuchsenring, pp. 435. Boloña, La Habana.

2013 [1959]   Letter from E. R. de Leuchsenring to Fidel Castro. In *Epistolario III*, edited by E. R. de Leuchsenring, pp. 513–514. Boloña, La Habana.

de Leuchsenring, Emilio Roig, and Daniel Sierra Boudet

1959   *Letters between de Leuchsenring and Daniel Sierra Boudet*. MINCULT Central Archive. Old Section of Education, La Habana.

de Quesada, Gonzalo, and Luis Bay Sevilla

1943   Dos informes sobre el monumento a Martí. *Arquitectura* 11(123): 395–401.

DeHaan, Heather D.
2013   *Stalinist City Planning: Professionals, Performance, and Power*. University of Toronto Press, Toronto.

del Castañal, Héctor
1913   Monumento a las víctimas del Maine proyecto y realidad. *Bohemia*:10.

Denton, Kirk A.
2005   Museums, Memorial Sites and Exhibitionary Culture in the People's Republic of China. *China Quarterly* 183:565–586.

Derrida, Jacques
1976   *Of Grammatology*. Johns Hopkins University Press, Baltimore.

Díaz Peláez, José Antonio
1979   Actividades escultóricas de nuestro proceso actual. *Revista de la Biblioteca Nacional José Martí* 21(2):133–138.

Díaz Pendás, Horacio
1990   *Aprendiendo Historia en el Museo: Material de Estudio correspondiente al Curso de Metodología de la Enseñanza de la Historia en los Institutos Superiores Pedagógicos*. Pueblo y Educación, La Habana.
2008   *El museo en la enseñanza de la Historia*. Pueblo y Educación, La Habana.
2010   *Apuntes martianos para las clases de Historia de Cuba y otras ideas*. Pueblo y Educación, La Habana.

Dihigo, Juan M.
1937   *Elogio del Dr. Mario García Kohly (fundador de esta corporación): Leído por el Dr. Juan M. Dihigo y Mestre, en la sesión solemne celebrada en la noche del 8 de febrero de 1937*. Siglo XX, A. Muñiz y Hno., La Habana.

Dirks, Nicholas B.
1992   Introduction. In *Colonialism and Culture*, edited by N. B. Dirks, pp. 1–26. University of Michigan Press, Ann Arbor.

Domínguez, Jorge I.
1978   *Cuba: Order and Revolution*. Belknap Press, Cambridge.

Donghai, Su
1995   Museums and Museum Philosophy in China. *Nordisk Museologi* 2:61–80.

Donham, Donald Lewis
1999   *Marxist Modern: An Ethnographic History of the Ethiopian Revolution*. University of California Press, Berkeley.

Duany, Jorge
1997   From the Cuban Ajiaco to the Cuban-American Hyphen: Changing Discourses of National Identity on the Island and in the Diaspora. *Cuban Studies Association Occasional Papers* Paper 16.

Eliseo, Alberto
August 5, 1979   Un friso en la Plaza. *Verde Olivo*:56–57.

Equipo Coordinador
2013   *Proyecto de uso cultural para el Palacio de Segundo Cabo: Centro para la*

interpretación de las Relaciones Culturales Cuba-Europa. OHCH, Unpublished.

Estévez, Reynaldo

1953a   El Fórum sobre la Plaza Cívica. *Espacio* 2(9):36–44.

1953b   Ponencias presentadas en el Fórum, Arquitectos Porro, Beale, Caleache, Nicolás Quintana. *Espacio* 2(9):45–48.

Fairweather, Ian

2006   Heritage, Identity and Youth in Postcolonial Namibia. *Journal of Southern African Studies* 32(4):719–736.

Featherstone, Mike

1996   Localism, Globalism, and Cultural Identity. In *Global/local: Cultural Production and the Transnational Imaginary*, edited by R. Wilson and D. Wimal, pp. 46–77. Duke University Press, Durham, N.C.

Fernández, Damián

2000   *Cuba and the Politics of Passion.* University of Texas Press, Austin.

Fernández Mayo, Graciela, and Nuria Nuiry Sánchez

1986   *Pensamiento y política cultural cubanos: Antología 1.* Pueblo y Educación, La Habana.

Fernández Retamar, Roberto

1974   *Calibán: Apuntes sobre la cultura en nuestra América.* Abejón Mono, Bogotá.

Flikke, Michelle A. T.

2006   Cuban Museums and Afro-Cuban Heritage. Fragments and Transition in Daily Life. Ph.D., Harvard University.

2008   Three Interpretations of Materiality and Society Afro-Cuban Heritage and the Cuban Slave Route Museum. In *Six Essays on the Materiality of Society and Culture*, edited by H. Glørstad and L. Hedeager, pp. 87–126. Bricoleur, Lindome, Sweden.

Fonts Catá, Caridad

1995   Un rescate de la cultura nacional: El monumento a José Martí en el Parque Central de La Habana y su autor. *Bohemia*:18.

Fornet, Ambrosio

2009   *Narrar la nación: Ensayos en blanco y negro.* Letras Cubanas, La Habana.

Fornet, Pablo

1998   *El Centro Histórico en transformación: La Plaza Vieja.* CENCREM, La Habana.

Foucault, Michel

2007   *Security, Territory, Population: Lectures at the Collège De France, 1977–78.* Palgrave Macmillan, République Française, Basingstoke, New York.

Fraga, Jorge

1963   ¿Cuántas Culturas? Carta abierta a la compañera Mirta Aguirre. *La Gaceta de Cuba* 2(28):10–12.

Franqui, Carlos
1984   *Family Portrait with Fidel: A Memoir*. Random House, New York.
Frederik, Laurie
2012   *Trumpets in the Mountains: Theater and the Politics of National Culture in
            Cuba*. Duke University Press, Durham, N.C.
Freyre de Andrade, Fernando
1919   No es un español, no puede ser un español el llamado a perpetuar en
            bronces y mármoles el genio y la gloria de nuestros caudillos. *Heraldo
            de Cuba*.
G. C.
1910   G. O. Decreto presidencial #732, 1 de agosto de 1910. Gobierno de Cuba,
            La Habana.
1913   G. O. Decreto #503, 10 de mayo de 1913. Gobierno de Cuba, La Habana.
1976a   *Constitución de la República de Cuba*. Ministerio de Justicia, La Habana.
1976b   *Ley 23 de Museos Municipales de Cuba, 19 de Mayo de 1976*. Gobierno de
            Cuba, Asamblea Nacional del Poder Popular, La Habana.
1977   Ley número 1 ley de protección al patrimonio cultural. Gobierno de
            Cuba. Asamblea Nacional del Poder Popular, La Habana.
1985   Decreto 129. Sobre el desarrollo de la escultura monumentaria y ambi-
            ental. Consejo de Ministros, La Habana.
Galalova, K. M.
1987   Problemas del perfeccionamiento de la dirección de museos. In *Experi-
            encias del curso para cuadros de la esfera de museos*, edited by Instituto de
            adiestramiento y calificacion de cuadros. Ministerio de Cultura; Direc-
            ción Patrimonio Cultural, Moscú.
Galkina, P. I., V. K. Gardanov, I. P. Ivanitkin, K. G. Miteaev, G. A. Novitki, and N. N.
            Plavilscikov
1957   *Bazele Muzeologiei Sovietice*. Romanian Ministry of Culture, Bucharest.
García Buchaca, Edith
1961   *La teoría de la superestructura: La literatura y el arte*. Consejo Nacional
            de Cultura, La Habana.
García Castañeda, José
1945   *Como logar la efectividad de la labor educacional encomendada a los museos*.
            Sanchez y hermano, Holguín.
García Molina, José Antonio
1989   *Museo etnológico del grupo Guamá una institucion que debe ser rescatada*.
            Biblioteca Nacional José Martí, La Habana.
García Santana, María Mercedes
2010   Surgimiento, Evolución y Desarrollo del Coleccionismo y los Museos en
            Cuba, Museología, Colegio Universitario San Jerónimo, master's the-
            sis, unpublished.
García Serrato, Nelson
1938   La oficina del Historiador de la Ciudad: Contenido cívico de su obra.
            Carteles 29(1):36.

García Valdés, Pedro
1923   *Enseñanza de la historia en las escuelas primarias.* Librería J. Albela, La Habana.

Geertz, Clifford
1973   *The Interpretation of Cultures: Selected Essays.* Basic Books, New York.

Giebel, Christoph
2004   *Imagined Ancestries of Vietnamese Communism: Ton Duc Thang and the Politics of History and Memory.* University of Washington Press, Seattle.

Gill, Graeme J.
2011   *Symbols and Legitimacy in Soviet Politics.* Cambridge University Press, Cambridge.

Gómez Iglesias, David
Ca. 1985   *El Museo, contribución a la educación patriótica e internacionalista: Museo provincial, Holguín.* CNPC Archive, La Habana.

Gonçalves, João Felipe
2001   The Apostle in Stone: Nationalism and Monuments in Honor of José Martí. In *The Cuban Republic and José Martí: Reception and Use of a National Symbol,* edited by M. A. Font and A. W. Quiroz, pp. 18–33. Lexington Books, Lanham.

González Aróstegui, Mely
2003   Fernando Ortiz y la polémica del panhispanismo y el panamericanismo en los albores del siglo XX en Cuba. *Revista de Hispanismo Filosófico* (8):5–18.

González del Campo, Loredano, and Fanny Azcuy
1950   *Metodología de los estudios sociales.* Cultural S.A., La Habana.

González Manet, Eduardo
1960   Transfomará la revolucion las costumbres del cubano. *Bohemia* 53(35):75.

González Quintana, Gualberto
1978   *Letter from G. González Quintana to P. Álvarez Tabío Longa concerning the construction of the monument to the landing of Granma. Sig. 07–4/79.* Oficina de Asuntos Históricos del Consejo de Estado, La Habana.

Gordon-Nesbitt, Rebecca
2012   To Defend the Revolution Is to Defend Culture: The Cultural Policy of the 1959 Cuban Revolution. University of Strathclyde, Glasgow, Scotland.

Gould-Davies, Nigel
2003   The Logic of Soviet Cultural Diplomacy. *Diplomatic History* 27(2):193–214.

Groys, Boris
1992   *The Total Art of Stalinism.* Princeton University Press, Princeton.
1994   The Struggle Against the Museum; Or, the Display of Art in Totalitarian

Space. In *Museum Culture: Histories, Discourses, Spectacles*, edited by D. J. Sherman and I. Rogoff, pp. 144–162. Routledge, London.

Guerra, Charo

1999   Eusebio Leal: La ciudad es el hombre que la habita. *Gaceta de Cuba*.

Guevara, Ernesto

2005   Socialism and Man in Cuba. In *Manifesto: Three Classic Essays on How to Change the World*, pp. 147–168. Ocean Press, New York.

Guillén, Nicolás

1962   Report to the First National Congress of Writers and Artists. In *The Revolution and Cultural Problems in Cuba*. Ministry of Foreign Relations, La Habana.

Gutiérrez González, Aurelio, and Edel Morales Fuentes

Ca. 1985   *Los fondos del Museo Nacional de la Lucha Contra Bandidos: Museo Nacional de la Lucha Contra Bandidos, Trinidad*. CNPC Archive, La Habana.

Gutiérrez, Tomás Servando

May 1919   Monumento al Generalísmo: Zanelli, Dacci y los escultores italianos. *Malecón*.

Harrison, Rodney, and Lotte Hughes

2010   Heritage and Postcolonialism. In *Understanding the Politics of Heritage*, edited by R. Harrison, pp. 234–266. Manchester University Press, Manchester.

Hart Dávalos, Armando

1977   Discurso de clausura del 2° Congreso de la UNEAC. *Granma*:2. La Habana.

1981   *Letter from Armando Hart Dávalos to Fidel Castro, Including the Draft CODEMA Guidelines and a Tentative List of Monuments to be Built in the Following Years*. Correspondence with the PCC, CODEMA Archive, La Habana.

1983   *Cambiar las reglas del juego*. Letras Cubanas, La Habana.

1989   *Cultura e identidad nacional*. Ministerio de Cultura, La Habana.

Hartman, Joseph

2011   The Ceiba Tree as a Multivocal Signifier: Afro-Cuban Symbolism, Political Performance, and Urban Space in the Cuban Republic. *Hemisphere* 36:16–41.

Havel, Václav

1985   The Power of the Powerless. In *The Power of the Powerless: Citizens Against the State in Central-Eastern Europe*, edited by V. Havel and J. Keane, pp. 10–59. M. E. Sharpe, Armonk, N.Y.

Hearn, Adrian H.

2004   Afro-Cuban Religions and Social Welfare: Consequences of Commercial Development in Havana. *Human Organization: Journal of the Society for Applied Anthropology* 63(1):78.

Hedin, Astrid

2004   Stalinism as a Civilization: New Perspectives on Communist Regimes. *Political Studies Review* 2(2):166–184.

Hegel, Georg Wilhelm Friedrich

2010 [1812] *The Science of Logic*. Cambridge University Press, Cambridge.

Herrera Ysla, Nelson

1980   *Mausoleo a los mártires de Artemisa*. Letras Cubanas, La Habana.

Herzfeld, Michael

1992   Metapatterns: Archaeology and the Uses of Evidential Scarcity. In *Representations in Archaeology*, edited by J. Claude Gardin and C. Spalding Peebles, pp. 66–86. Indiana University Press, Bloomington.

1997   Anthropology: A Practice of Theory. *International Social Science Journal* 49(153):301–318.

2002   The Absence Presence: Discourses of Crypto-Colonialism. *South Atlantic Quarterly* 101(4):899–926.

2005   *Cultural Intimacy: Social Poetics in the Nation-State*. Routledge, London.

2012   The Crypto-Colonial Dilemmas of Rattanakosin Island. *Journal of the Siam Society* 100:209–223.

Hill, Matthew

2007   Re-Imagining Old Havana: World Heritage and the Production of Scale in Late Socialist Cuba. In *Deciphering the Global: Its Scales, Spaces and Subjects*, edited by S. Sassen, pp. 59–76. Routledge, New York.

2012   The Future of the Past: World Heritage, National Identity, and Urban Centrality in Late Socialist Cuba. In *Global Downtowns*, edited by M. Peterson and G. McDonogh, pp. 186–205. University of Pennsylvania Press, Philadelphia.

Horrego Estuch, Leopoldo

1954   *Juan Gualberto Gómez: Un gran inconforme*. La Milagrosa, La Habana.

Humphrey, Caroline

2005   Ideology in Infrastructure: Architecture and Soviet Imagination. *Journal of the Royal Anthropological Institute* 11(1):39–58.

Hyde, Timothy

2012   *Constitutional Modernism: Architecture and Civil Society in Cuba, 1933–1959*. University of Minnesota Press, Minneapolis.

Ibarra, Jorge

1995   Historiografía y revolución. *Temas* 1:5–17.

Ichaso, Francisco

1954   Museo y Bienal. *Boletín UNESCO* 3(6):1–2.

Iglesias Utset, Marial

2011   *A Cultural History of Cuba during the U.S. Occupation, 1898–1902*. University of North Carolina Press, Chapel Hill.

2014   A Sunken Ship, a Bronze Eagle, and the Politics of Memory: The "Social Life" of the USS *Maine* in Cuba (1898–1961). In *State of Ambiguity:*

Civic Life and Culture in Cuba's First Republic, edited by S. Palmer, J. A. Piqueras, and A. S. Cobos, pp. 22–53. Duke University Press, Durham, N.C.

Jubrías, María Elena
1989   *Historia Social del Arte V. 4*. Pueblo y Educación, La Habana.

Kaluza, Karoline
2014   Reimagining the Nation in Museums: Poland's Old and New National Museums. In *National Museums: New Studies from Around the World*, edited by S. J. Knell, pp. 151–162. Routledge, London.

Kapcia, Antoni
2000   *Cuba: Island of Dreams*. Berg, Oxford.
2005   *Havana: The Making of Cuban Culture*. Berg, Oxford.
2014   *Leadership in the Cuban Revolution: The Unseen Story*. Zed Books, London.

Kapferer, Bruce
1988   *Legends of People, Myths of State: Violence, Intolerance, and Political Culture in Sri Lanka and Australia*. Smithsonian Institution Press, Washington.

Kertzer, David I.
1980   *Comrades and Christians: Religion and Political Struggle in Communist Italy*. Cambridge University Press, Cambridge.

Khazanov, Anatoly M.
2000   Selecting the Past: The Politics of Memory in Moscow's History Museums. *City & Society* 12(2):35–62.

Kirillov, Vladimir
1918. *Gryadushcheye* 2:4.

Kirshenblatt-Gimblett, Barbara
1998   *Destination Culture: Tourism, Museums, and Heritage*. University of California Press, Berkeley.
2004   Intangible Heritage as Metacultural Production. *Museum International* 56(1–2):52–65.

Klausewitz, Wolfgan
1988   Introducción a la Museología: Contribución al trabajo teórico de los Museos. In *Diversos aspectos de la teoría museológica: Reunión Nacional de Directores de Museos; Matanzas, 14–17 de Septiembre de 1988*, edited by MINCULT and Dirección de Patrimonio Cultural, pp. 3–23. MINCULT, La Habana.

Kwon, Heonik, and Byung-Ho Chung
2012   *North Korea: Beyond Charismatic Politics*. Rowman & Littlefield, Lanham, Md.

La Futura Plaza Cívica
1950   La futura Plaza Cívica José Martí. *Revista de la propiedad urbana* 201:6.

Labatut, Jean
1952   Monuments and Memorials. In *Forms and Functions of Twentieth-Century Architecture*, edited by T. Hamlin, pp. 521–533. Columbia University Press, New York.

Lachatañeré, Rómulo
1992 [1942]   *El sistema religioso de los afrocubanos*. Ciencias Sociales, La Habana.

Laguna Enrique, Martha Elizabeth
2013   El museo nacional de bellas artes de la Habana y la colección de retratos de la pintura española del siglo XIX. Universidad de Salamanca, Salamanca.

Lauderman Ortiz, Gladys
1951   *Factores estilísticos de la escultura cubana contemporánea*. Editora de Publicaciones, La Habana.

Leal Spengler, Eusebio
April 29, 2010   *Fragmento de su intervención del durante el Taller de conceptualización Palacio del Segundo Cabo*. Museo de la Ciudad, La Habana.
1986   Palabras de clausura a cargo de Eusebio Leal. In *Memorias: IV Simposio de la Cultura de Ciudad de La Habana; Ciudad de La Habana, 14 de noviembre de 1986*. Divulgación, La Habana.
2006   La cultura, única certeza para un proyecto sostenible. In *Manejo y gestión de centros históricos: Conferencias de los Encuentros Internacionales II y III, La Habana Vieja, 2003 y 2004*, edited by C. Guerra and M. V. Pardo, pp. 13–25. Boloña, La Habana.

Lefebvre, Henri
1991   *The Production of Space*. Blackwell, Oxford.

Lenin, Vladimir Ilich
1972 [1913–1914]-a Critical Remarks on the National Question. In *Collected Works*, Vol. 20, *December 1913–August 1914*, pp. 17–51. Progress, Moscow.
1972 [1913–1914]-b The Heritage We Renounce. In *Collected Works*, Vol. 20, *December 1913–August 1914*, pp. 491–534. Progress, Moscow.

Levinson, Sanford
1998   *Written in Stone: Public Monuments in Changing Societies*. Duke University Press, Durham, N.C.

Leyva, Armando
1922   *Museo*. Arroyo Hermanos, Santiago de Cuba.

Light, Duncan
2000a   Gazing on Communism: Heritage Tourism and Post-Communist Identities in Germany, Hungary and Romania. *Tourism Geographies* 2(2):157–176.
2000b   An Unwanted Past: Contemporary Tourism and the Heritage of Communism in Romania. *International Journal of Heritage Studies* 6(2):145–160.

Limia, José
1978   *Museo Histórico 26 de Julio*. Oriente, Santiago de Cuba.
Linares Ferrera, José
2002   *Un centro histórico no debe ser una escenografía turística*. CONACULTA, México D.F.
Linares Ferrera, José, and MINCULT
1984   *Architecture Plan of the "Museo De La Lucha Contra Bandidos."* CNPC Archive, La Habana.
Lizaso, Félix
1953   *José Martí. Recuento del centenario: Tomo I*. Ucar García, La Habana.
Lodder, Christina
1983   *Russian Constructivism*. Yale University Press, New Haven.
Lomnitz-Adler, Claudio
2001   *Deep Mexico, Silent Mexico: An Anthropology of Nationalism*. University of Minnesota Press, Minneapolis.
Long, Colin
2012   Modernity, Socialism and Heritage in Asia. In *Routledge Handbook of Heritage in Asia*, edited by P. T. Daly and T. Winter, pp. 201–217. Routledge, Oxon.
2014   The Modern Capital of a Modern Nation: Heritage and Identity in Post-Socialist Vientiane. *Historic Environment* 26(3):14–24.
Longa, Rita
1984   *Letter to the People of Guantánamo*. CODEMA Archive, La Habana.
1993   *Informe CODEMA 1993*. CODEMA Archive, La Habana.
Ca. 1985   *Letter from Rita Longa to Marcia Leiseca*. CODEMA Archive, La Habana.
López, Alfred J.
2006   *José Martí and the Future of Cuban Nationalisms*. University Press of Florida, Gainesville.
Maleuvre, Didier
1999   *Museum Memories: History, Technology, Art*. Stanford University Press, Stanford.
Mañach, Jorge
1944   Voto del Dr. Jorge Mañach en el concurso de proyectos del monumento a Martí. *Arquitectura* 12(127):62–64.
1953   El Monumento a Martí (historia de un lauro frustrado). *Bohemia* 64:97–98.
Marín, Víctor
1990   *Informe sobre el avance y costos de las obras de la Plaza Vieja*. CENCREM, La Habana.
Marinello, Juan
1961   *Conversación con nuestros pintores abstractos*. Imprenta Nacional de Cuba, La Habana.

Marrero Oliva, Lelis
2004   *Historia del surgimiento de los Museos en la provincia de La Habana*. Unpublished manuscript.
Marris, Peter
1974   *Loss and Change*. Pantheon Books, New York.
Martínez Carmenate, Urbano
2010   *El coleccionismo en Matanzas: Del gabinete privado al museo público*. Ediciones Matanzas, Matanzas.
Martínez Heredia, Fernando
2005   *En el horno de los 90*. Ciencias Sociales, La Habana.
Martínez Inclán, Pedro
1925   *La Habana actual: Estudio de la capital de Cuba desde el punto de vista de la arquitectura de ciudades*. Imprenta P. Fernández, La Habana.
Martínez Riera, Magaly
1988   *Formas del Museo de la Lucha Clandestina de ejercer su influencia o contribución en la formación de hábitos y una conciencia político-cultural en niños y jóvenes: Museo de la Lucha Clandestina, Santiago de Cuba*. CNPC Archive, La Habana.
Maza, Aquiles, and Juan José Sicre
1953   Forum del Colegio de Arquitectos sobre la plaza de la república: Informes de Aquiles Mazas y Sicre. *Arquitectura* 21(241):317–334.
Mbembe, Achille
2001   *On the Postcolony*. University of California Press, Berkeley.
Medin, Tzvi
1990   *Cuba: The Shaping of Revolutionary Consciousness*. Lynne Rienner, Boulder.
Menéndez-Conde, Ernesto
2009   Arte Abstracto e Ideologías Estéticas en Cuba. Ph.D., Duke University.
Meskell, Lynn
2012   *The Nature of Heritage: The New South Africa*. Wiley-Blackwell, Malden, Mass.
Meyer, Hans
1972   *El arquitecto en la lucha de clases y otros escritos*. G. Gili, Barcelona.
MICONS
1962   *Report on the "Plaza Cívica."* Sig. *13239*. MICONS Archive, La Habana.
1962–1964   *"Plaza Cívica"—Architecture projects 3, 6, 10, 11, 12 and 16*. MICONS Archive.
Mignolo, Walter D., and A. Escobar
2009   Globalization and the Decolonial Option. In *Delinking: The Rhetoric of Modernity, the Logic of Coloniality and the Grammar of De-Coloniality*, edited by W. D. Mignolo, pp. 303–368. Routledge, London.
Mignolo, Walter D.
2000   *Local Histories/Global Designs: Coloniality, Subaltern Knowledges, and Border Thinking*. Princeton University Press, Princeton, N.J.

Mikoyan, Anastas

1960   *Mikoyan en Cuba.* Oficina de Prensa de la Embajada de la URSS, La Habana.

Miller, Ivor

2000   Religious Symbolism in Cuban Political Performance. *Drama Review* 44(2):30–55.

MINREX

1976   *La funcion cultural-educacional del estado socialista cubano.* Dirección de Prensa, Información y Relaciones Culturales, La Habana.

Miró Argenter, José

1918   *Discurso del General José Miró en el acto de la inauguracion del monumento a Maceo, el 20 de Mayo de 1916.* Sociedad Editorial Cuba Contemporánea, La Habana.

Mola Fernández, Claudia

1985   Emilio Roig de Leuchsenring y la Oficina del Historiador de la Ciudad. In *Memorias del 3er. Simposio de Cultura: Ciudad de La Habana, 14 de noviembre de 1985,* pp. 73–88. Dirección Provincial de Cultura, La Habana.

Montané Oropesa, Jesús

1982   *Letter from J. Montané Oropesa to A. Hart Dávalos.* Correspondence with the PCC, CODEMA Archive, La Habana.

Montenegro, Mauricio

1982   *Instrucciones Metodológicas.* Patrimonio Cultural, MINCULT, La Habana.

Moore, Carlos

1988   *Castro, the Blacks, and Africa.* University of California Press, Berkeley.

Moreno Fraginals, Manuel

1983   *La historia como arma y otros estudios sobre esclavos, ingenios y plantaciones.* Crítica, Barcelona.

1995   *Cuba, España, España, Cuba: Historia común.* Crítica, Barcelona.

Moreno García, José Ramón

1988   *Informe del asesor técnico internacional José Ramón Moreno, octubre de 1988: Proyecto PNUD-UNESCO CUB/86/017.* Grupo Técnico Asesor de la Campaña de la Plaza Vieja.

Moret, Enrique

1975   La escultura monumental en Cuba: Conferencia pronunciada en el II Simposio Nacional de profesores e instructores de artes plásticas. *El Caimán Barbudo* 89:19.

Museo de la Revolución

2013   *Proyecto para el remontaje de la exposición permanente del Museo de la Revolución.* Museo de la Revolución Archive, La Habana.

Ca. 1963   *Newspaper Clipping without References.* Museo de la Revolución Archive, La Habana.

Ca. 1988   *Unclassified Pictures and Texts from Previous Museum Exhibitions*. Museo de la Revolución Archive, La Habana.

Museo de Morón

1981   *Museo Histórico de Morón. Guión General*. Museo de la Revolución Archive, Morón.

Museo Nacional de Cuba and E. Heredia y Mora

1913   *Memoria del Comisionado Sr. Emilio Heredia, diciembre 5 de 1910 a 1 de marzo de 1913*. La Universal, Habana.

Myhrberg, Karin

2012   Heritage from the Communist Period in Albania—An Unwanted Heritage Today? Master of science, University of Gotheborg.

Naranjo Orovio, Consuelo

2001   La historia se forja en el campo: Nación y cultura cubana en el siglo XX. *Historia social* 40:153–174.

Navarro, Desiderio

2002   In medias res publicas: Sobre los intelectuales y la crítica social en la esfera pública cubana. *Revista del CESLA* 4:111–123.

Niell, Paul B.

2015   *Urban Space as Heritage in Late Colonial Cuba: Classicism and Dissonance on the Plaza De Armas of Havana, 1754–1828*. University of Texas Press, Austin.

Nora, Pierre

1989   Between Memory and History: Les Lieux De Mémoire. *Representations* 26:7–24.

1996   General Introduction: Between Memory and History. In *Realms of Memory: Rethinking the French Past*, Vol I: *Conflicts and Divisions*, edited by P. Nora, pp. 1–20. Columbia University Press, New York.

Novel, Ricart

1984   *Memorias de la primera Reunión del Grupo Asesor de la Campaña Internacional de Salvaguarda de la Plaza Vieja*. UNESCO, La Habana.

OHCH

2012   Cooperación en patrimonio cultural.

Oliva, Raúl

1963   Creación de la Comisión Nacional de Monumentos. *Arquitectura Cuba* 30(332):3–5.

Ortiz, Fernando

1948   La música y los areitos de los indios de Cuba. *Revista de Arqueología y Etnología* Época 2, Año 3(6–7):115–189.

1987   *Contrapunteo cubano del tabaco y el azúcar*. Fundacion Biblioteca Ayacucho, Caracas.

1987   *Entre Cubanos: Psicología tropical*. Ciencias Sociales, La Habana.

Ortiz García, Carmen

2003   Cultura popular y construcción nacional: La institucionalización de los estudios de folklore en Cuba. *Revista de Indias* 63(229):695–736.

Otero, Lisandro, and Francisco Martínez Hinojosa
1972   *Cultural Policy in Cuba*. UNESCO, Paris.
Parra Donet, Yadira
2008   Conjunto Monumental Plaza de la Revolución Mayor General "Antonio
            Maceo Grajales," una obra singular en la Tipología Plaza de la Revolu-
            ción. Maestría, Universidad de Oriente.
Patronato
1941   *Actas del Patronato Prorestauración y Conservación de la Catedral*. CEN-
            CREM Archive, La Habana.
PCC
1976   *Tesis y Resoluciones Primer Congreso del Partido Comunista de Cuba*. Co-
            mité Central del Partido Comunista de Cuba, La Habana.
1987   Resolución sobre la cultura artistica y literaria del II Congreso del PCC.
            In *Pensamiento y política cultural cubanos: Antología, v.4*, edited by G.
            Fernández Mayo and N. Nuiry Sánchez. Pueblo y Educación, La Ha-
            bana.
PCC Holguín
1978   *Creación y funcionamiento de los Salones de Historia en los Centros de Tra-
            bajo Fundamentales. Material mimeografiado*. PCC Holguín, Holguín.
Pereira, María de los Ángeles
1985   El Monumento a José Martí en la Plaza de la Revolución. In *Memo-
            rias del III Simposio Provincial de Cultura de la Ciudad de La Habana*, pp.
            24–36. Dirección Provincial de Cultura, La Habana.
1994   La Escultura monumentaria y ambiental en Cuba. Ph.D., Universidad
            de La Habana.
Pérez Beato, Augusto
1964   Monumento Playa Girón: Resultado del concurso internacional. *Arqui-
            tectura Cuba* 30(331):53–64.
Pérez, Louis A.
1980   In the Service of the Revolution: Two Decades of Cuban Historiogra-
            phy, 1959–1979. *Hispanic American Historical Review* 60(1):79–89.
1999   *On Becoming Cuban: Identity, Nationality, and Culture*. University of
            North Carolina Press, Chapel Hill.
Peters, Christabelle
2010   Identifying (with) "Carlota": Myths, Metaphors and Landscapes of Cu-
            ban Africanía, 1974–1980. Ph.D., University of Nottingham.
Petkova-Campbell, Gabriela
2009   *A Place in Europe: Bulgaria and Its Museums in "New" Europe*. Archaeo-
            press, Oxford.
2011   Uses and Exploitation of History: Official History, Propaganda and
            Mythmaking in Bulgarian Museums. In *Great Narratives of the Past.
            Traditions and Revisions in National Museums. EuNaMus conference pro-
            ceedings, Paris 29 June–1 July & 25–26 November 2011*, edited by D. Pou-

lot, F. Bodenstein, and J. M. Lanzarote Guiral, pp. 69–77. Linköping University Electronic Press.

Pichler, Adelheid

2012   The Dynamics of Heritage Choice and Heritage Regimes in the "Making of Old Havana." In *Heritage Regimes and the State*, edited by R. Bendix, A. Eggert, and A. Peselmann, pp. 39–60. Universitätsverlag Göttingen, Göttingen, Germany.

Plan Maestro

2012   *Luces y Simientes: Territorio y gestión en cinco centros históricos cubanos.* OHCH, La Habana.

Pogolotti, Graziella

2006   *Polémicas culturales de los 60.* Letras Cubanas, La Habana.

Ponte, Antonio José

2011   La Habana: City and Archive. In *Havana Beyond the Ruins: Cultural Mappings After 1989*, edited by A. Birkenmaier and E. Whitfield, pp. 249–269. Duke University Press, Durham, N.C.

Porro Hidalgo, Ricardo, Alberto Beale Alfonso, and René Calvache Suárez

1958   Ponencia Presentada por los Arquitectos Miembros del Ciam. Arqs. Ricardo Porro Hidalgo, Alberto Beale Alfonso, y René Calvache Suárez. *Espacio* 2(9):45–46.

Portieles Fleites, José Antonio

2005   *El apoyo de la Cooperación Internacional a procesos de desarrollo local en curso: La experiencia del Centro Histórico de La Habana.* OHCH, La Habana.

Portuondo, J. A.

1963a   En busca de la expresión estética de una "nación para sí." In *Estética y Revolución*, pp. 57–90. Unión, La Habana.

1963b   *Estética y revolución.* UNEAC, La Habana.

1979   *Itinerario estético de la Revolución Cubana.* Letras Cubanas, La Habana.

1982   *Martí, escritor revolucionario.* Editora Política, La Habana.

Postone, Moishe

2004   Critique and Historical Transformation. *Historical Materialism* 12(3):53–72.

Pratt, Marie Louise

1991   Arts of the Contact Zone. *Profession* 91:33–40.

Pupo Pupo, Rigoberto

2005   *Identidad: Emancipación y nación cubana.* Editora Política, La Habana.

Quijano, Anibal

2000   Coloniality of Power and Eurocentrism in Latin America. *International Sociology* 15(2):215–232.

Quintana, Augusto, and Catalino Cabrera

1982   *Report to Rubén Valle and CODEMA Concerning the Monument to Lenin.* CODEMA, La Habana.

Quiza Moreno, Ricardo
2014 New Knowledge for New Times: The Sociedad del Folklore Cubano during the "Critical Decade" (1923–1930). In *State of Ambiguity: Civic Life and Culture in Cuba's First Republic*, edited by S. Palmer, J. A. Piqueras, and A. S. Cobos, pp. 269–291. Duke University Press, Durham, N.C.

Rama, Angel
1996 *The Lettered City*. Duke University Press, Durham, N.C.

Rangel Rivero, Armando
2013 *Antropología en Cuba: Orígenes y desarrollo*. Fundación Fernando Ortiz, La Habana.

Răuță, Alexandru
2009 Civic Centers under Ceaușescu's Rule: The Failure to Articulate a Professional Discourse. In *Modern Architecture and the Totalitarian Project: A Romanian Case Study*, edited by I. Augustin, pp. 105–119. ICR, Bucharest.

Reyes Gavilán, Antonio
1960 Será un ejemplo viviente el Museo de la Revolución. *Carteles* 41(8):38–40, 80–81.

Riaño San Marful, Pablo
2002 *Gallos y toros en Cuba*. Fundación Fernando Ortiz, La Habana.

Rigol, Isabel
1986 *Proyecto de Informe sobre la Ejecución del Proyecto Cuba 81/017 PNUD-UNESCO 1982–1986*. CENCREM-MINCULT, La Habana.

2013 La recuperación del patrimonio monumental en cuba, 1900–1959. In *Conservación Patrimonial: Teoría y critica*, edited by A. Rojas Ávalos and I. Rigol, pp. 90–111. Universidad de La Habana, La Habana.

Rigol, Isabel, and Nancy González
1983 *La Plaza Vieja*. ECIGRAF, La Habana.

Ríos Marrero, Lucía N.
1984 *Museo de Ambiente Histórico Cubano*. Oriente, Santiago de Cuba.

Rivas Rodríguez, Jorge
2000 Buscar maneras atractivas de educar y elevar el nivel cultural de la sociedad. *Proceedings of the Trabajadores: III Encuentro nacional de directores municipales de Cultura*. La Habana.

Rodriguez Alomá, Patricia
2009 Gestión del desarrollo integral de los centros históricos: La metodología TESIS. Ph.D., CUJAE.

Rodríguez Alomá, Patricia, and Alina Ochoa Alomá
2002 *Desafío de una utopía: Una estrategia integral para la gestión de salvaguarda de la habana vieja*. OHCH; Colegio Oficial de Arquitectos Vasco-Navarro, La Habana; Pamplona.

Rodríguez, Carlos Rafael
1944 *El marxismo y la historia de Cuba*. Paginas, Habana.

Rodríguez Joa, Mariela

2009   *La escultura conmemorativa en Santiago de Cuba: 1959–2000*. Ediciones Santiago, Santiago de Cuba.

Rodríguez Morey, Antonio

1944   Museografía. *La Libertad*:6.

Rojas, Ángela

2000   Turismo y patrimonio: La práctica de la verdad. *Arquitectura y Urbanismo* 13(4):21–25.

Rojas, Rafael

2006   Otro gallo cantaría: Essay on the first Cuban Republicanism. In *The Cuban Republic and José Martí: Reception and Use of a National Symbol*, edited by M. A. Font and A. W. Quiroz, pp. 7–17. Lexington, Oxford.

2007   Diaspora and Memory in Cuban Literature. In *Cuba: Idea of a Nation Displaced*, edited by A. O'Reilly Herrera, pp. 237–252. SUNY, Albany.

2011   The Illegible City: Havana after the Messiah. In *Havana Beyond the Ruins: Cultural Mappings After 1989*, edited by A. Birkenmaier and E. Whitfield, pp. 119–134. Duke University Press, Durham, N.C.

Roldán Oliarte, Esteban

1940   *Cuba en la mano: Enciclopedia popular ilustrada*. Ucar, García y cía., La Habana.

Roniger, Luis Sznajder Mario

1998   *Constructing Collective Identities and Shaping Public Spheres: Latin American Paths*. Sussex Academic Press, Brighton, Portland.

Root, Deborah

1996   *Cannibal Culture: Art, Appropriation, and the Commodification of Difference*. Westview Press, Boulder.

Routon, Kenneth

2008   Conjuring the Past: Slavery and the Historical Imagination in Cuba. *American Ethnologist* 35(4):632–649.

Ruiz, Gervariso G.

1956   Una obra urgente el museo nacional. *Carteles* 37(44):54.

Sabio, Salomon

2011   Eusebio Leal, el germen capitalista y antidemocrático. Kaosenlared.net.

Salinas, Fernando

1985   *Pórtico del pueblo*. Revolución y Cultura. CODEMA Archive, La Habana.

Sánchez, Celia

1958   *Letter from Celia Sánchez to Fidel Castro, 13 May 1958*. Sig. 07–16/37. Oficina de Asuntos Históricos del Consejo de Estado, La Habana.

1959   *Letter from Celia Sánchez to Camilo Cienfuegos Gorriarán, 16 March 1959*. Sig. 07–1/33. Oficina de Asuntos Históricos del Consejo de Estado, La Habana.

1978a   *Letter from Celia Sánchez to Arturo Duque de Estrada*. Sig. 07–7/47. Oficina de Asuntos Históricos del Consejo de Estado, La Habana.

1978b   *Letter from Celia Sánchez to the Political Bureau of the Cuban Communist Party Concerning the Construction of Monuments in the Sierra Maestra.* Sig. 07–3/75. Oficina de Asuntos Históricos del Consejo de Estado, La Habana.

Sánchez, Juan

October 20, 1992   La cultura y sus filos. *Bohemia*:22–24.

Santovenia, Emeterio S.

1915   *Próceres occidentales: Apuntes sobre el proyecto de erigir seis bustos de patriotas de Vuelta Abajo.* La Universal, La Habana.

1928   *Libro conmemorativo de la inauguración de la Plaza del Maine en la Habana* [Memorial book of the inauguration of the Maine Plaza at Havana]. Obras Públicas; Sindicato de artes gráficas, La Habana.

Sartre, Jean-Paul

1961   *Sartre on Cuba.* Ballantine Books, New York.

Sarusky, Jaime, and Gerardo Mosquera

1979   *The Cultural Policy of Cuba.* UNESCO, Paris.

Scarpaci, Joseph

2000   Winners and Losers in Restoring Old Havana. *Cuba in Transition* 10:289–298.

Schildgen, Brenda Deen

2008   *Heritage or Heresy: Preservation and Destruction of Religious Art and Architecture in Europe.* Palgrave Macmillan, Basingstoke.

Schöpflin, George

1996   *Politics in Eastern Europe: 1945–1992.* Blackwell, Oxford.

Segre, Roberto

1970   *Cuba: Arquitectura de la revolución.* G. Gili, Barcelona.

1994   Tres décadas de arquitectura cubana: La herencia histórica y el mito de lo nuevo. *Revolución y Cultura* 3 (Época 5, Año 33):36–45.

1998   Encrucijadas de la arquitectura en Cuba: Realismo mágico, realismo socialista y realismo crítico. Paper presented at the La Habana, 1898–1998, Madrid.

2003   *Arquitectura antillana del Siglo XX.* Arte y Literatura; Universidad Nacional de Colombia, Havana; Bogotá.

Society of the Army of Santiago de Cuba

1906   *Dedication of the Battle Monument at El Caney, Cuba; Dedication of the First Landing Monument at Daiquiri, Cuba: Report of the Santiago Battlefield Commission.* Press of J. S. Bridges, Baltimore.

Stephen Thomas, William, and Antonio Rodríguez Morey

1954   *VIII Curso de museografía: El museo y el mundo moderno.* Sociedad económica de amigos del país, La Habana.

Suárez García, María Margarita

2006   Cultural Heritage Legislation: The Historic Center of Old Havana. In *Art and Cultural Heritage: Law, Policy, and Practice,* edited by B. T. Hoffman, pp. 239–241. Cambridge University Press, New York.

Tamames Henderson, Marcos A.

2012   *La cofradía de los signos urbanos*. Ácana, Camagüey.

Tasalov, Vladimir

1980   Diez años del problema de "lo estético" (1956–1966). In *Problemas de la teoría del arte*, edited by V. Ivanov, pp. 306–384. Arte y Literatura, La Habana.

Terrón, Grisel, and Laura García

2012   *Sala del Libro en Cuba: Proyecto de uso cultural del Palacio del II Cabo; Guión museológico y museográfico*. OHCH, unpublished.

Thrower, James

1992   *Marxism-Leninism as the Civil Religion of Soviet Society: God's Commissar*. E. Mellen Press, Lewiston.

Ticktin, Hillel

1992   *Origins of the Crisis in the USSR: Essays on the Political Economy of a Disintegrating System*. M. E. Sharpe, Armonk.

Tlostanova, Madina, and Walter Mignolo

2009   Global Coloniality and the Decolonial Option. In *Kult 6-Special Issue: Epistemologies of Transformation; The Latin American Decolonial Option and Its Ramifications*, pp. 130–147. Roskilde University, Roskilde, Denmark.

Torres, Aleyda, Laureano Llorente, Norys Rodríguez, and Luis Cordero

1984   *Historia del Museo de Cárdenas: Desde su fundación a la actualidad; Museo de Cárdenas, Cárdenas*. CNPC Archive, La Habana.

Torriente Govín, Diana Rosa

2012   El Museo y Biblioteca Pública de Cárdenas (1900–1921). Inicios de la Museología Moderna en Cuba. Ph.D., Historia, Universidad de La Habana.

Touraine, Alain

1983   *L'après-socialisme*. Grasset, Paris.

Trouillot, Michel-Rolph

2012   *Silencing the Past: Power and the Production of History*. Beacon Press, Boston.

Trujillo, José Miguel

1914   *La enseñanza de la historia*. Cuba pedagógica, La Habana.

U.P.01 Osvaldo Sánchez

1973   *Seminario internacional de construcciones escolares: La Arquitectura escolar de la revolución cubana*. Unidad Productora 01 Osvaldo Sánchez; Instituto Cubano del Libro, La Habana.

UNESCO Cuba

1962a   Museo Hemingway. *Boletín UNESCO* 1(3):8–9.

1962b   Museo Napoleónico. *Boletín UNESCO* 1(2):9–10.

1965   Museo de Historia Natural. *Boletín UNESCO* 4(11):9–11.

1967   El Museo de la Alfabetización. *Boletín UNESCO* 6(20):15–16.

1969   Seminario internacional de museología: Palabras de Marta Arjona. *Bo-letín UNESCO* 8(28):16.
1971   El museo viaja al campo. *Boletín UNESCO* 10(33–36):9–17.
1972   Los museos en el mundo de hoy. *Boletín UNESCO* 11(40):2–5.
1973   Museo y Archivo de la Música. *Boletín UNESCO* 12(45):5–10.
1983   Campaña internacional de salvaguarda de la Plaza Vieja de La Habana. *Boletín UNESCO* 24(91):3–31.

Universidad de La Habana
1970   *Ensayos sobre arquitectura e ideología en Cuba revolucionaria.* Centro de Información Científica y Técnica, La Habana.

USSR
1918   *On Republic's Monuments, April 12, 1918.* Council of People's Commissars, Moscow.
1977   1976 Law on the Protection and Use of Historic and Cultural Monuments. In *Museums in the USSR: Transactions*, edited by L. Godunava, I. G. Lupalo, and I. P. Verchovcev. Central Museum of the Revolution, Moscow.

Van-Hoof, Herman
2009   Palabras acto de firmas proyecto UNESCO-Comisión Europea Herman van-Hooff.

Varutti, Marzia
2014   The Aesthetics and Narratives of National Museums in China. In *National Museums: New Studies from Around the World*, edited by S. J. Knell, pp. 302–312. Routledge, London.

Veiga, José
1980   La escultura en Cuba, ¿Hallará la salida? *Revolución y Cultura* 98–99:41–47.

Veila González, Nelia
Ca. 1985   *La revolución cultural en relación al patrimonio del pais: Museo Polivalente, Centro Habana.* CNPC Archive, La Habana.

Verdery, Katherine
1995   *National Ideology under Socialism: Identity and Cultural Politics in Ceauşescu's Romania.* University of California Press, Berkeley.

Vergani, Amneris
1963   Prólogo a una conversación sobre el parque-monumento a los mártires universitarios. *Arquitectura Cuba* 30(335):19–28.

Villoldo y Bertrán, Julio
1938   *Las estatuas y los monumentos en los parques conferencia dada por radio, desde la Estación radioemisora de "La voz del aire," el día 3 de noviembre de 1935.* Imprenta Molina, La Habana.

Wertsch, James, and Doc Billingsley
2011   The Role of Narratives in Commemoration: Remembering as Mediated Action. In *Cultures and Globalization: Heritage, Memory and Identity*, ed-

ited by H. K. Anheier, Y. Raj Isar, and D. Viejo-Rose, pp. 25–38. SAGE, London.

Winter, Tim

2008   Post-Conflict Heritage and Tourism in Cambodia: The Burden of Angkor. *International Journal of Heritage Studies* 14(6):524–539.

Zéndegui y Carbonell, Gabriel

1957   Lo que significa el Museo Nacional y cómo aprovecharlo. *Revista Cubana* 31(3–4):119.

Žižek, Slavoj

2001   *Welcome to the Desert of the Real.* Wooster Press, New York.

INDEX

PABLO ALONSO GONZÁLEZ is postdoctoral researcher at the Institute of Social Sciences at the University of Lisbon (ICS-UL). He holds a Ph.D. in history from the University of León in Spain and a Ph.D. in archaeology and heritage studies from the University of Cambridge. His research addresses heritage as a political reality at the intersection between society and material culture from the past. Drawing on critical heritage studies, González analyzes processes of nation-building, musealization, public archaeology, gentrification, and, more recently, processes of civic participation related to heritage. From an initial interest in the relationship between heritage and nation-building in Spain and Cuba, his research has broadened to include visual anthropology (he has produced three documentaries) and the anthropology of food. More recently, Pablo has examined the heritage dimension of wine in Spain and Portugal.

Lightning Source UK Ltd.
Milton Keynes UK
UKOW04n1449191217

314767UK00001B/33/P